SNAKEHEAD

SNAKEHEAD

A Fish Out of Water

Eric Jay Dolin

Smithsonian Books

Washington and London

To my children, Lily and Harry

Editorial proofreader: Laura Starrett
Production editor: Robert A. Poarch
Designer: Brian Barth

Dolin, Eric Jay.
    Snakehead : a fish out of water / Eric Jay Dolin.
        p.   cm.
    Includes bibliographical references (p.   ).
    ISBN 1-58834-154-2 (alk. Paper)
    1. Northern snakehead—Maryland—Crofton.
    2. Nonindigenous aquatic pests—Control—Maryland—Crofton.
I. Title.
QL 638.C486D66 2003
598'.7—dc21

                                                                      2003045571

British Library Cataloguing-in-Publication Data is available

Manufactured in the United States of America
09 08 07 06 05 04 03   5 4 3 2 1

CONTENTS

Acknowledgments   vii

Preface   xiii

1   Mystery Fish   1

2   "The Baddest Bunny in the Bush"   33

3   Then There Were Two   52

4   Spawn of Frankenfish   78

5   Poison 'Em   115

6   Going in for the Kill   152

7   Aftermath   206

8   Making Sense of the Summer of
the Snakehead   242

Bibliography   253

Index   263

ACKNOWLEDGMENTS

It is the lucky author who has the opportunity to write an exciting book literally fall into his lap. For this book, I was lucky indeed. In early August 2002 I was talking to Vince Burke, the Science Editor at Smithsonian Books, about a book I had recently written for Smithsonian titled the *Smithsonian Book of National Wildlife Refuges*. As I was preparing to hang up the phone, Vince asked if I had been following the stories about the snakehead fish found in Crofton, Maryland, a location that was, at the time, a mere thirty miles from my home. I had seen a couple of articles but really didn't know too much about it, and I told him so. Vince's next query nearly knocked me off my seat. "Are you interested in writing a book about the snakehead?" I immediately said yes, not wanting him to recant his implied invitation, which in my mind had already morphed into a signed book deal. Then I asked, "What, in particular, about snakeheads would the book cover?" The more Vince told me about the phenomenal media coverage the snakehead had been receiving and Smithsonian Books's desire to document the evolving summer of the snakehead, the more excited I became. Two weeks later, I submitted a formal book proposal. Two weeks after that I signed the book contract. And six months later I submitted the manuscript. All I can say is thank you, Vince. It was great fun writing this book. Anytime you (or any other publisher) have an idea for a book, just give me a call.

I was very fortunate that numerous individuals shared their time, thoughts, and perspectives with me. A special thanks is due to Dr. Walter Courtenay Jr. (a.k.a., "Dr. Snakehead"), with the U.S. Geological Survey's Center for Aquatic Resources Studies, who gave freely of his time and expertise, always with enthusiasm and good cheer. Similarly, Steve Early, with the Fisheries Service at the Maryland Department of Natural Resources (DNR), was extremely helpful in answering my many questions about the summer of the snakehead. Steve's colleagues at the DNR are also due heartfelt thanks. They include Angel L. Bolinger, Ron Klauda, Bob Lunsford, Heather Lynch, Eric Schwaab, Ann Schenk, Jill Stevenson, John Surrick, Edith Thompson, Beth Versak, and Lisa Warner. Not only did they provide me with valuable information, but they also offered examples of why dedicated government employees are one of our most precious resources. Other government workers whose assistance was critical to this project are Kari Duncan, Sharon Gross, Mike Slattery, and Julie Thompson, all with the U.S. Fish and Wildlife Service; and Paul Shafland, with the Florida Fish and Wildlife Conservation Commission.

A number of people generously shared their thoughts, their images, and in some cases, their music with me, helping to make the book more complete as well as visually attractive. They include Erin Berkshire; William Berkshire; Michael Cooke; David Cotton; Paul DiMauro; Stephanie Drummond and the Kirk, Mark & Lopez Morning Show on 98 Rock Baltimore; Joe Gillespie; David Goldin; Jean Francois Helias; Johnny Jensen; Christian Kanele of www.snakeheads.org; Steve Koorey; Chris Ramsey; Janice Saul; Charles Somerville; and Richard Thompson. Thank you.

Other very helpful people to whom I am indebted include Sue Bents, Peter Bergstrom, Don Boesch, Maureen Booth, Jude Brennan, Geoff Brown, Scott Burke, Christine Carlson, Raegan Carmona, Bill Davis, Lucy Erickson, George Franchois, Anita Huslin, Rachel Indek, Elizabeth Jackson, Don Kemp, Jennifer Klang, Michael Letourneau, Leon Liu, Paul Loiselle, Mark Lotwis, Elizabeth Low, Danny MacQuilliam, Kathy Mavrikakis, Leo Nico, Peter Ng; Todd Richards, Judy Smith, Mike Smith, Eric Smith, Hank Stuever, Mike Thomas, Candy Thomson, Susan Tobin, Jerry Trice II, Lavonda Walton, Jim Williams, and Jeremy Weiner.

While virtually everyone that I asked for help gave of their time and expertise freely, there were a couple of individuals who never responded to my entreaties, despite numerous attempts to gain their cooperation. They know who they are, and all I have to say to them is, may menacing snakeheads with very large teeth haunt your dreams.

My thanks also goes to the folks at Smithsonian Books, including Brian Barth, Donald Fehr, Kiki Forsythe, Matt Litts, Robert Poarch, and Nicole Sloan. Once again you have made publishing a book a pleasure.

Although I would rather write full time, a man's gotta eat, and the only way I was able to write this book while working a regular job was with the undying and unstinting support of my wife, Jennifer, daughter, Lily, and son, Harry. Jennifer, in particular, gave me the emotional and physical permission to cut down on my family time to pursue my infatuation with snakeheads. And Jennifer was not a jealous lover, although there were moments when she did have some choice words for the snakehead and me. Lily, five, and Harry, three, followed my progress with great interest. Lily was always visiting me in the basement with words of encouragement, such as, "Daddy, when are you going to get off the computer and let me play my computer games!" Harry thought the snakehead pictures were cool, but not as cool as his trucks. And the two of them loved the song, "Spawn of Snakehead," which was sent to me in CD-form by David Cotton, one half of the band BrainFang. After hearing the song for the first time, Lily and Harry made me play it six times over, while they sang and danced around the room. And that wasn't the last time they requested it. Whenever I needed a laugh while writing, all I had to do was recall the image of Lily and Harry jumping about singing their favorite refrain, "spawn of snakehead, get 'em outta here!"

Near the end of this project, I knew it was time to wrap up things quickly, and not just because my editor kept reminding me of the deadline in my contract. For the first time I can recall, I had a nightmare about what I was writing about. In it, I was typing at the computer when the right side of my desk was suddenly transformed into a swamp, and out crawled a northern snakehead, teeth bared. He didn't say anything, and I probably wouldn't have heard him if he had, because as soon as I saw him rise out of the murky waters I bolted from my desk and ran up the stairs. The last thing I remember about the dream was being worried that the snakehead, big and hungry, was following right behind. As soon as I awoke, I went downstairs to my computer, with a renewed determination to finish the book. While most of my attention was focused on the monitor, every once in a while I looked to my right, just in case.

Finally, I want to thank the northern snakehead, *Channa argus*. Without you there would have been no story. You da fish! Now, get on outta here.

PREFACE

Often the most unusual tales have humble beginnings. On a warm and muggy day in May 2002, two men went fishing at a small totally unremarkable pond in Crofton, Maryland, just a short drive from the nation's capital. One of them caught a fish that looked like nothing he'd ever seen. Before throwing it back, he snapped a few pictures and later shared them with state fisheries biologists. They too were puzzled, but after some sleuthing they identified the fish as a northern snakehead. It didn't belong in the wild in Crofton, or Maryland, or the United States for that matter. It was an alien, a potentially invasive species from Asia with sharp teeth, a predilection for dining ravenously on other fishes, a primitive lung, and apparently and most amazingly the ability to walk over land to a new body of water whenever the mood struck it. Should snakeheads establish themselves in Maryland, officials feared they could wreak havoc on the local ecosystem. In late June and early July, more northern snakeheads were caught in the pond. Their presence became a major event, covered internationally in newspapers and magazines, and on radio and television. With astonishing speed, the northern snakehead, variously labeled a "Frankenfish," "killer fish," "pit bull with fins," "Chinese thug fish," "X-Files fish," and the "fish from hell," became an indisputable media superstar. But the snakeheads' days were numbered; come September they were gone, done in with poison administered by the state of Maryland.

Coverage of the snakehead story ranged from serious and thoughtful to silly and sensational. At its base lay the persistently troubling issue of invasive species and their ability to harm the environment and the economy. But that story line alone, while perhaps good for an article or two could not sustain the media frenzy that ensued. No, this fish story had everything—shadowy origins, illegal activity, misinformation, exaggerations, epic battles between man and fish, the specter of ecological doom, earnest bureaucrats, wanted posters, bounties, late-night talk-show hosts, early-morning talk-show hosts, a blue ribbon-panel, poison, hilarious satire, snakehead entrepreneurs, purported links to terrorism, theme songs, culinary concoctions, medicinal connections, and most importantly a fish that pound for pound surely ranks as one of the most vilified creatures on earth. Just as the summer of 2001 was called the summer of the shark, the summer of 2002 became the summer of the snakehead. This is the story of that fascinating fish and how it captured our imagination and took us all on a wild ride.

ONE

MYSTERY FISH

On Tuesday May 14, 2002, Paul DiMauro and his buddy, James Griffith, got off early in the afternoon from their construction jobs in Washington, D.C. It was sunny and warm with the mercury in the mid-eighties. Rather than head for home the two decided to go fishing. They drove twenty miles east to a small pond in Crofton, Maryland, tucked behind a strip mall just off Route 3. DiMauro had heard about the pond three years ago, and he and Griffith had been there many times. They parked in the small lot behind the bank, grabbed their fishing gear, and walked a short distance down a steep slope to the edge of the water.

The pond is unimpressive. Covering four acres and averaging only four to five feet in depth, it was created in the early 1960s when the area was excavated to provide sand and gravel for local con-

Taken in the fall, a view across the surface of the pond where Paul DiMauro and James Griffith went fishing on May 14, 2002. Courtesy Eric Jay Dolin.

struction projects. The shallow pit that was left behind filled with groundwater and has remained so ever since. Over time the pond became a destination for local anglers in search of largemouth bass, black crappies, chain pickerel, and yellow perch. The pond was owned by the MacQuilliam Organization, a development and realty company that also owned and managed the adjacent strip mall. Although the pond was officially off limits to fishing and its perimeter was dotted with no trespassing signs, the rules were not enforced. Years of anglers circling the pond to find a good spot had left a well-worn trail a few feet from the water.

DiMauro and Griffith walked along the trail a third of the way around the pond to the clearing where they usually fished. The pond's surface was covered in green. Vast mats of aquatic vegetation, including white waterlily, slender pondweed, bladderwort, and duckweed, competed for space with pinched expanses of open water. Beneath the surface, the vegetation was just as dense. Fishing in this watery jungle required special lures that wouldn't get tangled in the weeds. That's why DiMauro was using his Moss Mouse, a lure manufactured, appropriately enough, by a company called Snag Proof. The Moss Mouse looks like its namesake, complete with a long, skinny tail, ears and whiskers, and two hooks that roll up around its back. According to the company's literature, this lure is "perfect for fishing in the slop where the big ones [bass and pike] hide and feed."

On his first cast, DiMauro caught a fourteen-inch bass, reeled it in, and threw it back. Soon after the lure hit the water a second time, DiMauro saw something moving rapidly toward the mouse,

Part of the Route 3 Center strip mall. The pond where the northern snakeheads were found is behind the portion of the mall at the right of the picture. Courtesy Eric Jay Dolin.

leaving a wake in its path. "If you've ever seen a beaver in the water," said DiMauro, "it looked like that." Whatever it was jumped out of the water, missing the lure by a couple of inches, and then disappeared. "On the next cast," DiMauro recalled, "I hit the same spot and the fish came from maybe thirty feet away and you could see the lilies actually moving where it was coming through. And I stopped my mouse and it ate it. It didn't fight real well. It went down and I took a little drag."

DiMauro reeled in the fish, and by the time he pulled it ashore it was covered with weeds. He figured it was a bass, but after brushing the weeds aside, both he and Griffith knew it wasn't. It was about eighteen inches long, with fins running most of the length on its top and bottom, and dark brown bars and splotches on its side. They stared at it for a while wondering what it was. Then DiMauro bent down and pushed open the fish's mouth only to find a formidable set of teeth, the sight of which caused him to jump back. The fish's jaws then clamped tight around the lure, according to DiMauro, "almost like a pit bull." He thought about keeping the fish because it was so unusual, but that didn't square with his catch-and-release philosophy, which he said was based on the idea that fishes "have their own little spirit. Who am I to take that from them? I'm there for the sport, and I figure that you can come back later and catch them again."

DiMauro had another reason for wanting to release the fish— it looked pregnant. He remembers thinking, "I didn't want to be the one to kill the fish and all those little babies." At the same time, he wanted to document the catch so he could identify it later. Fortunately, either he or Griffith always brought a camera along when fishing, in case they caught something worth recording on film, like the twenty-four-inch bass DiMauro had once pulled from the pond. Griffith pulled out his camera and snapped three pic-

As the sun sets behind
him, Paul DiMauro
holds up the northern
snakehead he caught
and released. Courtesy
Paul DiMauro and
James Griffith.

tures; one with the fish on its side on the grass, and two with
DiMauro holding it aloft dangling at the end of the line. Now
came the tricky part, getting the lure out of the fish's mouth.
Throughout the photo shoot, the fish's jaws had remained shut
tight. Remembering the teeth, DiMauro didn't want to get his fin-
gers too close. Instead, he used pliers to wrench the lure free, and
then he slipped the fish back into the pond, where it quickly disappeared into the murky, weedy water.

To add an extra element to their fishing trips, DiMauro and
Griffith competed to see who could catch the biggest fish, the most
fish, or the most different types of fish. Although DiMauro called
it quits for the day, Griffith, not wanting to be bested by his friend,

continued to cast his line into the pond, but he came up empty. Even if Griffith had caught five sizeable bass and a few pickerel, DiMauro still would have emerged victorious. As DiMauro later deadpanned, "I think I got him with species."

DiMauro wanted to develop the pictures immediately so he could show them to people and hopefully identify the fish. Griffith also wanted to develop the film, but not before he had finished the roll, which still had a ways to go. DiMauro offered to buy the camera but Griffith wouldn't sell. In the meantime, the two of them searched the Internet for images that looked like the fish. Having no luck with that approach, DiMauro called the Maryland Department of Natural Resources (DNR) and was connected to Bob Lunsford, a biologist in the Fisheries Service. DiMauro described the fish and Lunsford said it might be a bowfin, a freshwater species commonly found in Maryland. Armed with this information, DiMauro went back to the Internet and searched for pictures of bowfins. Although there were similarities in terms of shape and coloration, DiMauro was sure that his fish wasn't a bowfin.

Finally, in early June Griffith finished the role of film and brought it in for developing. As soon as the fish pictures came back, DiMauro took them to a tackle store near his house in Edgewater, Maryland. A guy in the store said it looked like a snakeheaded eel. DiMauro laughed and told the guy he was out of his mind. DiMauro next showed the pictures to a couple of his buddies, but they were stumped as well. Then, on the morning of Friday, June 14, a month after he had caught the fish, DiMauro visited the DNR. He was directed to Beth Versak, a Fisheries Service biologist, who along with a few of her colleagues studied the pictures. It clearly wasn't a bowfin, or any other native species they had ever seen, but what was it? Some of them thought it might be a discard from someone's aquarium, a common route by which exotic species make it into local waterways. Versak and her colleagues tried to match DiMauro's fish with images in reference materials to no avail. As DiMauro recalls, "We were in there forever looking at the picture and looking at books." Before DiMauro left, Versak scanned his three pictures into her computer and labeled them "mysteryfish" 1, 2, and 3. That way she could send the images to other fish experts for their opinions.

Soon after DiMauro left, Versak remembered that her colleague, Lisa Warner, had not only worked in pet stores before coming to the DNR, but also had at one time twenty-one aquariums in her bedroom. If the fish was an aquarium discard, perhaps Lisa would recognize it. It was Lisa's day off, so Versak sent an e-mail, with the pictures as attachments, to Lisa's home computer. About the same time, another fisheries employee, Ann Schenk, sent an e-mail to a colleague that captured the current thinking on the mysteryfish. "We've looked at the pictures here," wrote Schenk, "and decided we agree with Mr. DiMauro that the fins aren't right for a bowfin. Jay thinks it may be a burbot. Everyone thinks that it is probably a discard fish, maybe from a fisherman's out-of-state catch or an aquarium dump. In any case, can you name that fish in 3 pictures?"

When Warner looked at the pictures she thought it was a snakehead, but didn't know which species. She had seen different types of snakeheads in the pet stores where she worked, but never one that looked exactly like this. Armed with this piece of information, Versak went to the Internet to one of the best sites for exotic or nonnative species, the U.S. Geological Survey's database on nonindigenous aquatic species. There she soon landed on an information page for *Channa micropeltes*, also known as the giant snakehead. The picture didn't exactly match the fish DiMauro had landed, but it was clearly

This picture of the fish caught by Paul DiMauro was the one that DNR Fisheries Service biologist Beth Versak scanned into the computer as "mysteryfish1." Courtesy Paul DiMauro and James Griffith.

within the same genetic ballpark and quite likely of the same genus, although not the same species. The write up for the giant snakehead stated that its native range was Southeast Asia and that individual specimens had been found in Maine, Massachusetts, and Rhode Island, all of which were likely the result of people releasing the fish into the wild once they got too big for their aquaria, something that could easily happen given that this species grew to more than three feet in length and over forty pounds. When Versak scrolled to the bottom of the page she found a clickable link to its author, Leo Nico, a research biologist at the U.S. Geological Survey's Center for Aquatic Resources Studies, located in Gainesville, Florida. Versak sent Nico an e-mail with the scanned image of the fish lying on its side ("mysteryfish1"), and asked him if he knew what it was.

Versak had come to the right place, but Nico felt he wasn't the best person to answer the question, so on June 17 he forwarded the request to two of his colleagues, Jim Williams, an aquatic biologist, and Walter Courtenay Jr., an ichthyologist. As soon as Williams saw the picture, he sent an e-mail to Nico and Courtenay saying, "*Channa argus* all the way!!"—in other words, the northern snakehead. Courtenay concurred and offered some advice. "Leo," he wrote, "see if you can get the other two photos, any information as to where and when it was caught, and recommend that MD Dept. of Nat. Res. get out to that pond and shock the hell out of it." By shocking, Courtenay meant using either backpack- or boat-based equipment that sent electricity through the water to temporarily stun the fish in the area and cause them to float to the surface, where they could be collected and inspected by biologists. If there were snakeheads in the pond, a thorough shocking would likely uncover them.

Courtenay's concern about the discovery of a northern snakehead in a Maryland pond was born of experience that he relayed in an e-mail to Versak on June 18, which read, in part,

> Leo Nico asked me to reply to your message of 6/14. I am in charge of preparing a risk assessment analysis on snakeheads on behalf of USGS for the U.S. Fish and Wildlife Service, and I've learned a lot about this family of fishes since starting this project last September.
>
> The fish in the photograph you sent to Leo is the northern snakehead, *Channa argus*, a species native from the Yangtze River of China northward to the Amur River basin on the China/Russia border. It has a temperature range of 0–30° C and can live under ice. Like other snakeheads, it is a lie-in-wait thrust predator, preying mostly on other fishes. Adult northern snakeheads can reach a length of almost one meter. This species is the most available snakehead being sold in ethnic (typically Asian) food markets that sell live fishes, and has been showing up in open waters in the past couple of years. Two were caught by hook and line in the St. Johns River, Florida, between Sanford and Titusville in 2000, and

another was taken by electrofishing in a pond in central Massachusetts last October. We believe another was captured by electrofishing from a reservoir in southern California in 2000, but California Fish and Game personnel did not save the specimen. Of the 28 recognized species of snakeheads, this species has the capability to become established throughout most of the U.S. and perhaps into southern Canada.

. . . It would be most worthwhile if Maryland Department of Natural Resources would electrofish that pond to see if there are more snakeheads present. Frankly, it wouldn't surprise me that they might be reproducing there, although I would hope the individual that was caught is the only snakehead in that pond.

The risk assessment Courtenay referred to was designed to help the U.S. Fish and Wildlife Service determine whether snakeheads, all twenty-eight species, should be placed on the federal list of injurious wildlife and thereby be barred from importation into the country and transport between states. For many years biologists, especially ichthyologists, had been concerned about the introduction of snakeheads into American waters. In their native ranges, primarily in Southeast Asia, snakeheads are an integral part of freshwater ecosystems, and many species are prized as a sport fish and for eating, with the most sought-after species being raised on fish farms to supplement natural populations. In some areas, freshly killed snakeheads served on their own or in soup are considered to have medicinal properties. There are even reports of snakehead extracts being applied after surgery to reduce scarring. But outside of their native ranges, snakeheads are often viewed with alarm. As aggressive and large predators with a preference for other fish, snakeheads introduced into new environments could potentially rearrange food chains and negatively impact populations of valuable recreational and food species.

Snakeheads get their name from their shape, which is elongated and in some species tends toward the tubular; from the large scales on their head, which look similar to the scales present on the heads of snakes; and from the location of their eyes on the sides near the top and forward part of the head. Although the twenty-eight species of snakeheads share many characteristics, they also vary greatly. For example, while most of the species are found in Southeast Asia, three live in tropical Africa. Snakeheads range in size from barely seven inches to nearly six feet. Some are cultured for sale as food both within their native countries and overseas in food markets, where they are often sold live. Only a few of the snakehead species have made their way into the aquarium trade, those being mainly the smaller ones that are brightly colored, and juveniles of some of the larger species, which are also quite attractive. While popular with some fish hobbyists, snakeheads are an unusual pet. They are very aggressive, rarely play well with other fishes, have large appetites that can be expensive to satisfy, and the brightly colored juveniles of larger species tend not only to become much less attractive as they age, but they also can quickly outgrow their aquaria. As a result there have been instances in which fish hobbyists, initially enamored with their snakeheads, have lost interest over time and released them into the wild. *The Encyclopedia of Tropical Fishes* offers would-be owners of the Chinese snakehead, *Channa asiatica*, clear advice. "The young can grow with amazing rapidity," the entry reads, "and the only problem encountered is that of keeping their terrific appetites satisfied. If you like your fish big and nasty, this is the fish for you!"

The northern snakehead is one of a small number of snakehead species that have established breeding populations outside of their native range. In the early 1920s, northern snakeheads were inten-

Channa orientalis, one of the smaller species of snakeheads that can be found in the aquarium trade. Courtesy Johnny Jensen.

tionally introduced to Japan, and have since expanded their range to cover most of the country's prefectures. "Japan was the first country in the world," said Courtenay, "to complain about the introduction of the northern impacting native species." In the early 1960s, northern snakeheads were accidentally introduced into the former Soviet Republics of Kazakhstan, Uzbekistan, and Turkmenistan, coming as hitchhikers in shipments of carp from Asia. According to Courtenay, when the northern snakehead "hit the former Soviet Republics, it just took off like a scalded dog. It expanded its range dramatically and still is." While northern snakeheads are mainly viewed as a nuisance fish in Japan, in the former Soviet Republics they have become a popular sport and eating fish.

Even before the formal risk assessment of snakeheads had begun, more than a dozen states had banned the possession of live snakeheads, with Texas being the first way back in the 1960s. The main impetus behind the assessment, however, was not state actions, but the discovery, in March 2001, of a breeding population of bulls-eye snakeheads (*Channa marulius*) in Florida. This wasn't the first case of breeding snakeheads in the United States; Hawaii lays claim to that distinction. The blotched snakehead (*Channa maculata*) was intentionally introduced in the late 1800s into a small number of reservoirs on Oahu, Hawaii, and has been breeding there ever since. And the chevron snakehead (*Channa striata*) was introduced on Oahu in the early 1990s, where it is being raised as a food fish. While breeding populations of snakeheads were welcomed in Hawaii, a state that has no indigenous freshwater species of fish, the prospect of breeding populations of snakeheads in the continental United States, where there are huge numbers of indigenous fresh-water fish species, is another story entirely.

The discovery in Florida greatly concerned Williams and he shared his concern with his peers on the Risk Assessment and Management Committee of the Aquatic Nuisance Species Task Force, an intergovernmental organization co-chaired by the U.S. Fish and Wildlife Service and the National Oceanic and Atmospheric Administration that is dedicated to preventing and controlling aquatic nuisance species. The committee felt that the potential threat

Drawing of northern snakehead by artist Susan Trammell. Courtesy U.S. Geological Survey.

This is the image of the bullseye snakehead (*Channa marulius*) that appeared in the March 22, 2001, Florida Fish and Wildlife Conservation Commission press release letting the public know that Florida had a new, reproducing exotic fish in state waters. In the press release, Paul Shafland, director of the Non-Native Fish Research Laboratory with the Florida Fish and Wildlife Conservation Commission was quoted as saying, "We hope the public doesn't overreact as was the case with the media-inspired hysteria regarding the appearance of the walking catfish back in the 1960s and even the swamp eel a few years ago. The presence of this species immediately places it into the unwelcome and undesirable category, but more importantly it clearly demonstrates that illegal introductions of exotic fishes continue in Florida. In fact, this is the sixth exotic fish that has been documented reproducing in Florida waters since 1992." Courtesy Florida Fish and Wildlife Conservation Commission.

posed by all twenty-eight snakehead species merited a formal risk assessment. The U.S. Fish and Wildlife Service agreed, and contracted with Williams and the U.S. Geological Survey to perform the assessment. Williams, in turn, coaxed Courtenay out of retirement to head up the project. Courtenay's bona fides included more than thirty years as a professor of zoology at the Florida Atlantic University in Boca Raton, Florida, where he specialized in ichthyology and the management of nonindigenous fish species. For someone with this specialization, Florida was the place to be. As Courtenay and two of his colleagues wrote in a 1970 paper on exotic fishes and other aquatic organisms, "One of the unique natural North American communities, that of tropical Florida, has become a biological cesspool of introduced life." If you ranked the states based on the number of nonindigenous species of all forms of wildlife, not just fish, Florida would likely be at the top of the list, or perhaps runner-up to Hawaii.

Nonindigenous or introduced species are neither inherently bad nor good. It all depends on their impact once they become established outside of their native ranges, and more importantly on how people view such impacts. For example, an introduced species of fish might set off a cascade of events, such as outcompeting a native species of fish and causing its local extinction or significantly altering the food chain by eating large quantities of aquatic organisms. This local ecosystem, left to its own devices, will absorb the new species and continue to evolve, albeit perhaps changed in fundamental ways. It is only with the overlay of human perspective that the changes in ecosystems wrought by introduced species gain a subjective and normative component. Labeling the impacts of introduced species as good or bad, positive or negative, welcome or unwelcome, is something that only human beings can do. Similarly, the decision about whether anything should be done to eradicate or control the spread of an introduced species is a purely human choice.

Before human beings wandered the earth, species moved from places where they were to places where they weren't. But the introduction of species was usually a slow process, a gradual creep across the landscape, often impeded by natural barriers such as mountains and water. With the advent of humans and their subsequent migrations, the process sped up. Traveling humans often brought with them, either wittingly or unwittingly, biological pieces of the areas they had left behind. And some of those pieces established themselves in the new lands. The history of the United States, from the time of the first colonists up through the present, offers innumerable examples of species introduction aided by humans. For the most part, such introductions have been beneficial. Honeybees, peaches, oranges, soybeans, tomatoes, domestic cattle, chickens, wheat, and rice are all introduced species, and it would be hard to imagine modern life without them.

But some introduced species have caused considerable damage. An Office of Technology Assessment report on the subject found that "approximately 15 percent of the NIS [nonindigenous species] in the United States cause severe harm," and that such species affect a range of national interests, including agriculture, industry, human heath, and the environment. The same report concluded that between 1906 and 1991, just seventy-nine nonindigenous species caused documented losses totaling $97 billion. A more recent study by David Pimental, et al., at Cornell University, concluded that nonindigenous species cause "major environmental damages and losses adding up to more than $138 billion per year."

Harmful nonindigenous species are often referred to as invasive species, the term that is used here. The formal definition of this term is found in Executive Order 13112, which established the National Invasive Species Council, and was signed by President William J. Clinton on February 3, 1999. According to that order, "'Invasive species' means an alien [nonnative] species whose introduction does or is likely to cause economic or environmental harm or harm to human health." There is a huge and fascinating literature on invasive species, covering how they get introduced, what they have done in their new locations, and what humans have done to manage or, at least, cope with them. The goal here is not to offer a cross-section of that literature, or even a significant slice. Rather, what follows is a summary of highlights and, hopefully, enough information to help place the snakehead in a broader context. (For those readers interested in learning more, the bibliography contains a list of excellent resources to get started.)

The avenues or "pathways" by which invasive species arrive in the United States are quite diverse. Some are brought here with the best of intentions only to pose problems later on. For example, in 1877, the U.S. government imported carp from Europe with high hopes that they would become a favorite food and sport fish. According to George Laycock's account, in *The Alien Animals*, so popular were the carp that in subsequent years politicians fought hard to make sure that their constituents got a fair share of this "wonder fish." In 1883, the distribution of 260,000 carp was so widespread that all but three of the 301 congressional districts received an allotment. People marveled at the carp's appetite and growth rate. One happy constituent in Texas wrote a letter to the U.S. Fish Commission, in which he crowed, "My carp . . . are doing well. They grow like China pigs when fed with plenty of buttermilk." The fish loved their new homes well enough, and reproduced and spread rapidly, but as they did their welcome quickly wore out. It turned out that Americans didn't much care for the taste of carp, nor were they seen as worthy game fish. And the carp's eating habits tended to muddy up the waters, reduce visibility, and, in general, degrade valuable habitat important for sustaining native game fish and waterfowl. By the turn of the century, the same people who had been clamoring for carp when they first became available were demanding that action be taken to control or get rid of the fish. But it was too late. The carp were here to stay, and have remained with us ever since, notwithstanding numerous and often quite expensive efforts to get rid of them.

Another famous invasive invitee is kudzu, often called the "vine that ate the South." It first made its appearance on U.S. soil in 1876 at the Japanese Bazaar at the United States Centennial Exposition in Philadelphia. Visitors were beguiled by its beauty and astounded at its rate of growth, which was so prodigious— up to a half inch an hour—that one could literally watch it grow day after day; and, in fact many repeat visitors did just that. When the exposition ended, the Japanese left their kudzu behind and it was soon being promoted as an ornamental and a forage crop. For many years, it was not considered a problem species, although its propensity to drape itself over any stationary object, dead or alive, including houses, did alarm some. During the 1930s and 1940s the government strongly encouraged farmers to plant kudzu as a way of stemming erosion, a task that the plant performed exceptionally well. But by mid-century, whatever benefits kudzu may have bestowed were greatly outweighed by its negatives. Kudzu outcompetes virtually all other plants in its path, covering them over in an almost impenetrable armor of stems and leaves, which kills the plants by cutting them off from the sun. Kudzu can also kill by girdling woody plants and by breaking branches or uprooting trees it has covered as a result of the vine's great weight. Worse, kudzu, which has a tap root that can reach seven inches in diameter and extend nine feet into the ground, is extremely difficult to control, much less completely eliminate from an area. The plant's unsavory fame led poet James Dickey to write a poem titled "Kudzu," a snippet of which reads,

Japan invades. Far Eastern vines
  Run from the clay banks they are

Kudzu enveloping the edge of a forest in Georgia. Courtesy George
Gentry and the U.S. Fish and Wildlife Service.

Supposed to keep from eroding,
Up telephone poles,
Which rear, half out of leafage,
As though they would shriek.

According to Georgia legend, Dickey wrote, "You must close your
windows at night to keep it out of the house." Today, kudzu covers
an estimated 7 million acres in the southeast and ranges as far West
as Oklahoma and north to Connecticut. And it's still spreading, day
by day, often despite massive efforts to keep it in check.

Many invasive species sneak into this country unseen, as freeload-
ers. The zebra mussel, a native of Russia, is the most famous or, more
accurately, infamous example of this. It arrived in the Great Lakes
Region in the ballast water on a ship during the mid to late 1980s, and
rapidly colonized and spread to all the Great Lakes, and beyond into
the Mississippi, Ohio, Hudson, and Tennessee river basins. The mus-

sels have a phenomenally high reproductive rate and they attach themselves to stationary and moving objects, both animal and human-made, in incredibly thick colonies, some of which have densities of over 1 million individuals per square meter. The mussels have fouled boats and clogged intake pipes for drinking water supplies, power plants, and manufacturing facilities. Zebra mussels are also very efficient filter feeders and, given their huge numbers, through their combined feeding they can strip the water clean of the phytoplankton and zooplankton that are critical to the survival of other organisms. Zebra mussel control expenditures are estimated to be in the hundreds of millions, if not billions of dollars annually, and as the species spreads farther and farther across the country those costs will surely rise.

There are invasive species that are brought into the country on purpose and in confined conditions, but then escape into the wild. The poster species for this type of introduction is the gypsy moth caterpillar. In 1868, Ettiene Leopold Trouvelot, an astronomer and amateur lepidopterist, living in Medford, Massachusetts, imported European gypsy moth eggs for use in an experiment. According to Kim Todd's excellent account of this episode, in her book, *Tinkering with Eden*, Trouvelot hoped that by breeding the gypsy moths with local species, the new hybrid "could jump-start the silk industry in the United States and boost his own fortunes as well." That summer, possibly as a result of a storm knocking over the cage where they were housed, a few of the gypsy moth caterpillars escaped, and almost immediately, no doubt, started eating leaves on the trees close to Trouvelot's house. The caterpillars and their progeny prospered, much to the dismay of local residents, who, in the decades to follow, complained bitterly about the destruction wrought by these small, furry eating machines. In 1882, for example, a Medford woman wrote, "the caterpillars were over everything in our yard and stripped all our fruit trees." A few years later, another resident observed that, the caterpillars "were so thick on the trees that they were stuck together like macaroni." The Commonwealth of Massachusetts and the federal government launched an all-out assault on the caterpillars around the turn of the century, but they were not victorious. Since that time, gypsy moth caterpillars have become one of the worst forest pests there is, defoliating millions of acres and spreading throughout the northeastern United States and beyond, down to North Carolina and west to Michigan and Ohio, with reported pockets of infestation in some Pacific Coast states. Management efforts aimed at controlling the caterpillars have been both extensive and expensive.

Some species that are imported to battle invasive species become invasive species themselves. One of the best examples of so-called "counterpests" gone awry is the establishment of the rosy wolf snail in Hawaii. In 1958, state officials imported these snails to control the rapidly expanding population of the giant African snail. Reaching lengths of eight inches and weights of up to a pound, the giant African snail lives up to its name. According to Laycock, this large mollusk first landed on Hawaii's shores in 1936, courtesy of a young woman who brought two specimens back from a trip to Taiwan, thinking that the snail's pretty markings would add to the beauty of her garden. From that point forward the rapidly reproducing giant African snail ate its way through local crops, becoming a major agricultural pest. It was thought that the smaller but highly predaceous rosy wolf snail would soon have the invasive giant African snails on the run, but instead of targeting the intended victims, the rosy wolf snail began feasting on native snails. In short order, the rosy wolf snail ranked as an invasive species that was as bad, if not worse than the giant African snail it was sent to conquer. The rosy wolf snail's predatory preferences have contributed to the extinction of many native snails.

Profiling invasive species becomes more complicated when one takes into account the impact of location and human perspective. One person's invasive species can be another person's idea of a valuable addition to the local flora or fauna. For example, purple loosestrife, first introduced from Europe in the early 1800s, is a beautiful plant, especially in bloom, and is regarded as such by many who use it as an accent in their gardens. However, that same plant is considered one of the worst invasive species there is in the wild, where it is a serious wetland weed that forms dense mats that crowd out native grasses and flowers, creating a degraded habitat for waterfowl and other wildlife. Similarly, hydrilla, a fast-growing aquatic perennial herb that was introduced into American waterways in the middle of twentieth century as a discard from the aquarium trade, is viewed favorably by some anglers because it creates habitat conducive to bass. But to most people the plant is seen as a problem, disrupting boating, swimming, and other waterborne activities. And like purple loosestrife, hydrilla becomes so dense that it outcompetes many native plant species, often by cutting off their access to light.

Not all of the invasive species in the United States were imported into the country. Sometimes when a species from one part of the country is introduced to another part of the country it becomes invasive. For example, species of mosquitofish (*Gambusia*) have been transplanted throughout much of the country in an effort, not surprisingly, to control mosquito populations. While *Gambusia*'s mosquito control abilities have been seriously questioned in the literature, the fish's ability to negatively impact other species of native fish has not. In some areas of the southwest, where a species of *Gambusia* was introduced, its aggressive and predaceous ways have caused a dramatic decline in the populations of other small native fishes, many of which are on the U.S. endangered species list.

To the group of invasive species mentioned above could be added hundreds of others. Some are famous by dint of reputation and the amount of media coverage they have received, including the Africanized honeybee (killer bee), the fire ant, and the West Nile virus. Others, while not as widely known are also very damaging and despised by those who have to deal with their onslaught on a daily basis; for example, salt cedar, leafy splurge, garlic mustard, and round gobies. The types of damage wrought by invasive species are almost as diverse as the species themselves, and broadly include parasitism, defoliation, disease, death, and the rearrangement of food chains and other established biotic relationships within ecosystems. According to one estimate, up to 46 percent of the species on the endangered species list have been negatively affected by invasive species. And invasive species are not only a problem in the United States. Most if not all of the countries in the world are negatively impacted by such species.

If invasive species are such a problem in the United States, then one could reasonably ask why not just keep them out in the first place? This would be a great solution, but part of the problem is that it is not easy to identify which new species will become invasive when they are taken away from their natural habitat and placed in an alien one. Although scientists are working on predictive models that could supply such information, these models are very rudimentary and not much practical use and may never be. Scientists who have studied ecosystems for decades often have difficulty accurately predicting the outcomes of mild perturbations to the environment. Asking them to predict what might happen if a new species arrives on the scene moves the difficulty meter up a few notches. Thus, targeting invasive species in advance remains a tricky proposition.

Of course, another alternative is to ban the importation of all nonnative species, not just those that are potentially invasive. Theoretically that might be a foolproof policy for keeping invasive species out of the country, but it is one that is so far removed from the current policy regime as to be almost inconceivable. Even if it were implemented, given the various routes by which nonnative species enter the country, stanching their flow would be very difficult, if not impossible. And a policy of excluding nonnative species would not only keep out the potentially invasive species, but also potentially beneficial ones.

If barring all invasive species from entering the country is not an option, what about eradicating them as soon as they do invade, thereby preventing them from becoming established? This is clearly the preferred alternative, but it is often difficult to implement for a number of reasons. First, invasive species often don't become a problem, or at least become a known problem, until they are already reproducing and firmly established in a particular area. This could take years and by then eradication is often no longer possible. Even if a potentially invasive species is discovered soon after it is introduced, and is limited to a small geographic area, it still might be difficult to eradicate, because to succeed one needs to be sure that all the individuals are captured or killed. If one pair capable of breeding escapes, the species could make a comeback. Once eradication is no longer a viable option, management of the invasive species is the next line of defense. There are many instances in which such activities have worked, but effective control is also often very expensive and time consuming. And as the examples above attest, even when management measures are employed, they might have limited success in halting the species' spread.

Maryland has long been coping with a wide array of invasive species, including mute swans, nutria, water chestnut, green crabs, rapa whelks, purple loosestrife, and phragmites. Nutria, for example, a large rodent originally from South America, has been reproducing prolifically in the Chesapeake Bay area for decades, displacing native muskrats and destroying thousands of acres of marshland vegetation. Nutria is particularly destructive because it eats the roots of plants, rather than leaves. Because the roots hold the soil in place, once they are gone the marshlands themselves simply wash away. There are ongoing and extensive efforts to manage and, possibly, eradicate nutria in the region. A major part of this offensive revolves around the work of a team of fourteen full-time trappers, who kill huge numbers of nutrias yet still cannot keep up with burgeoning population.

Given the long and troubling history of invasive species in the United States, and more locally in Maryland, it is not surprising that when the biologists at the DNR heard from Courtenay that there was a nonindigenous and potentially invasive species of fish swimming in the pond just off of Route 3 that not only grew to impressive size but also ate other fish and could survive in Maryland waters, they immediately began assessing the nature of the potential threat and how to address it. Courtenay's e-mail was sent at 11:19 A.M. on June 18, and opened shortly thereafter by Versak. Soon, word of the fish spread via e-mail to an ever-widening circle of biologists inside and outside of the DNR.

Versak sent the e-mail to Schenk and a few others, noting that "Lisa was right, it is a snakehead. The USGS guys strongly suggest shocking that pond. Any ideas on that? I'll call the guy who caught it and let him know. Pretty cool." Schenk, in turn, forwarded Courtenay's message to others. After briefly recounting the events relating to DiMauro catching the fish and trying to get it identified, Schenk ended her note saying, "Unfortunately for the other fish in the pond, he put it back." One of the people on Schenk's list was Ron Klauda, another biologist at the DNR, who forwarded the news to Lunsford. Klauda asked Lunsford if the DNR had the authority to apply rotenone, a widely used piscicide, or fish poison, to the pond. Rotenone would likely kill all the fish in the pond and, at the same time, tell the DNR whether there were other snakeheads lurking there. "Might be able to snuff out a potential problem," Klauda wrote, "before it spreads."

Lunsford responded first thing in the morning on June 19 as follows.

> Believe it or not this guy [DiMauro] called me and tried to describe this fish over the phone. I could not (from his verbal description) have ever come up with a snakehead. It's not a matter of do we have the authority at this point, it's a matter of permission from the landowner and do we really want to expose the Little Patuxent to a possible rotenone kill? I can bring a crew in to shock IF there is a launch/retrieve site or IF there is no outlet we could look at rotenone and a total kill. Let me know your recommendations on this one.

By "Little Patuxent" Lunsford meant the Little Patuxent River, which flowed by less than seventy-five yards from the edge of the pond. Lunsford's e-mail not only went to Klauda, but also Eric Schwaab and Jill Stevenson, the director and deputy director, respectively, of the DNR's Fisheries Service, as well as Steve Early, Lunsford's boss and program director for Restoration and Enhancement. Early was on vacation at the time and Lunsford was acting in his stead. Thus, at this point, many of the key people within the Fisheries Service knew about the snakehead in Crofton and were already considering response options. Less than two hours later, the net of communication grew wider. Klauda e-mailed Edith Thompson, an exotic/invasive species biologist with the DNR's Wildlife and Heritage Service.

> Are you aware of this recent discovery? What do you think DNR Fisheries Service folks should be encouraged to do? See Walt Courtenay's comments below. He thinks we should find out how many snakeheads are in this gravel pit pond and then try to get rid of them before they escape into the Patuxent River system, if they haven't done so already. I haven't seen the pond yet so it's not clear what our eradication options might be, if any. However, before I get back to Bob Lunsford with some recommendations, I'd like to hear what the Bay Program's Invasive Species Workgroup has to say. Bob thinks that the fish was probably introduced by someone who purchased it at an aquarium shop and it outgrew its tank. It's possible that the fish that was caught (and returned to the pond) is the only one there. On the other [hand], there may be more in the pond. And, if the pond is periodically inundated during high river flow periods, an escape route to the Patuxent is possible. I await your comments.

Just after noon that same day, Thompson forwarded Klauda's e-mail to the members of the Invasive Species Working Group, asking them what they thought, adding that "we can go ahead and shock the pond to assess the extent of the problem and maybe put a stop to it before it gets into the system." One of the recipients of that e-mail was Julie Thompson, a biologist with the Chesapeake Bay Field Office of the U.S. Fish and Wildlife Service. She, in turn, forwarded the e-mail to her boss, Mike Slattery, the Coastal Program Leader for the field office. Slattery, a biologist with considerable background in dealing with aquatic invasive species, was quite familiar with snakeheads, if only by reputation. He was well aware of the snakehead risk assessment that was underway and had attended various professional meetings where the potentially damaging impact of snakehead introductions was discussed. When he read the series of communications from the DNR, his response, in the form of an e-mail sent just before 3 P.M. on June 19, was characteristically intense and clear. The recipient list included a raft of DNR employees, both ones that had and had not been involved in the electronic chain of communication thus far. That e-mail read, in part, as follows.

Indulge me and allow me to reconvene the Ecosystem Council for this one. Here's my advice. . . . .

If the pond is configured so that comprehensive electroshocking is feasible, with 100% assurance that all fish in it will be observed (doubtful), then shock it this evening and see if there are any more snakeheads, and KILL THEM IMMEDIATELY and keep looking for more in the area. If 100% coverage is not possible, then get an emergency public meeting together with local angling clubs and interested citizens for this weekend, advertise it loudly and broadly, make sure that Bill Burton and Candy Thomson come, try to get TV press there, and explain that:

1) you are the qualified scientists who have determined that there is an unacceptable risk to Patuxent recreational fisheries;

2) you are the appropriate agency to make this decision;

3) it would be irresponsible of you as scientists, fisheries managers and public servants not to take appropriate action;

4) you would be derelict in your responsibility to the citizens of Maryland and the Chesapeake Bay watershed if you did not rotenone the pond and all like it in close proximity, followed by a robust stocking of largemouths and bluegills by DNR;

5) it would not be necessary to do this except for the irresponsible actions of whoever released it;

6) it is your duty to accomplish the task on Monday.

Make sure you have lots of ugly, fierce-looking pictures of snakeheads. Be very empathetic if people express opposition, but be firm that it must be done . . . . and CONVEY A GENUINE SENSE OF URGENCY AND VILLIFY SNAKEHEADS!!

Try to get Maryland B.A.S.S., T.U. and/or Friends of the Patuxent to volunteer to assist in the rotenone deployment.

This is a chance to portray yourselves as an agency that is capable, decisive, responsive and right on top of things. You can turn this into an opportunity. If you rotenone and get more snakeheads, you've "done the necessary and responsible thing" and can "look forward to restarting the recreational fishery in this pond." If you rotenone and no other snakeheads turn up [you can say,] "this is exactly what we had hoped to learn. The angler's and environmentalists of Maryland should be very pleased and relieved with this result. In this instance drastic measures were required, and that's unfortunate in the very short term, but the prospect of gambling on a snakehead population possibly becoming established in an open river system with a natural fish community as important to the Chesapeake Bay as the Patuxent's alarms the environmentalist in me greatly. We're just glad that, very fortunately, this issue could be put to rest for now without inflicting any long-term impact on the recreational fishery that existed here. We just couldn't afford not to find out for sure."

If you choose to do this, know that I will be at the meeting, awash in USFWS emblems, defending your decision.

Don't forget to use the restocking event as a PR and image building event too.

This is a serious issue. Snakeheads are not fish with which we should trifle. Whoever let that thing go, if caught, should be bound, stripped to the waist and deserted on Barren Island (still bound) on a warm, still summer evening as greenhead bait. Couldn't they have been satisfied with a bowfin? They're nearly as cuddly as snakeheads.

Anyone can feel free to call me if you'd like to know my true feelings on this. . . .

According to Slattery, the DNR's response to his e-mail was, "'Whoa, whoa, you're overreacting. We're going to try to keep this quiet. We don't think this is a significant thing.' They were trying to blow it off essentially." While the DNR certainly didn't want to pursue Slattery's very public course of action, it didn't view that decision as implying that they weren't concerned about the snakehead and its potential to become a serious problem. Rather than sound the alarm, the DNR preferred to do what they usually did when reacting to the discovery of an invasive species. Namely, assess the magnitude of the threat, develop a range of responses, and implement the one that was most appropriate. The DNR took the first step down this road early the next morning, when Lunsford, accompanied by Slattery, visited the pond for the first time. Upon returning to the office, Lunsford sent an e-mail to the growing group that was following the situation. He described the surface of the pond as being almost 80 percent covered in vegetation, and noted that beneath the water's surface there was a variety of species of submerged aquatic vegetation. The berm around the edge of the pond was a couple of feet high, and he and Slattery had noticed only one low area, about twelve-feet across, where the pond appeared to overflow at high water. Although Lunsford didn't mention it in the e-mail, this low area was the part of the pond closest to the Little Patuxent River. The two saw no outfall structure or pipe through which fish could escape. In talking to some people at the nearby strip mall, they had learned that there might have been a pet shop there that had recently gone out of business. The unsaid implication being that the snakehead could have been discarded before the shop went under. Lunsford concluded the e-mail saying, "We both agree that it would not be possible to shock the pond, with regular shocking vessels [in part because of interference from the vegetation], and that the use of rotenone would not be advisable, due to the SAV [submerged aquatic vegetation]. The SAV would trap any fish poisoned below it and make any recovery effort impossible."

Visiting the pond caused Slattery to reevaluate his position. Given the prolonged drought cycle the area was experiencing, he felt it was unlikely that there had been a flooding event that could have caused the pond and the Little Patuxent River to come together, creating an exit route for the fish. Thus, it appeared as if, for the time being, the snakehead, or possibly snakeheads, was not going anywhere. And killing the fish with rotenone, yet not being able to collect them, didn't appear to be a viable option. As Slattery noted in a follow-up e-mail, "The prospect of . . . acres of rotting fish immediately behind a busy business center seemed as though it had the potential to undo any positive PR we might generate." As a result, Slattery agreed with Lunsford that the best course of action would be to place sandbags across the low area, monitor the pond, and reevaluate the situation and available eradication options in the fall when the vegetation in the pond died back. Slattery even offered the services of his staff to keep tabs on the situation, "particularly during gully-washers between now and early winter (presuming that we have any)." To provide others with additional background on the northern snakehead, Slattery appended an excerpt from briefing materials provided for the February–March 2002 meeting of the Aquatic Nuisance Species Task Force. The excerpt discussed how, despite Texas's long-standing ban on live snakeheads, the Texas

Department of Parks and Wildlife had as recently as the summer of 2001 found live northern snakeheads being sold in ethnic food markets. It went on to say that the northern snakehead's "potential length of nearly a yard, aggressive behavior, and toothed jaws, suggest an obvious ability to negatively impact local aquatic resources. It should be noted that Texas restrictions do not preclude the sale of dead snakeheads on ice or frozen, only of living individuals that are potential ecological threats. Luckily, no snakeheads have been reported from Texas waters to date."

Nobody within the DNR or the larger group of interested observers disagreed with Lunsford's suggested approach. Thus, on Thursday, June 20, two days after finding out that they were dealing with the northern snakehead, the DNR had a plan. If it worked as expected, they, with the U.S. Fish and Wildlife Service's assistance, would decide when and how to eradicate this potentially invasive species before it gained a foothold in Maryland. There would be no big media event nor any attempts to vilify the northern snakehead. Rather, the DNR would go about its work quietly. But events were taking place that would cause the evolving saga of the snakehead to explode onto the public scene and to take on a life of its own. The story was going to be anything but quiet.

TWO

"THE BADDEST BUNNY IN THE BUSH"

Candus (Candy) Thomson, the outdoor writer for the *Baltimore Sun*, loves a good story, the more unusual the better. So, it was no surprise that she was fascinated when Julie Thompson told her about the nuclear worm, a semiterrestrial polycheate (read "worm") imported from Vietnam. It's an impressive creature—for a worm—brilliant red in color, thick as a pencil, with hundreds of tiny feet, and reaching a length of well over a meter. One could imagine that the name was applied by someone who looked at a particularly large specimen and speculated that it had started life as a plebian, run-of-the mill worm only to be irradiated by tunneling through uranium tailings, whereby it was transmogrified into a nuclear worm. But, according to Thompson, the name is a marketing ploy on the part of the wholesale distributor. If that is the case, it has worked brilliantly. The nuclear worm has been sold in bait shops in Maryland since 1994 and it is doing quite well. Just cut an inch off the end, slap it on a hook, and the fish come running, er, swimming. And with a worm that is over a meter long, this is bait that keeps on giving.

The problem with the worm, from Thompson's perspective, is not that it might colonize the area and become invasive. Being a semitropical species, it is highly unlikely that the nuclear worm could survive in Maryland. The real problem is that the worm isn't clean. In the early years, the worms were shipped to the United States packed in soil from their native Vietnam. Being that they are worms, and worms like to scrounge around in muck, and muck often has high levels of organic material, and in a lesser developed country like Vietnam such organic materials might contain some nasty stuff, people like Thompson, whose job is to be on the look-out for new organisms entering the country, became worried and began looking at muck samples under the microscope. And they found the bacterium *Vibrio*, which can cause cholera. The worms are no longer packed in soil, but because worms eat dirt and could just as easily transport nasty stuff in their gut on their trip halfway around the world, the U.S. Fish and Wildlife Service is still concerned and monitoring the situation.

Candy Thomson had long had an interest in invasive species and how they impact the environment. The nuclear worm not only had an invasive species angle, but was also a fun story. That is why, on June 19, 2002, a little after lunch, Thomson was on the phone with Julie Thompson pumping her for information. Thompson was bemoaning the fact that there was not enough public outreach on invasive species, especially the need for people to be more careful about what they do with exotic species once they are no longer wanted. A prime example of this was dumping bait buckets, containing nuclear worms, into local waterways. According to Thompson, Thomson said that she wanted to use the nuclear worm story to help get the word out about handling exotics in a responsible manner. Thompson also said that Thomson was astonished that the worm came all the way from Vietnam. "You'd be surprised about what comes into the country," Thompson responded. With that segue, she told Thomson about the snakehead that had just been found in Crofton, Maryland, and the theory that it was an aquarium discard. "This happened," Thompson added, "because somebody didn't know better. Joe Public has a fish and he thinks, oh, rather than kill it I will go put it in the pond and save it." Thomson wanted to know more and Thompson obliged by e-mailing her many of the e-mails on the snakehead that had been going around, along with some other information about snakeheads taken off the Internet. The time was 3:23 P.M.

Thomson read the e-mails and said to herself, "Holy cow." What really got her attention was the background information that said that the northern snakehead could breathe air, live out of water for days, and move short distances over land. Thomson remembers thinking, "It walks; it breathes. I couldn't have made up a scarier fish, that's for sure." The nuclear worm story would have to wait. She immediately dialed Chuck Porcari, a spokesman for the DNR, and told him that she had to speak to someone now. When Porcari asked why, Thomson said "because you have a northern snakehead in a Crofton pond." When he expressed doubt, Thomson told him to check with some of his field biologists. Porcari did and when he called Thomson back about twenty minutes later he said she was right and told her to call Bob Lunsford for more information.

Thomson interviewed Lunsford twice on Thursday, June 20, early and late in the day. She asked Lunsford if the northern snakehead was an aggressive predator that could breath air, walk over land, and survive out of the water for up to three days, to which, Thomson remembers, Lunsford responded yes on all counts. At one point, Lunsford said of the northern snakehead, "This is one tough customer. If I had to be a fish, this the fish I'd be." Hearing that, Thomson perked right up. At that point, Thomson recalled, she was "convinced that this was a big story, because Lunsford has been around forever and he had never seen anything like this." The quote also reconfirmed Thomson's admiration for Lunsford as a man, she said, "who gives good quote." After finishing the interviews, Thomson remembers "sauntering over to the editors late in the day to tell them the story and when I got to, 'and it could breath out of water and get across land,' they all looked at me and said, 'and you're writing this for page one.'" That posed a bit of a problem because that weekend was Thomson's mother's seventy-fifth birthday celebration and Thomson and her husband had to drive to her mom's house in New Jersey early the next day. So, on Friday, as her husband drove, Thomson wrote the story on her laptop in the front seat while the highway zipped by. When they arrived, Thomson told her mother, "I love you dearly, I got to go send this story."

The story, titled "It Lurks in Crofton's Waters," ran on the first page of the *Baltimore Sun* on Saturday, June 22. The story's opening sentences set the tone. "It sounds like a critter from a cheap science fiction movie, a companion for the Creature from the Black Lagoon. But this fish is real and it's living in a pond in Crofton." Readers were told that the northern snakehead came from China, could grow to be eighteen inches long, was aggressive ("gobble up every other fish in sight"), could breath air and "walk short distances on their extended fins," and that scientists were "worried" about the ability of the fish to "negotiate" the distance between the pond and the river and that, once in the river, the fish might "eat its way" down river to a nearby wetlands sanctuary. Thomson discussed the content of the e-mails that she had seen, including the various concerns voiced by biologists at the DNR and the U.S. Geological Survey. Lunsford's "tough customer" quote was used and Thomson told about the bankrupt pet shop in the mall and Lunsford's related concern that more than one fish might be in the pond. A quote from Schwaab added that, "the presumption is that we are dealing with a small number. We want to make sure we get all of them. Controlling this could be a costly undertaking." Thomson mentioned the various control options being considered, including poisoning the pond and applying herbicide to kill off the vegetation so that the pond could be effectively electroshocked. Using herbicides might create a problem, Lunsford thought, because it would lower the oxygen level in the pond and the snakehead might "run away."

The only problem with this story was that one of the things that made it so dramatic and compelling, the northern snakehead's ability to "walk" over land, turned out to be incorrect. Only a few of the twenty-eight different species of snakeheads can move over land, using a wiggling type motion, and the northern isn't one of them. But neither Thomson nor Lunsford knew this. Indeed, Walter Courtenay, who was an expert on snakeheads didn't know at the time that the northern wasn't mobile over land. As Courtenay later recalled, "When I was at Florida Atlantic University I used to teach ichthyology to graduate students and I always mentioned the family *Channidae* [snakeheads]. I said these fish are known to breathe air and several of them are capable of moving over land from one pond to another and I just assumed mistakenly that the northern was one of these." It wasn't until later in the summer of 2002 when Courtenay corresponded with one of his colleagues,

Professor Peter Ng, from the University of Singapore, that he learned the truth. Ng, an ichthyologist who has considerable experience with snakeheads, told Courtenay that the chevron snakehead and the giant snakehead could move over damp or wet land, with the latter even being able to move on dry land. But Ng said the northern does not possess the same skills. In discussing Ng's comments, Courtenay was quick to add that although adult northern snakeheads could not move over land, very small juveniles could move short distances. And, of course, adult northern snakeheads could flop around like most other fish and, hence, move some distance over land, but that is not really equivalent to the type of walking indicated in the article. The only way that a northern snakehead is likely to move any significant distance between two bodies of water is if those bodies of water establish a water connection, due to flooding, or if the fish can find a watery slurry of mud to slither through from one location to the other.

While Thomson apparently had read some literature about the northern that, in hindsight, was incorrect, Bob Lunsford's belief that the northern could move over land was, like Courtenay's, the result of a mistaken assumption. Soon after learning that the fish DiMauro caught was a northern snakehead, Lunsford began surfing the Internet to find more information on the species. He found a number of sites, including a few that talked generically about the characteristics of snakeheads. For example, one site he looked at, called "Le Fish Corner," contained the following under the heading, "Asian Snakeheads": "The snakehead is tolerant of anaerobic conditions because it is endowed with an air-breathing apparatus. Their air-breathing capabilities allow them to 'walk' on land from one body of water to another by lateral undulations of the body." When Lunsford talked to Thomson he drew on the many bits and pieces of information he had quickly collected on snakeheads, including the northern, and mistakenly concluded that the northern was one of the "walkers." It was a form of guilt by association.

There were two other items in Thomson's story that while not necessarily incorrect were unqualified and, as a result, could leave the reader with the wrong impression about the northern snakehead. One was its ability to live three days out of water. Like any other fish, if a snakehead were taken out of the water on a hot sunny day, it would quickly dry out and die, regardless of its ability to gulp air. If, on the other hand, a snakehead out of water is kept wet, it can, according to many knowledgeable observers, live as an air breather for up to three days. Indeed, the Chinese refer to snakeheads as *sang yee*, which is Cantonese for fish of life, on account of the fish's reputation for surviving out of water for long periods of time. Similarly, the northern snakehead's propensity to "gobble up every other fish in sight" was arguably too extreme. Northern snakeheads, like many other species in this family, are aggressive predators that have a strong preference for other fish. Yet, while northern snakeheads clearly could have a major negative impact on other fish in any body of water that they populate, it is highly unlikely that they would wipe out all the other fish. Indeed, in the former Soviet Republics and Japan, both areas where introduced northern snakeheads have been breeding and spreading for decades, there are still plenty of native fish in evidence, despite the fact that some local fish species have certainly taken a hit, sometimes serious, from the new fish on the block.

No doubt many of the people who read the article in the *Baltimore Sun* envisioned a gruesome, invading fish that might, after eating its way through the pond in Crofton, simply pull itself out of the water and walk to the Little Patuxent River, and then continue chomping its way through the region. It was the kind of story that captures your attention. One person who was drawn in was Marshall Yaap, the Saturday editor of the *Capital*, a newspaper based in Annapolis, Maryland, which covers most of Anne Arundel County, including Crofton. This being a local story with real color, Yaap knew that the *Capital* had to cover it. The newspaper's environment reporter was on vacation, so Yaap called Scott Burke, a community reporter whose beat included Crofton.

Burke's phone rang as he was driving some friends on Interstate 295 from Baltimore to Washington, D.C. Burke doesn't normally answer his cell phone while driving, but he reached for it anyway, perhaps because the ringer was set on high. Yaap asked Burke if he had seen the article in the *Baltimore Sun*. Burke hadn't, so Yaap told him about the "alien fish found in Crofton." At first, Burke didn't believe him, partly because Yaap was not only the Saturday editor, he was also Burke's roommate and was fond of joking. Burke thought Yaap was pulling his leg. When it became clear that wasn't the case, Yaap said that the Associated Press had picked up on Thomson's piece and that he was going to hold it until Monday morning to see what Burke could add to it.

His curiosity piqued, Burke visited the pond on Sunday. "I couldn't see anything," Burke said. "Nobody was there, and I'm just looking at this ugly, weed-choked pond." On Monday morning, after calling the DNR to get more information, Burke filed his story, which appeared that afternoon under the headline, "Alien Fish Raises Concerns at DNR." It repeated much of the information that Thomson had uncovered, including Lunsford's quote about the snakehead being "one tough customer," but Burke also added a few new twists. John Surrick, the DNR's Media Relations Manager, told Burke that biologists from the DNR were heading to the pond that day to pull traps they set the previous Friday to see if any of them caught a snakehead. Burke also learned that the DNR had placed sandbags in the low area of the pond to minimize the chances that a storm could cause the pond to overtop and flow into the Little Patuxent River. Eric Schwaab told Burke that "this is a fish that will feed on other fish. You don't really know when you introduce it to other native species what impact it will have. It's the potential risk that gives us the most cause for concern. Our plan is to wait until the vegetation clears in the fall, which will then allow us to take a more comprehensive and more aggressive sampling and catch."

Burke visited the pond Monday afternoon when the DNR and U.S. Fish and Wildlife Service personnel were checking the traps. He got in a canoe with Lunsford and Slattery and watched as trap after trap turned up turtles and other native species of fish but no snakeheads. Burke did notice a local television channel filming, but other than that, nobody was there. The next day, Thomson visited the pond with Lunsford to look around. It was an odd experience for her. She had fished this pond many times before and now it was the subject of her reporting. Thinking back on the scene, Thomson mused that "it was the last time that summer that there were only two people at snakehead pond."

Although Thomson and Lunsford were alone that day, there was clear evidence around the pond that a snakehead was nearby. The DNR had tacked up wanted posters for the fish, reminiscent of the type one would see in the Wild West, when nasty outlaws like Jesse James were on the loose. At the center of the poster was DiMauro's picture of the snakehead on its side. The poster's text was enough to cause any angler's pulse to rise. It gave the impressive dimensions of the fish—"length up to 40 inches, weight up to 15 pounds"—and said that it "could cause serious problems if introduced into our ecosystem." Underneath the picture it read, "If you come across this fish, PLEASE DO NOT RELEASE. Please KILL this fish by cutting/bleeding as it can survive out of water for several days." Anglers who encountered the fish were asked to contact the DNR immediately, via phone, fax, or e-mail.

Thomson's next article, on Wednesday, June 26 was titled, "Search Continues for Predatory Fish in Crofton Pond." By now, Thomson had spoken to Courtenay, who told her that "of the twenty-eight species of snakehead, the northern snakehead is the most hardy and has the highest reproductive rate." Courtenay added that, "they are voracious predators that can easily tolerate Maryland winters." The article also laid low the theory that the fish had made it into the pond as an aquarium discard, with Courtenay pointing out that although some species of snakehead appear in the aquarium trade, the northern usually isn't one of them. Instead, he speculated that the fish had been bought to eat, but the would-be diner changed his mind and dumped it in the pond. Thomson further clarified the size issue as well, noting that an unnamed angler caught and released an eighteen-inch fish the previous month, but that this species could get as large as thirty-six inches. As for the DNR's management options, two appeared to be out of contention. The article noted that shocking the pond earlier in the week had been unsuccessful and that pumping water out of the pond could give the fish entrée to the river. One management option still on the table was applying the fish poison, rotenone.

Later that day, Anita Huslin, the environmental reporter for the *Washington Post*, got a call from one of her editors asking if she had seen "the really funny little story in the *Baltimore Sun*" about the fish. Huslin hadn't, but when she read it she became interested. As Thomson recounted it, Huslin walked into the office of Bob Thomson, an editor at the *Washington Post*, who just happens to be Candy Thomson's husband. Huslin reportedly said, "This is a great story, but the *Sun* underplayed it," to which Bob Thomson responded,

Northern Snakehead

Distinguishing Features
Long dorsal fin • small head • large mouth • big teeth • length up
to 40 inches • weight up to 15 pounds

HAVE YOU SEEN THIS FISH?

The northern snakehead from China is not native to Maryland
waters and could cause serious problems if introduced into our
ecosystem.

**If you come across this fish,
PLEASE DO NOT RELEASE.**
Please KILL this fish by cutting/bleeding
as it can survive out
of water for several days and REPORT all catches to
**Maryland Department of Natural Resources
Fisheries Service. Thank you.**

Phone:	410 260 8320
TTY:	410 260 8835
Toll Free:	1 877 620 8DNR (8367) Ext 8320
E-mail:	customerservice@dnr.state.md.us

The wanted poster posted by the DNR. Courtesy Maryland
Department of Natural Resources.

"Oh you didn't see Candy's first story, on Saturday, which ran on page
one." Huslin read that one too and started digging.

Huslin's first article on the snakehead appeared the next day,
Thursday, June 27, under the headline, "Freakish Fish Causes Fear in
Md." It covered much of the territory of its predecessors and then
some. In a stylistic turn that would reverberate throughout the sum-

mer, Huslin labeled the snakehead "a nasty Frankenfish, as far as U.S. officials are concerned . . . dreaded by fish biologists, it is capable of clearing out a pond of all living creatures and then wriggling on to new hunting grounds on its belly and fins." Thus, now the snakehead was not only capable of eating every fish in sight, but every single living creature in sight. The snakehead was moving up in the world. The article also said that the snakehead could survive not just three, but up to four days out of water. Lunsford lived up to his reputation as a quotable man and gave Huslin a real winner. "The fear is," Lunsford said, "this thing could hop from the pond, across the floodplain and into the river, and then all bets are off. It's the baddest bunny in the bush. It has no known predators in the environment, can grow to 15 pounds, and it can get up and walk. What more do you need?" Later in the article, Lunsford echoed the message of the wanted poster, saying, "If you catch it, kill it. It's not a dead or alive thing, we want it dead." Courtenay weighed in too. "I don't know of anything admirable about these fish. The only recourse they've got is to either get rid of the vegetation or wait until winter when it dies back, and kill all the fish in the pond."

Even though Huslin's article ran on the third page of the B section, it caused quite a stir. The *Washington Post* is a widely read, major national paper, and clearly a lot of people took notice of the article. The DNR's John Surrick said that the snakehead story "really took off after Anita's story in the *Post*, because she was a little bit sensational." The *Milwaukee Journal Sentinel* reprinted Huslin's article the same day, titling it, "Ferocious Fish: Foreign Intruder Worries Biologists in East." The NBC affiliate in the Washington area, Channel 4, ran a story on the nightly news that began with, "Word is spreading in Crofton about the killer fish that's lurking in a pond behind businesses along Route 3."

Snakehead hunters, tipped off by the media coverage, came to the pond in search of glory. Burke was there and recorded their quest. One of the teens on hand had a hockey stick, to "beat" the snakehead if he caught it. His buddy claimed that if they got the snakehead, they'd "be the heroes of Crofton." In the pursuit of glory, the two teens hung around the pond most of the day, in the sweltering heat, casting their fishing lines into the water. Their bait was ham, but the snakehead wasn't biting. A mother, with her ten-year-old daughter and two of her friends in tow, told Burke they "wanted to say we've been to the pond where the walking Chinese fish lives." Another indication that the story was growing could be found around the edge of the pond. The wanted posters that the DNR had tacked up just days earlier were gone. They had already become collector's items. Not wanting to lose the initiative, the DNR soon replastered the area with posters.

At the Thursday morning staff meeting at the Washington, D.C., offices of National Public Radio the group was batting around ideas for stories when someone mentioned Huslin's article and the strange fish. Enough said. Soon correspondent Lynn Neary was on the phone with Lunsford. The four-minute piece, titled "Evil Fish," aired later that day on the show "All Things Considered." It began with Neary intoning, "They are calling it the Frankenfish." During the interview, Lunsford added a new feature to the snakehead's growing repertoire of capabilities, one that was drawn from the information he had gathered earlier while cruising the Internet for data. "It has these lobed, muscular pectoral fins," said Lunsford, "that allow it to kind of hop and hold itself up and move at least short distances on land." As it turns out the northern snakehead's pectoral fins are not lobed, nor are they unusually muscled. In fact, they look very much like and operate in a similar fashion to the run-of-the-mill pectoral fins that one might find on a bass or trout. Toward the end of the interview,

Lunsford expressed the concern that the snakehead could get to the Little Patuxent River and feed on the fish there. Neary asked, "Is it possible that it's already gotten there?" Lunsford responded, "At this point, yes," and then Neary raised the specter of the fish being the proverbial "one that got away." Lunsford laughed and said, "I hope if it is the one that got away, that it was one that got away."

Meanwhile, a covert operation was taking place in the Little Patuxent River. While the biologists at the DNR had no reason to believe that any snakeheads had made their way into the river, they wanted evidence. The best way to get that would be to shock the river and see what floated to the surface. But the DNR had no interest in making this a public spectacle. As Eric Schwaab said later, "We absolutely reached the conclusion early on that to overtly go to the Little Patuxent and shock and look for fish would have suddenly created a new level to the media speculation that frankly wasn't warranted at that point." As Mike Slattery recalls, Schwaab "told his staff no one is to go shocking the Patuxent." But the DNR still wanted the information. So Schwaab and Slattery agreed that the latter would quietly visit the river with other U.S. Fish and Wildlife Service personnel, do some shocking, and report back to the DNR. Slattery did this and found plenty of fish, but no snakeheads, and everyone's confidence that the problem was contained in the pond rose.

On Friday, June 28, NBC Channel 4 ran another story, in which Lunsford reiterated a number of his earlier comments, but again added a few new twists. "This particular species has the ability to hop across the land or crawl across the land. It has rudimentary legs . . . it's a tough critter that's going to be difficult to eradicate." Then, drawing a comparison between another very famous invasive species, Lunsford commented that the snakehead "could be the gypsy moth of the water world." Two days later, Thomson poked fun at the snakehead story in her regular outdoors column. "Just what we need," the piece began, "a

The Little Patuxent River. Courtesy Eric Jay Dolin.

fish with Tony Siragusa's appetite, Osama bin Laden's looks, William Donald Schaefer's hardiness and Gale Sayers's mobility." (Siragusa is a six-foot-three, 342-pound, former defensive tackle for the NFL's Baltimore Ravens, well-known for his love of food and voracious eating habits; Schaefer, currently the comptroller for Maryland, is an octogenarian who has served in public office for more than forty-five years at the state and local level, including terms as governor and mayor of Baltimore.) Noting that the northern snakehead was the top issue at the DNR, Thomson ventured that the agency might "have to amend its name to include the unnatural." She said that *Channa argus* was Latin for "my, what big teeth you have." And to solve the problem, Thomson proposed a "snakehead tournament" with top-name anglers, sponsors, and prizes. Thomson's article was also notable because she talked at some length about Paul DiMauro and his role in the snakehead story. While virtually all of the earlier press reports had mentioned that an angler caught a snakehead in May, few mentioned the angler's name or covered his story in any detail.

Cartoon by Eric Smith, which appeared in the *Capital* on June 28, 2002. Courtesy *Capital-Gazette*.

On the same day as Thomson's outdoor column, the *Capital* ran an article titled, "No Fish Tale: Anglers Take Hunt Seriously." In it Burke shared details of e-mails he had received from Joan Griffith, the mother of James Griffith, DiMauro's fishing buddy. Like DiMauro, Griffith was upset about the DNR's plans to kill the fish. Joan Griffith wrote that her son was "distressed about the fallout. . . . Fishing is such simple pleasure. James likes to catch his fish and return them to the ponds so he can catch them again. The snakehead apparently was a real fighter once it was hooked, and James and his friend, Paul DiMauro, admired the spirit of the fish." Burke's article ran on page one, and included a sidebar that posed a question and a challenge: "Want to test your fishing skills against the mysterious Chinese walking fish—and win a gift certificate in the process?" If you were the lucky angler to land the mighty snakehead and provide proof that you had actually caught the fish in question and not a look-alike species, the *Capital* would bestow upon you a $100 gift certificate for use at a local fishing supply store. The snakehead now had a bounty on its head.

William Berkshire, a longtime resident of Crofton, was following the snakehead story with great interest. He, too, wanted to make money off the snakehead, but not by catching it. He had much grander designs. "I had a lot of experience," Berkshire said, "with what was promotional and what was not. This [the snakehead] was. From the first time I read the article, I knew that this would be something that was very significant." In fact, he thought the snakehead was a "promoter's dream." Berkshire's background had prepared him to make this assessment. He had been promoting various moneymaking ventures his entire adult life. While a special agent with the U.S. Secret Service between 1965 and 1975, Berkshire not only protected the nation's leaders, but he also started, with a few of his fellow agents, the Lancer Corporation, named after John F. Kennedy's Secret Service code name. As it turned out, he and his colleagues had a lot of down time flying around the country, in between all the public appearances where their services were required. To fill that time, the men of Lancer Corporation began playing the market, doing their own analyses, and buying and selling stocks.

In 1973, Berkshire accompanied Vice President Spiro Agnew, who was going to a testimonial for John Wayne in Newport Beach, California. Just as the motorcade was ready to leave the airport, the two regular secret service follow-up cars broke down, forcing the agents to borrow the White House communications car. In a motorcade, agents often have to jump out of the cars while they are moving. Berkshire was adept at doing this with the regular follow-up cars, but not with the communications car, which differed in design. Thus, when Berkshire jumped out of the communications car, the door didn't open up as much as he had expected and it knocked him to the pavement, whereupon one of the rear tires rolled over his legs and smashed one of his knees. He stayed in the Secret Service for two more years, but the constant wear and tear on his damaged knee led him to retire in 1975.

The Lancer Corporation carried on, and through it and other ventures, Berkshire continued to expand his business and promotional activities. He was involved in the creation of the short-lived company called Ms. America Tennis Incorporated, which ran a professional women's tennis circuit. He bought the Crofton Country Club and raced thoroughbreds. He started up a restaurant on Route 3, called Uncle Nicky's Fish'n Hole that sells ribs, chicken, and catfish. One of the best sellers at Uncle Nicky's are catfish nuggets and Berkshire, sensing a marketing opportunity, tried to trademark the name "catfish nuggets," but it didn't get approved because it was too generic. Had he gotten rights to the name, Berkshire planned to sell catfish nuggets worldwide. Over the years Berkshire has also lobbied to build a six-story hotel and a ten-story casino and hotel and family amusement complex, both in Crofton.

Berkshire was not only interested in the snakehead because of its promotional potential; he also had a more personal stake. Years ago, he purchased a six-acre tract of land, just off of Route 3, that had two ponds and backed up to the Little Patuxent River. One of the ponds is next to the pond where the snakehead was caught. They are separated by a strip of land less than twenty feet wide—just a hop, skip, and a jump for a "walking" snakehead. Berkshire bought the land as a present for his grand, half-uncle, Nicholas R. Rick, or Uncle Nicky as he was commonly called. Uncle Nicky took in Berkshire, his siblings, and his mother when Berkshire was very young, and became the only father Berkshire ever knew. Uncle Nicky loved to fish and Berkshire hoped that one day Uncle Nicky would fly from California to Maryland to visit the pond and indulge his passion. The present was going to be a surprise, but, unfortunately, by the time Uncle Nicky visited Crofton, he was already ill with bone cancer. Not wanting to make Uncle Nicky feel any worse, Berkshire didn't tell him about the pond. Instead, Uncle Nicky went back home and soon died. The restaurant, Uncle Nicky's Fish'n Hole, is named in his honor.

Soon after Berkshire read the initial articles on the snakehead he recommended to his two daughters, Erin and Chris, both in their thirties, that they consider starting a business to sell snakehead-related items, such as T-shirts and caps emblazoned with an image of the snakehead and wording such as "Crofton Snakehead" or "Frankenfish." Berkshire said he "knew right off that this would be a major local or national story," but he also was confident that it would peak fast, and that is why he urged his daughters to act quickly. Erin and Chris didn't need much coaxing, and they immediately began taking the steps necessary to launch their snakehead-based business. Berkshire was not surprised by his daughter's eagerness. We are a "typical entrepreneurial family," he said.

In the little more than a week since Thomson had broken the story, it had grown considerably in size. The snakehead had been depicted as a multitalented fish that threatened serious consequences to the ecosystem should it venture out of the pond, notwithstanding that fact that its ability to wander was, like rumors of Mark Twain's death, greatly exaggerated. Still, it was clear that the story had legs, even if the fish didn't. And the story was about to start walking really fast all over the place.

THREE

THEN THERE WERE TWO

During the week Joe Gillespie of Crofton repairs computers, automatic teller machines, and cash registers as a technician for Fujitsu. But outside of work, especially on the weekends, Gillespie spends a lot of time hunting and fishing. Evidence of his success, in the form of skulls, feathers, mounts, and photos is scattered throughout the house he shares with his wife, Julie, daughter, Caitlin (fourteen), and son, Mark (eleven). Gillespie also loves skateboarding, and that is why on Saturday, June 22, he took his kids to a skatepark in Baltimore, Maryland. After Gillespie signed in, the man at the counter said, "You're from Crofton, where they found that weird fish." Gillespie asked him what he was talking about, at which point the man flipped over his copy of the *Baltimore Sun* to reveal Thomson's first article on the snakehead, complete with a map to the pond.

Gillespie had fished at the pond many times before, and the article brought back memories of a day the previous October when he went there with his son, his brother, and his brother's son. Late in the afternoon, gliding along the surface of the pond in a canoe, they spied what they thought were air bubbles from a turtle. But as they got closer, they realized that they weren't air bubbles, but what looked to be "tons of little minnows" circling, creating a cylindrical column of fish. Out flew Joe's nephew's lure into the center of the column. A big fish immediately hit the lure and let go. Then Gillespie threw his lure, and the fish nailed it. For fifteen minutes Gillespie fought the fish, playing it gingerly because he didn't want the four-pound-test line to snap. At one point during this tug of war, the canoe moved close to where the fish was holed up in the weeds. Gillespie's brother leaned over to move the plants out of the way, and perhaps grab the fish, but it wasn't going quietly. The fish shot up and out of the water, right through Gillespie's brother's outstretched arms. Gillespie reckons it flew four feet through the air before splashing back into the water and breaking free of the line. Caught off guard by this turn of events, Gillespie's brother fell back into the canoe and let out a yell, leading his son to say, "Dad, I'm embarrassed." Although there was interest in pursuing the fish, it was getting dark and windy, and a thunderstorm was moving in, so the anglers left the pond and the fish behind.

During their encounter, Gillespie and his companions had gotten a few glimpses of the big fish, but weren't sure what it was. Joe said it looked "like an anaconda coming out to the water." Given the bar-like markings on its side, the fish might have been a chain pickerel, but that didn't make sense. It was much bigger than any pickerel any of them had ever seen, and if it were a pickerel, Gillespie thought, it would certainly be a state record. What it really looked like was a tiger muskie. Upon hearing back from the DNR that the state hadn't stocked the pond with tiger muskies, the four anglers went back to their original hunch. It must have been huge chain pickerel. In honor of the fish's massive size, they dubbed it Moby Pick.

The four of them visited the pond one more time, before the story of the snakehead broke, to see if they could catch Moby Pick, but came up empty. Now, reading the article at the skatepark, Gillespie was sure he had solved the mystery—Moby Pick must have been a northern snakehead. But something was wrong. The article said the northern snakehead only grew to eighteen inches. Joe knew that Moby Pick was bigger than that. Later in the summer, he would recall that the fish he had seen that October day was "humongous" and as "big as a golf bag," although he was quick to admit that its size might have been amplified by the weeds wrapped around it.

Over the next week, Gillespie followed the snakehead story with great interest, oftentimes thinking back on his encounter with Moby Pick. On Sunday, June 30, he had planned to go fishing in the Little Patuxent River with his son, Mark, and his son's friend, Jake Harkey (thirteen), choosing that location because he thought the kids would have more fun fishing the open, fast-moving river rather than the heavily weeded and stagnant waters of the nearby pond. But the boys had seen the front page of the *Capital* that morning and they wanted to go after the bounty on the snakehead, which they promised to split fifty-fifty if either one of them caught the fish. Gillespie compromised. He and the boys first fished the river, then walked over to the pond.

Their method of fishing in the pond that day was unconventional. Instead of casting from the shore or going out in a canoe, they rode low to the water on Gillespie's two sailboards, minus the sails. The boys climbed on one with their fishing rods and kayak paddles, and Gillespie got on the other, carrying his fishing rod, a bucket of minnows for bait, a paddle, and a fishing net. They decided to paddle out to the area where Gillespie had hooked Moby Pick, on the far side of the pond, away from the parking lot. However big the snakehead might be, Joe thought he was ready. Not only did he have a sizeable net to scoop up the beast, but he also had brought his sturdy surf rod with fifteen-pound-test line, a serious step up from the ultralight rod and the four-pound line he had had last October.

While the boys were fishing in relatively open water toward the center of the pond, Gillespie paddled slowly along the edge among the weeds, looking for the telltale column of "minnows," and he soon found them. "The water was bubbling and churning," Gillespie said, and "they kept moving away, moving away." They were also exhibiting some unusual behavior, for a minnow that is: jumping out of the water, wiggling across lily pads, and then plopping back in. While watching this odd display, Gillespie said he saw a big fish pop its head out of the water like a turtle, look at him, and then disappear under the surface.

Gillespie was paddling strategically now, with the goal of getting the mass of small fish to the perimeter of what he described as a "little peninsula of floating weeds." This accomplished, Gillespie stationed his sailboard close by, and that's when he first saw the impressive size of the big fish as it moved slowly through the water to where the small fish were congregated. Gillespie wanted to get the big fish out into the open water where the boys were, so he used his paddle to sever the peninsula of weeds from the larger weed mat, and then pushed the now free-floating weeds toward the boys. The small fish followed, and for a short time the big fish was out in the open, but then it too followed the floating weeds.

Gillespie could see the big fish hovering in the water and he dropped his bobber and baited hook on that spot. The fish darted toward the surface. "I could see the whole mouth take the bobber,"

Gillespie remembers, "and, *boom*, down it went." The fish pulled and then released the bobber, which floated back to the surface. For the next twenty or thirty minutes, Gillespie and the boys cast time and again without a single hit. The fish even boldly swam up to Gillespie on a couple of occasions, knocking into his paddles and feet. Gillespie saw the fish many times and he was convinced it was a snakehead.

Gillespie was excited, but the boys were getting nervous. "The first time the boys saw him," said Gillespie, "they lifted their feet up onto the sailboard, and started arguing with each other, saying, Don't push me, don't push me." To keep the fish away from the boys, Gillespie splashed the water with his paddle and kicked his legs. When the fish came toward him, Gillespie threw in his line, then the fish would go over to the other side of the floating weeds, closer to the boys, and Gillespie would tell them, Here it comes. "Daddy, don't tell me," yelled Gillespie's son, as his and his friend's feet flew out of the water, "I don't want to know. I don't want to see him."

At one point, Jake Harkey cast his line and got a hit right away, but the fish quickly released. Gillespie immediately threw his line to the same place, got a hit, and set the hook. The battle was on. "He was pulling me pretty good," Gillespie recalls. "I was almost standing and leaning way forward and starting to lose my balance." The fish would pull away then come back, at times stopping directly under the sailboard, then pull away again. As Gillespie tried to dip the net on the fish he remembers there being a big splash, then the line went slack. For a moment, he thought he might have lost him, but then all of a sudden the line was taut and the end of the rod bowed way down. Gillespie was worried that the fish was going to snap the line. He slowly pulled the fish toward his net, closer, closer, and then when the net was under the fish Gillespie lifted the net and hauled his catch out of the water and onto the sailboard. To keep the fish from escaping, Gillespie used his left elbow and hand to pinch the top of the net closed and hold the fish tight against his body.

> The fish's head was down by my fingers [Gillespie said]. He was still kicking and my arm was kind of flapping like a chicken. The hook is still in his mouth and the fishing pole is laying down on the sailboard. The boys grabbed my windsurfer and pulled me in. While we were coming back across the pond, the thing is chomping. It ripped through two of the nylon squares on the half-inch netting. I had a little Gerber diver's knife on my hip. That's what I brought it out for, to dispatch the fish if we got a hold of him. So I stuck him in the head and I'm pretty sure he was mortally wounded at that point. Later, I thought that I should have brought him up on shore, but I didn't know if I was going to make it with the boys pulling me. The fish was still kicking a bit [after I stabbed it], but no more biting.

When Gillespie and the boys got to shore, Janice Saul and Michael Cooke greeted them. Saul, a math teacher at an alternative middle school in Baltimore County, and Cooke, a telecommunications salesman, were at the pond at Cooke's urging. An avid outdoorsman and self-avowed amateur news-event hound and stormchaser, Cooke liked to go to big events and happenings, and the snakehead story was shaping up to be a real winner. So, on their way to visit friends in Annapolis, Cooke led Saul on a short detour to the increasingly infamous pond. In fact, Cooke had already been there earlier that week to catch the fish himself. Now he was back for another try. While Cooke fished from the edge of the pond, Saul, who claims she "could barely identify a fishing rod," read a book in the shade. Other than Gillespie and the boys, Saul and Cooke were the only ones at the pond. The snakehead's celebrity and its having

A picture of the pond taken by Michael Cooke on the day he and Janice
Saul witnessed Gillespie capture a northern snakehead. Notice how
thickly the plants cover the surface. Courtesy Michael Thomas Cooke.

a price on its head, apparently, were not enough to lure more anglers
on this hot and muggy Sunday afternoon, with temperatures creeping into the nineties.

Because the pond was relatively small, both Cooke and Saul
could hear Gillespie and the boys talking to each other as they pursued the snakehead. Saul heard Gillespie yell, "There it is," and tell
the boys to pick up their feet. She remembers thinking, "There's
no way they're talking about that fish." Cooke too heard them talking, and he didn't know, he said, "whether they were stalking the
fish, or the fish was stalking them." As the circling of combatants
went on, Cooke doubted that they would hook a fish. "I figured,"
he said, "that the chance of anybody getting anything in this weed-
choked pond was slim." By now, Saul, who was closer to Gillespie
and the boys than Cooke, was intently listening to and watching

what was playing out on the water. When she saw Gillespie catch the fish she screamed over to Cooke that they had caught the snakehead. Cooke had seen Gillespie's rod bend and even saw him land what appeared to be a sizeable fish, but he couldn't believe it was *the* fish. Cooke recalls telling Saul, "Get out of here, no they did not." Saul then screamed to Gillespie, Did you catch the snakehead, and he said yes. Cooke and Saul watched as the boys towed Gillespie and the fish ashore. When the victorious trio got out of the water, they gave each other a round of high fives.

Saul remembers that the two boys "were shocked, scared, and happy. . . . I could have cried. I mean I couldn't believe it was that fish. I thought, What more could a father and son ask for? It was the most beautiful story, the most perfect simple story, that of a father and son fishing" and catching the prize fish. The scene reminded Saul of the movie *On Golden Pond*, which she and Cooke had recently watched. The movie, which stars Henry Fonda and Katharine Hepburn, is a touching story about growing old and coming to grips with complex and often frustrating family relationships. In it Norman (Fonda) and his wife, Ethel (Hepburn), return for their forty-eighth and quite possibly last summer at their cottage in Maine on the edge of Golden Pond. Their daughter, her fiancée, and his thirteen-year-old son show up to celebrate Norman's eightieth birthday. One of the movie's themes is the evolving relationship between Norman and the thirteen-year-old boy and their efforts to catch "Walter," the biggest trout in the lake, which Norman had been trying to land for years. Norman named the fish Walter, he said, because it reminded him of his wife's brother Walter—"fat, lazy, and ugly." On their last day at the cottage, Norman and the boy venture forth one more time in search of that "crafty old son of a bitch," Walter, and to their delight, the boy catches him. As Gillespie and the boys pulled their sailboards onto the bank, Saul

Gillespie with his famous catch in the net, just after the fish was caught.
Courtesy Michael Thomas Cooke.

said to Cooke, "This is just like *On Golden Pond*, they caught the snakehead, they caught Walter." There was, however, one big difference between the fate of these two fish. Norman and the boy let Walter go because he had lived this long and they thought they should "let him keep on living." The snakehead wasn't so lucky.

Saul ran to get her camera and then took a few pictures of Gillespie and the boys and the fish, which was twenty-six inches long. She also ripped one of the wanted posters off a nearby tree. It said to call the DNR if you caught the fish, and she did. According to Saul, the woman who answered the phone said that nobody was there and that Saul would have to call back on Monday. Although it was Sunday, not a normal workday, Saul was surprised that nobody was there; in fact, she said she was "in shock." After all, the fish was big news, it had been in the papers and on television, and there were wanted posters up all over the place. Wouldn't the DNR have someone available in case the fish were caught? She turned to Cooke and said, "You're not going to believe this, they hung up on me." At Cooke's urging, Saul called back. When the same woman answered, Saul said, "You don't understand what fish this is perhaps," and she proceeded to explain. The woman wasn't able to offer much more than she did during the first call, but before hanging up Saul could hear someone in the background yelling, "Kill it, make sure you kill it."

While taking pictures, Saul told the boys that they were certainly going to have something to write about when their teachers asked them what they did during their summer vacation. Saul said she was making a big deal of the catch because she thought that it was going to be the end of the story. Reflecting on all that transpired afterward, Saul laughed a bit at her naivete. "The story," she said, "just never stopped."

Within minutes of Gillespie and the boys coming ashore, Gillespie's wife and daughter arrived. They hadn't been called; rather, their curiosity brought them down to the pond to see if the guys had been lucky. Gillespie's daughter pulled out her digital camera and began documenting the scene, not realizing that her photographs would soon be seen not only from coast to coast, but around the world. Gillespie and the boys lugged their sailboards and their trophy to the parking lot behind the bank building. As they were packing up, a few other people, unaware of Gillespie's success, arrived to try their luck at catching the fish. One elderly gentleman was in the process of getting his canoe off his truck, when he saw Gillespie holding the snakehead aloft and posing for pictures. Undaunted, the gentleman announced, "Well, I'm going after another one," and off he went. Soon other people showed up, some of whom had been tipped off by excited cell

Gillespie displays his catch. The small light circle in the middle of the fish's head is where Gillespie stabbed it with a knife. Courtesy Cait Gillespie.

phone calls from the parking lot. Gillespie estimated that about twenty to thirty people arrived before he got in his car and drove the mile or so to his house. Soon after he got home, neighbors, friends, and assorted out-of-town guests began coming by for an informal viewing of the strange fish. Gillespie willingly obliged the visitors and regaled them with stories of his and the boys' adventure at the pond.

Gillespie already knew he wanted to mount the fish, so that night he wrapped it in plastic and placed it in the freezer. That way, when the fish was thawed it would still be in good shape for the taxidermist. Shortly after seven the next morning, Gillespie called the DNR and spoke to Heather Lynch, in public affairs, who asked him to bring in the fish. The boys had been there for

Gillespie's northern snakehead on the grass. Courtesy Cait Gillespie.

the dramatic capture, and Gillespie wanted them to be there for the identification as well. After all, if the fish were positively identified as a northern snakehead, the next stop would be the *Capital* to collect the $100 bounty. Gillespie grabbed the frozen fish, placed it gingerly in his cooler, and drove the fish and the boys to the DNR in Annapolis, which was fifteen minutes from his house.

Nobody was there to greet him at the entrance to the DNR and Gillespie and the boys wandered the halls for a short while before someone pointed them in right direction. Although it was early on a Monday, many people in the Fisheries Service were already at work, and word had begun circulating that an angler was coming in, possibly with a snakehead. Slattery, too, was there, alerted by Lunsford's boss, Steve Early, who was just back from vacation. Lunsford had briefed Early about the events of the last two weeks and Early was frankly puzzled at the level of media interest in the story. The DNR had dealt with a number of aquarium dumps and other releases of nonindigenous species before, including giant snakeheads and piranhas. "I didn't think a whole lot of it," Early recalled. "I thought, well somebody's dumped a couple of fish."

Gillespie, the boys, and the fish were escorted into Director Eric Schwaab's office, along with a small group of DNR staffers and Mike Slattery. Gillespie hoisted the black, rock-hard fish out of the cooler and placed it on the small conference table in front of Schwaab's desk. Like a coroner readying for an autopsy, Steve Early donned light purple-plastic gloves and approached the deceased. A little warm water was drizzled onto the fish to tease apart the fins, which were frozen hard against the body. Early looked at the fish from top to bottom, taking note of its features. He also pulled off a couple of scales for later investigation. There was little doubt among those in the room as to the fish's identity, but to be sure they later shared pictures and information about the fish with Courtenay, and he verified that it was, indeed, a northern snakehead.

While Early and the others inspected the fish, Gillespie told them of the sequence of events leading up to its capture, and about the "minnows," which Gillespie now suspected were baby snakeheads. Gillespie thought he wasn't communicating the minnow part of the story very well, but as it turned out the DNR folks heard what he said, and it made them anxious. They knew that northern snakeheads guard their young, raising the possibility that the column of minnows was actually a column of baby snakeheads being guarded by a protective parent or parents. That would certainly explain the fish's desire to stay near the small fish and its aggressive actions in the pond that day. Adding fuel to that speculation was the question of size. The fish DiMauro caught was estimated to be eighteen inches; Gillespie's catch was twenty-six inches. Northern snakeheads grow fast, but nobody believed one could grow roughly eight inches in a little over a month.

If those were baby snakeheads, then there was almost certainly a breeding pair of adults in the pond.

At the end of the meeting, which lasted over an hour, Gillespie wrapped up his fish, put it back in the cooler, and drove home with the boys. He was supposed to start work by nine, but he wasn't going to make it. Someone tipped off the media. As soon as Gillespie got home the calls started. Reporters from a slew of local radio and television stations and newspapers wanted to see the fish and hear the story. And in short order those reporters started arriving at Gillespie's doorstep. Rather than entertain the quickly growing mass of media in his living room or backyard, Gillespie decamped to the pond, bringing the fish and the cooler with him. By this time, DNR staff, as well as Slattery and a few of his colleagues had also arrived on the scene. They were there to see if they could catch more snakeheads, either the old-fashioned way, by fishing, or with additional traps set throughout the pond.

Gillespie didn't get to work that day until noon. For the remainder of the week, he was in the eye of a developing media hurricane. Calls poured in day and night for interviews, and when he wasn't working or eating or sleeping, he would invariably be talking about the fish, at his house or down by the pond. Whenever a photographer wanted a money shot, Gillespie hauled out the fish. And many times, the photographers didn't have to ask, Gillespie would often take out the fish before the interview began, using the slab-o-snakehead as a prop. You could tell that Gillespie was having a good time. Schwaab said that Gillespie "was very much sort of enjoying the limelight." According to Thomson, Gillespie "was unavoidable for comment. If you wanted to talk to Joe, no problem. He knew what he had." But the intensity of the assault on Gillespie's time began to take a toll on his patience and enthusiasm for riding the media wave. "I got tired of telling the story over and over again," said Gillespie. "It got kind of redundant after fifty interviews." It also started to interfere with Gillespie's work.

While Gillespie was tiring of repeating himself, the media couldn't get enough of the story. In the week after Gillespie caught the fish, the snakehead coverage radiated outward in ever-widening circles. Local, regional, national, and international news outlets relayed the story under a dizzying array of shocking headlines.

JULY 2

Feared Fish Finds Its Way into Anglers' Net (*Washington Post*)

Maryland Wages War on Invasive Walking Fish (*National Geographic News*)

JULY 3

Wanted Dead: Voracious Walking Fish ("CBS Evening News")

Maryland's Most-Wanted (*Newsday*)

Fishy Invader Sets Off Alarms in Maryland (MSNBC)

Stop That Fish! (*Washington Post*)

Freaky Fish Story Flourishes (*Washington Post*)

JULY 5

Terror from the Deep (*Bangkok Post*)

JULY 6

"Frankenfish" in Maryland Pond Horrifies Anglers and Environmentalists (*Kansas City Star*)

JULY 7

Snakehead Must Not Be the One That Got Away (*South China Morning Post*)

JULY 8

Asian Alien Strikes (*Baltimore Sun*)

One could almost see the editors at newspapers and radio and tel-

Cartoon by Eric Smith, which appeared in the *Bowie Blade–News* in early July. Courtesy *Capital-Gazette*.

evision stations licking their lips at their fortune for having such a great story fall in their laps during the traditionally slow summer season. A *Baltimore Sun* editor was surely speaking for many of her peers when she said to Thomson, "This is the story that is going to get us through the summer, thank you."

A local radio station saw the snakehead story as a way to have some fun. The day after Gillespie brought the fish to the DNR, the station told its listeners of a "Freakish Fish Festival!" taking place that day at the pond and implored them to come by and help "Save the Fish." A few loyal listeners did just that, hoping to picket for the

The parking lot behind the bank. This picture was taken in the fall, well after the poisoning of the pond, but the orange fencing is still up and can be seen at the far edge of the parking lot. Courtesy Eric Jay Dolin.

cause and also do some partying. But upon discovering that there was no music or food, the protestors took off, seemingly willing to leave the fish's fate hanging in the balance. Anita Huslin interviewed one of the spurned protestors, who complained, "There's no one down here but reporters!"

One of those reporters was Candy Thomson, who remembers pulling into the parking lot behind the bank and thinking, "Holy #$@%! There's television trucks and photographers and people talking into cell phones." Slattery, who was there checking traps, had never seen anything quite like what he witnessed at the pond that day. "It was an absolute three-ringer," he said. "There were people everywhere. There were skate rats asking me where the half-pipe is. There were people showing up with bags of goldfish from Wal-Mart trying to use them as bait. There were people elbow-to-elbow around the pond, most with fishing rods. People with hot dogs as bait." At one point a gaggle of reporters coalesced around Surrick. What did the DNR think about all this, they wanted to know?

This cartoon by Richard Thompson appeared in the Style section of the *Washington Post* on July 7, 2002. Courtesy Richard Thompson for the *Washington Post*.

"There's poor John [Surrick] standing in a sea of reporters," recalled Thomson. "John smokes, and I could tell the man needed a cigarette bad."

The reviews of Gillespie's catch weren't pretty. Jim Vance, anchor for Washington's NBC Channel 4 news, pronounced the northern snakehead "one ugly dude," and later said it was "a mean dude with attitude." The *Capital*'s Eric Smith called it a "pug-ugly creature. It's not a tasty rockfish, a graceful swordfish or a colorful parrotfish. It looks like a moray eel with a bad haircut." Reporters on Channel 13 and Channel 2, both out of Baltimore, called the northern snakehead, "kind of ugly" and "one ugly fish," respectively. The word "ugly" got so much airtime that it easily qualified as the adjective du jour when describing the snakehead.

To many reporters the story was more science fiction than non-fiction. One newscaster on Channel 13 called it "the invasion of the walking fish," while her colleague said he expected to see Rod Serling of "Twilight Zone" fame arrive on the scene any moment. A reporter on the "CBS Evening News" said the northern snake-head was "like the Loch Ness monster of this little pond." An in-studio anchor for Channel 2 news warned her pond-side colleague of the dangers of staying in the area too long. "With that killer fish on the prowl," she said, "we don't want you there after dark, so go home, okay." After listening to a colleague rattle off the northern snakehead's more alarming characteristics, Wendy Rieger of Channel 4, in Washington, D.C., expressed one of the most unusual knocks against the fish, saying, "It's probably not even paying its taxes, so, you know, we don't like it."

Naturally, the stories during this week presented a lot of the same information, including the concerns about there being more than one snakehead the pond, the possibility of them mating, and, of course, numerous renditions of Gillespie's battle with the fish. And virtually every report commented on the snakehead's amazing skills. For exam-ple, Brad Bell, of Channel 7 news out of Virginia, ended one of his reports stating that snakeheads have the "potential to take over the ecosystem, devouring all native fish; and here's the spooky part, it can travel over land." But many of the stories also added their own twists. *National Geographic News* tied the snakehead to the larger issue of invasive species. The article quoted Paul Shafland, director of the Non-Native Fish Research Laboratory with the Florida Fish and Wildlife Conservation Commission, a man who has decades of experience managing nonindigenous species in that state, and who would later in the summer play an important role in managing the snakehead situation in Crofton. "Obviously we need to do more," Shafland said, "to educate the public about the serious ecological consequences that the illegal release of exotic species represents. People need to understand that once exotic species are established they're impossible to eliminate and the consequences can be catastrophic. Releasing them into the wild is not humane and it's not smart." In one of Thomson's articles, Walter Courtenay raised another concern; namely that the fish Gillespie caught was much bigger than northern snakeheads one is likely to see in a fish market, "which is about 12-14 inches." This led Courtenay to speculate that the fish had "been in there for a while." The *Bangkok Post* chimed in with a culinary perspective, noting that the snakehead, called *pla chon* in Thailand, is a common item in Thai restaurants. For those intent on eating, not retreating from the snakehead, the newspaper offered three options: drop chunks of the fish in a spicy, lemony soup; make it into fishcakes; or steam it whole with onions, scallions, garlic, and shiitake mushrooms.

What some of the articles and reports that came out this week shared, other than the basic information, was a developing sense of humor. Even if the snakehead could potentially cause serious harm to local ecosystems, it was fun writing about this ugly invader that appeared to have been engineered by mad scientists intent on scaring us out of our wits. Thomson's June 30 column on the snakeheads was probably the first to try to get a laugh from the snakehead story.

Now, such efforts were multiplying. On July 2, CBS News senior political editor Dotty Lynch ran a column titled "summer stories," and the snakehead made the list. She briefly recounted the very basics of the story, then wondered, "Will Kathleen Kennedy Townsend [Democratic candidate for governor of Maryland] send her lieutenant governor pick, four-star admiral Charles Lawson, off to fight the snakeheads? Will her gubernatorial opponent, Republican Bob Ehrlich, blame them on too many years of Democrats in the Statehouse?" The next day, Ken Ringle, wrote in the *Washington Post* that "as if global warming, Islamic terrorism and Britney Spears's midriff weren't enough to worry about, we have received, wafting in from Crofton, reports of snakehead fish marching on Washington." He interviewed a chef in Bethesda, Maryland, who offered two tantalizing snakehead recipes, one of which included a sauce made in part from green mangoes. The chef knew just what she would do should a wandering snakehead detour into her restaurant—give it "the mango treatment." On July 7, Maureen Dowd, in a *New York Times* op-ed piece titled "Have You Seen This Fish?" informed readers what the snakehead was and what it was not. "It's predatory, voracious and creeps on the land, but it's not a C.E.O.," wrote Dowd. "It's a snakehead, but it's not James Carville." She added, "The snakehead is as sneaky as the head snake Osama; it can burrow beneath muck, hiding for months." Lunsford's now famous "baddest bunny in the bush" quote made an appearance, as did the snakehead's best known alias, Frankenfish. Dowd ended with a warning, guaranteed to resonate with fans of "Saturday Night Live." "So if there is a knock at your door and a strange voice says, 'Candygram,' don't open it."

One person watching the evolving snakehead saga who was not at all amused was Paul DiMauro. He was interested in telling more people about his story of catching the first snakehead, and he definitely wanted credit for being the first to haul one in. But even before Joe Gillespie caught his fish, DiMauro had not gotten much media coverage. Once Gillespie and his fish became the story, DiMauro's tale faded even further into the background, and soon disappeared entirely. "This whole thing is kind of irritating to me," DiMauro said, "because I never got anything from it. This Joe Gillespie guy went off, but I never got anything from catching the snakehead. . . . They got their hero, I guess. That's Joe 'the snakehead' Gillespie. I laughed to myself but it made me angry." According to Burke, DiMauro's part of the story faded because "the press moved on. Maybe he [DiMauro] was mentioned in the last paragraph." Thomson said, "I feel kind of sorry for DiMauro because he ended up not being able to market himself. Here's this poor guy, nice guy, and just a few people wanted to talk to him." DiMauro was not only upset about the press's coverage of his role, but also the use of his pictures. The picture the DNR scanned in on that day in the middle of June, for identification purposes, ultimately made its way into the hands of newspaper reporters, and then the Associated Press and other wire services picked it up and it appeared all over the world. But, DiMauro insists, he "never gave them permission to the use the photograph. . . . I never made the photograph public domain." And he never got any compensation for the use of the image either.

In the midst of all this activity, Eric Schwaab took a moment to reflect on recent events. "It's an oddity," Schwaab told Scott Burke. "I think what's happening here is the combination of the unusual and the unknown sort of coming together to excite an interest." Schwaab later added, "Nobody has reacted to the zebra mussels in the way they have to the snakehead. There's a sort of mythology to it. Some of this is just a commentary on our culture." Schwaab was already concerned about the tenor of many of the news reports, which were getting more sensational by the day. In an effort to place the threat in perspective, Schwaab wrote about the snakehead in his "Director's Corner" article, which appeared on the DNR's website in early July.

As I write, the northern snakehead is all anyone wants to talk about.... We have worked to assess the scope of the problem and the threat posed by this non-native fish, considered various options for eradication of the fish from the pond, and generally worked with the media to separate fact from the growing fiction surrounding the fish. In the end, our goal will be to eliminate the threat to our native fish populations and use the attention brought to bear by this event to remind people of the dangers associated with careless introductions of non-native species into our waterways.

Like many other non-native species, the snakehead has the potential to disturb functioning natural ecosystems. As a top-level predator it can quickly impact local fish populations through predation or displacement. While many non-native species can spread rapidly, impacting an ever-broadening area (think of zebra mussels, gypsy moths and mute swans to name a few), the snakehead's ability to spread is limited by its mobility and habitat requirements. Although it has been reported as a walking fish, the real threat is its ability to live for days out of water and potentially wallow its way to other water bodies, or be spread by human intervention or flood. While there is a concern that it could spread to the nearby Patuxent River system, there is no evidence that such spread has occurred. Additionally, the species is not tolerant of salinity, so it is unlikely to threaten broad areas of the Chesapeake Bay region.

Schwaab was also quick to educate the public about the real risks of the snakehead in his growing interactions with the media. For example, during an interview on Channel 11 out of Baltimore Schwaab said, "The story has taken on a life of its own. . . . They do have a potential to displace other top line predators. . . . Do we view it as a walking fish, per se, no; could this fish live for long periods of time out of the water, yes; could it potentially wallow its way to other territories, yes." Apparently, Schwaab's efforts at education and reducing the hype were lost on the reporter who penned the story. As a lead-in to the segment featuring Schwaab, the reporter said, "The fish is a sharp-toothed monster able to swim in water and walk on land. Lurking in this Crofton pond it eats just about everything in its path, taking on almost mythical proportions."

Despite the media hype, Schwaab remained confident that there was no need to rush to rid the pond of snakeheads. Instead, the DNR planned to continue to monitor and assess the situation, and evaluate eradication options. Schwaab told Burke and other reporters that although the DNR wanted to capture the snakeheads as soon as possible, the risks associated with not being able to do so until the fall when the vegetation died back, were "minimal."

While the press was having a field day, the DNR was baiting hooks and setting traps to no avail. The DNR had set more than a dozen traps on Monday, July 1, laced with 9-Lives cat food to lure unsuspecting snakeheads to their doom. Although cat food might seem an odd choice, it wasn't. Cat food is what is technically referred to by fish biologists and anglers as stinky bait. Its oils quickly disperse into the water column, leaving a trail of odors that serve as a dinner bell for fish. Appropriately, cat food works wonders for attracting catfish. Perhaps it would do the trick with snakeheads as well. That hope, however, was in vain. When the traps were pulled the next day, there was nothing in them except for a snapping turtle that was quickly returned to the pond. The lack of fishing prowess on the part of state and federal officials was starting to raise eyebrows. DiMauro and

Gillespie had each caught a snakehead, after all, why couldn't the DNR or the Fish and Wildlife Service? Toward the middle of the week, the DNR retreated for the moment. "We're a bust," Lunsford was reported as saying in one of Thomson's articles. "We're pulling everything out for the Fourth of July weekend and letting the local experts—the guys who fish this regularly—take over. . . . This is definitely going to be a lengthy process."

Scores of anglers came in search of glory. They were a hardy bunch, braving soaring temperatures that flirted with the hundred-degree mark. It wasn't the heat that was bothering them, however, nor the humidity, but rather the lack of snakeheads. It is safe to say that the lowly pond off of Route 3 had never had as many people trolling its depths with hooks and lures as there were during these days in early July. And never had so many tried so hard, for so long, and come up with so little. Perhaps, offered a few observers, the snakehead was not only voracious but also smart. That nobody was catching anything led one angler to muse that the snakeheads must have eaten every other fish in the pond. While all of the anglers shared the same goal of catching a snakehead, their motives varied. Some thought it would be great to have the fame that would no doubt rain down on the head of the angler who caught another snakehead, even if that fame were likely to be fleeting and, well, fishy. Others just wanted to kill the dreaded demon in hand-to-fish battle. *Baltimore Sun* reporter Alec MacGillis caught up with a teenager from Glen Burnie, Maryland, who said, "This thing walks on land and has teeth sharper than a piranha. It doesn't belong here. If I get that [fish], I'm going to stab the heck out of it and kill it." Still others viewed the snakehead as money in the bank. MacGillis interviewed two teenagers who said that if they captured the snakehead, they would keep it alive and auction it off on eBay. One of them said they would start the bidding at $500. But what if the DNR wanted the fish, asked MacGillis. Well, replied one of teen entrepreneurs, "Then we can sell it to them. They can bid on it like everyone else."

The teens weren't the only entrepreneurs working to capitalize on the snakehead. William Berkshire and his daughters were forging ahead with their plans for a snakehead merchandising empire. The first and easiest step had already been taken. If you're going to start a new business on the fly and you want to get the word out quickly all over the country and the globe, one of the best and cheapest ways to do it is to publish a website on the Internet. A key to a good website is having a catchy and meaningful name. The Berkshires tried to grab www.snakehead.com, but that had already been taken, for what purpose, though, was unclear because the site had yet to be developed. Frankenfish.com was also gone, taken by the FrankenFish Racing Team, which seems to be a group that shows and races 1967 Plymouth Barracudas, a.k.a. the FrankenFish. Other sites were available, including croftonsnakehead.com, croftonfrankenfish.com, and snakeheadstuff.com, the last being the one the Berkshires decided to use. But a website is only as good as the products it offers, so during the first few weeks of July, the Berkshires designed a range of T-shirts and began the search for a graphics shop to produce them. With all the notoriety the snakehead had garnered, the Berkshires were already thinking big. It might be possible to sell thousands of T-shirts. It depended on what happened next.

FOUR

SPAWN OF FRANKENFISH

Toward the end of the first week of his newfound fame, Joe Gillespie took the snakehead out of the freezer and handed it over to Don Kemp to have it mounted. Kemp, a full-time florist and part-time taxidermist, was self-taught and had years of experience. Gillespie requested a skin mount, a complicated and lengthy process. First, the fish is cut open on one side and the meat and bones are taken out. Then the skin is cured in denatured alcohol and water for two weeks, making it hard; next, it is soaked in warm water and laundry detergent for five to ten minutes to make it pliable again. To further cure the skin and enable it to age well, other chemicals are applied, at which point a mannequin constructed by the taxidermist is placed inside the skin to give form to the fish. The skin is then sewn up, the fins are splayed, and the mount is left to dry for as many as four months. Finally, the fish is painted to look as if it had just been taken out of the water.

When Gillespie brought in the fish, Kemp couldn't tell him how long it would take to finish the mount. Part of the uncertainty had to do with Kemp's schedule. He would have to fit in the work when he could. But most of the uncertainty lay with the snakehead itself. As Kemp later recalled, "I've done hundreds of rockfish, hundreds of bluegills and other fish, but with a new fish like this one, I'm walking there blind." The biggest unknown surrounding the preparation of a skin mount for the snakehead centered on the drying process. For this type of mount, it is especially important that the taxidermist gets all the meat and fat out of the fish; if he doesn't, the mount might drip later on. Having never mounted a snakehead before, Kemp would have to monitor the drying process for some time before he was confident that it wouldn't drip and that he was handing over a quality product. "That's my name on it," Kemp said, "I don't want Joe [Gillespie] coming back two years later and saying she turned yellow."

Gillespie was excited about the prospect of having the fish mounted, but many of his thoughts were still focused on the pond. In the week since catching the snakehead, he kept wondering about the "column of minnows" he had seen and how the snakehead hung around them. Gillespie was convinced that they were baby snakeheads, and to prove his point, he went back to the pond on Sunday, July 7, to catch some. There were other people there, casting from the shore, hoping to hook another snakehead, but because Gillespie was in search of much smaller quarry, he knew he needed to use a very different fishing technique. He got on his sailboard and paddled out into the pond, net in hand, while his wife stood on the shoreline and used binoculars to locate where the "minnows" were

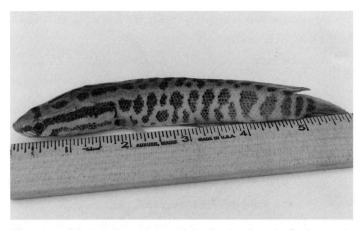

This is one of the juvenile northern snakeheads taken from the Crofton pond by the Maryland Department of Natural Resources. Courtesy Tom Darden.

bubbling up. After a half hour of wife-to-husband direction and multiple thrusts into the water, Gillespie netted one fish, which, judging by the bars on its side and other features, he felt sure was a baby northern snakehead. He brought the fish home, but there was a problem. Gillespie didn't have a fish tank, so his wife went out and bought him one, and in went the fish, which they dubbed Frank Jr., after Frankenfish of course.

Gillespie and his family admired the new addition to their kitchen, and watched Frank Jr. swim around the tank and devour guppies. Word traveled fast and a stream of people came by to see the fish. One visitor was Bonnie Coombs, a close friend of Gillespie's daughter. That night, while eating dinner with her family, Bonnie told her dad that "Mr. Joe" had caught a baby snakehead. This piece of information, while of interest, probably wouldn't have elicited much more than an "oh really, that's neat" from most fathers in Crofton, but Bonnie's dad wasn't just any father. He was Francis B. Coombs Jr., the managing editor of the *Washington Times*. "My news antenna went up instantly," said Mr. Coombs. The next morning, he instructed the metro news editor to call Gillespie, who confirmed that he had indeed caught a baby snakehead. Could a reporter and photographer come by to get the story, inquired the editor? "Sure," said Gillespie. By the time the folks from the *Washington Times* arrived, Gillespie was back at the pond. During the day, a number of his friends had come over to see the fish and a few wanted to have a Frank Jr. of their own, so off to the pond Gillespie went, in search of more babies. Gillespie's luck was better this time; he caught seven.

Tuesday morning, the *Washington Times* had the scoop on the all the other media outlets. "We stripped the story across the top of page one," recalls Coombs, "with a four-column color cutout of the fish, and the rest is history." Titled "Spawn of 'Frankenfish'?" the article chronicled Gillespie's capture of the babies. In addition to the outsized picture of the baby snakehead on page one, the article had an even larger shot of Gillespie standing knee-deep in the pond, net in hand, poised to strike, looking intensely into the weed-covered water for snakehead fry. Gillespie told reporter Jeff Barnes that he wasn't worried about keeping the snakehead babies. "They seem more like a puppy. They seem to have a lot of personality. Plus, it's a souvenir. If they poison the pond, at least I got a snakehead out of it." As to the measure of celebrity he had achieved by dint of catching the larger snakehead a week earlier, Gillespie said, "It's like winning the lottery and hooking 'jaws' all at once. It feels like a dream." When reached for comment, the DNR's John Surrick offered a measured response to the news of the purported, but as yet unconfirmed, newborns. "It's certainly something that's been a possibility and concern all along. There's no reason to believe it's becoming more widespread, but we think it's probably doing OK in the [pond]." With respect to the widespread media attention that the snakehead had garnered, Surrick added, "some people have called it 'Frankenfish,' but that's certainly not applicable. It certainly sells more newspapers."

Staff from the DNR visited Gillespie and the fish on Tuesday morning. As to why this visit didn't occur sooner after the fish were caught isn't clear. According to Gillespie, when he called the DNR on Monday, he was told that everyone was in a meeting and that they would come by the next morning to see the fish. Surrick claims that the folks at the DNR asked to come by right away, but Gillespie said that that was "not convenient now." Regardless of which version is correct, the DNR didn't see the babies until Tuesday morning, after the article in the *Washington Times* was on the street.

When the DNR arrived at Gillespie's house at 8:15 there was already a sizeable crowd of media folks milling around, all hoping for some time with Gillespie and one or more of the babies. Everyone knew that the snakehead story had just jumped a few notches higher on the newsworthy scale and they wanted in on the action. According to Schwaab, "Up until then, I think Gillespie was very much sort of enjoying the limelight, but the reality of having the media camped out in front of his house suddenly hit home." And the media weren't content to just sit quietly on the lawn. "It was wild," Gillespie said. "People were all over, knocking on the front door, knocking on the back door, and the phone [which had started ringing at 6:30 that morning] kept ringing. I was trapped in the house, there were about twenty cars and news vans out front." Eric Schwaab recalls Gillespie's wife asking him, "Can't you do something to make them go away?" Schwaab told Gillespie, "If you want to have the media circus to move away from the front of your house you need to stop talking to them at every opportunity." While certainly a reasonable long-term strategy, it did little to help the current situation.

With the intent of giving the Gillespie's some immediate peace and quiet, and answering the media's numerous questions, Steve Early placed one of the baby fish in a plastic bag and walked to the front yard, whereupon he informed the media throng that he and his colleagues would be going to the pond for a press conference. Like moths to a flame, the reporters gathered around Early, and then followed the small DNR motorcade to the pond. Gillespie seized the moment. "I waited until DNR left with the baby fish I gave them, and most of the news people followed. I still had to run to my truck and zoom out before the rest of the reporters realized I was leaving. I had a lot of work to do that day and was already running late." The reporters who stayed behind didn't give up, and they were joined by reinforcements. Throughout the day, Gillespie's wife called him with updates about reporters banging on the front door and not going away when they were told he was not home and that, no, they couldn't come in and take pictures. The phone rang so often that morning that Gillespie's wife turned off the ringer and let the answering machine take over.

One of Gillespie's neighbors became curious, and a little concerned, about the cars idling in the street. When the neighbor approached one of the cars and asked the occupants who they were and why they were hanging around, they said they were reporters waiting for Gillespie to come home. And they were very patient reporters because they were there all day.

Although it would be two days before Walter Courtenay positively identified the small fish as baby northern snakeheads, the DNR proceeded on the assumption that that was what they were. After all, they looked like miniature northern snakeheads and they certainly weren't the young of any other fish normally found in the area. This discovery changed everything. "The presence of juvenile fish," said Schwaab, "certainly upped the control ante for us. Suddenly, instead of dealing with one or two fish we are dealing with hundreds or thousands of fish. We've got a different control responsibility and problem now."

One of DNR's first actions, on the day that the *Washington Times* article appeared, was to work with the landowners, the MacQuilliam Organization and Berkshire, to close off the ponds to public access. Before the babies were found, anglers were viewed as a welcome partner in ridding the pond of adult snakeheads. The existence of babies, however, altered the DNR's perspective. According to Schwaab, closing the pond "eliminated or at least minimized the danger of a whole bunch of fisherman being in there and possibly transmitting viable eggs or young, by accident, that could be spread to other ponds. . . .With nonnative species introduction, more often than not, by the time you're aware of the problem it's too late to eradicate it, you are simply into a long-term control strategy. At this point we had a reasonable expectation that we could eradicate the population before it spread to other nearby bodies of water." To help keep the public out, the DNR erected an orange plastic fence along the edge of the parking lot next to the pond, and also posted no trespassing signs. That same day, the DNR created a panel of experts to explore ways to eradicate the snakeheads and recommend the best strategy to pursue. DNR Secretary, J. Charles (Chuck) Fox tapped Professor Donald Boesch, director of the University of Maryland Center for Environmental Science, to head the panel.

Two days later all of the speculation about the source of the northern snakeheads in Crofton stopped. At a press conference, the DNR announced that they knew the person responsible for the introduction. Acting on a tip, the Maryland Natural Resources Police had interviewed a local man of Asian descent who confessed to the deed, expressing great remorse for his actions. He said that he had purchased two live snakeheads from a New York fish market to make snakehead fish soup for his ailing sister, thinking that fish's curative powers would help her get better. Before he could make the dish, his sister got better, and instead of eating the fish, the man decided to keep them in an aquarium. Soon, however, the fish outgrew the aquarium and/or the man got tired of sating their appetite through daily and expensive feedings of up to twelve goldfish. To rid himself of the fish he dumped them in the Crofton pond—not in 2002, not in 2001, but in 2000. Because the statute of limitations had run out, the man could not be brought up on charges of violating the Maryland's ban on introducing nonindigenous species into state waterways. Even if he had been charged, the penalties for such actions were relatively minor, at most a $500 fine. Schwaab used the press conference as a forum for spreading the larger message about introduced species. "This situation again points out the responsibility," Schwaab said, "we all share to refrain from purposeful release of fish to our waterways and to take great care to prevent even accidental introduction of nonnative bait, plants or other species when we go fishing, boating, or otherwise venture into the natural environment."

On the day of the press conference, DNR and U.S. Fish and Wildlife staff were at the pond, electroshocking and dipnetting in the hope of landing more babies. Other anglers were there as well, including Gillespie. While he was giving a pond-side interview, Gillespie looked into the water and saw what he thought were baby snakeheads just a few feet from the shoreline. A guy from the U.S. Fish and Wildlife Service said they were mosquitofish, but Gillespie insisted they weren't. When the Service guy caught one and saw that it was a baby snakehead, he excitedly yelled over to his DNR colleagues, "You guys have to buy the doughnuts, we caught the first fish." By the end of the day, state and federal officials had captured ninety-nine three-inch baby northern snakeheads. According to Gillespie, "When those little babies came up to me when I was doing that interview at the pond, they were all teasing me that I must have gotten pheromones on me from the mother fish. That is the only way I could catch those babies. A few people said the babies were coming after me for revenge." Whatever the reason for the appearance of the babies that day, Gillespie was glad it happened. "I was happy when they caught the baby ones," he said, "because I was beginning to get these odd looks like how come Joe's the only one catching fish out of there."

The number of babies captured that day surprised few of the biologists. Northern snakeheads are prolific breeders. Mating occurs as many as four or five times a year, with females producing 100,000 eggs or more during that cycle. And because northern snakeheads actively protect their broods, survival rates are relatively high. Given these characteristics, it would have been more surprising had there been only a few babies in the pond. According to Surrick, "We've said all along that if there are juveniles in there, there would be hundreds or thousands of them."

The week following Joe Gillespie's capture of the babies was arguably the craziest of the summer for the folks at the DNR. The day the juveniles were found, John Surrick recalled, "Things really hit the fan." He and Heather Lynch were fielding dozens of media calls a day, and DNR biologists were also getting called directly. The snakehead saga had taken another evolutionary leap and the press was there to relay every detail to the growing national and international audience that had been watching the story unfold. Once again, headline writers were working overtime generating banners that were sure to lure readers.

JULY 9
"Frankenfish" Has Spawned (NBC 4, Washington, D.C.)

This cartoon was drawn by Charles C. Somerville (Who Else?®), a freelance writer and designer, who lives in Washington, D.C. Although this cartoon was never published, Somerville sent it via e-mail to folks at the Maryland Department of Natural Resources, the U.S. Environmental Protection Agency, and the Chesapeake Bay Foundation, as well as other organizations that were involved in one way or another in the snakehead story. Somerville said, "It was a natural to send the cartoon along to them . . . after all, they are the ones that really 'get it' when it comes to the threat of such pests." Many of the people who received the cartoon, in turn, sent it to their colleagues, and in that way the cartoon received wide distribution. One of the recipients was the author of this book.

JULY 10

Killer Chinese Fish Surfaces in Maryland (WPVI TV
Channel 6, Philadelphia)

JULY 11

Police Identify Killer Fish Culprit (NBC 4, Washington,
D.C.)

Alien Killer Fish Were Pets (CNN)

JULY 12

Flesh-eating Fish Stalks U.S. Residents (*The Independent*,
South Africa)

Maryland Suffers Setback in War on Invasive Walking Fish
(*National Geographic News*)

Giant, Meat-Eating Chinese Fish Worry Maryland Officials
(Fox News)

Freak Fish Have Spawned! Oh My! (CBS News)

Shocked: 99 Alien Fish Snagged in Pond (CNN)

"Frankenfish" Terrorizes MD Countryside; Well, Maybe Not, But
Creature Devours Contents of Entire Ponds (*Seattle Times*)

JULY 13

"Frankenfish" Threatens U.S. (New24.Com, South Africa)

Battling an Alien Predator in a Suburban Pond (*The New York
Times*)

Asian Snakehead, Dubbed "Frankenfish," Panics U.S.
Naturalists (*Agence France Presse*)

In Foreign Parts: Lurking Under the Lilypads, the Mystery of
Ole Snakey Is Finally Solved (*The Independent*, United
Kingdom)

Juvenile "Frankenfish" Raise Odds of Alien Invasion
(*Washington Times*)

JULY 15

Frankenfish, Voracious Eater that Can Grow Very Quickly,

Gillespie and his son, Mark, paddle out onto the pond for the benefit of the ABC News film crew, which had asked the pair to re-create their hunt for the snakehead. Courtesy Cait Gillespie.

Can "Walk" on Its Fins and Live on Land for Days (*Straits Times*, Singapore)

"ABC Nightly News" anchor, Peter Jennings, told listeners that the snakehead was "a peculiar fish that can also travel on land, is extremely aggressive, and always hungry. Most recently it has showed up in Maryland where it is causing great alarm because nobody knows how it got there." Jennings then turned the story over to reporter Bill Blakemore, who ended the segment with some advice. "If you're out fishing on a summer day by a pond or a stream," he said, "and happen to catch one of these [a northern snakehead], do not, repeat, do not throw it back." Gillespie, his son, Mark, and Mark's friend, Jake Harkey, remember the ABC spot very well. In preparing the piece, an ABC crew filmed the trio at the pond for nearly two hours and had them bring along Gillespie's sailboard and fishing rods to re-create and talk about their battle with the snakehead.

On NBC's "Today" show, Katie Couric and Matt Lauer turned to reporter Virginia Cha to tell the story. After running through the basic details, Cha asked, "How did this bloodthirsty fish native to China get here?" and quickly responded that "the answer" lay "200 miles away in New York's Chinatown where snakeheads can be purchased as a delicacy or as pets." Wendy Rieger, of Washington's NBC Channel 4 said that the story thus far "sounds like a script for a B-movie. But scientists say this isn't Godzilla." Schwaab then came on the air. "It's not a monster fish," he said. "It's a top-level predator that's not native to this area and therefore there are risks, most predominantly to the natural ecosystem. There are others [invasive species] that certainly don't have the allure, the media attention, or the mythology around them that the snakehead does but are perhaps just as, if not more, threatening in the long run." Reiger wasn't biting. "But face it," she said, "the dreaded zebra mussel isn't going to draw a crowd."

The *Washington Post* reporters Anita Huslin and Michael E. Ruane began their story with a lead-in worthy of a B movie: "Beneath the murky water that bubbles and smells like a cauldron of menace, where the blue dragonflies hover and the bottom tugs at unsuspecting feet, the monster fish may be multiplying." Despite the fact that the pond was officially off-limits to fisherman, Huslin and Ruane found that there were many who walked right past the orange barrier fencing and disregarded the newly posted no-fishing signs. One teenage angler boasted that he and his buddies would "conquer the snakehead. It doesn't matter how big it is, how tough it thinks it is. We'll destroy that snakehead."

Jennifer Harper of the *Washington Times*, in an article titled "'Frankenfish' Sets Off Feeding Frenzy," reflected on the snakeheads' growing notoriety and fame. "So, does the fish have an agent yet?" she wrote. "Crofton, Maryland's notorious northern snakehead fish has created a global splash, a veritable media feeding frenzy of camera crews, reporters, biologists, gawkers and—yes—anglers, who have besieged the four-acre Maryland pond, now home to a rogue family of *Channa argus*." Harper quoted Lynch as saying, "It has been a zoo. This is a top-of-the-line predator fish. It's not like covering, say, the invasion of mute swan or nutria, which are water rats." Harper noted that interest in the snakehead had risen high enough to merit airtime on the popular morning talk show, "Live with Regis and Kelly." The article also touched upon the question of who invented the term "Frankenfish." Someone at a local radio station claimed to have coined the term by using it earlier in the summer to describe the snakehead, but Harper set the record straight, noting that others had applied that moniker to genetically engineered salmon years earlier.

According to Stephanie Griffith, with the *Agence France Presse*, "the marauding invader, with its voracious appetite and seemingly supernatural powers, aroused fears from the moment it presence in the United States first became the subject of a news headlines and local television broadcasts. . . . Practically overnight the northern snakehead fish has come to be seen as one of the most dangerous interlopers to threaten any US ecosystem. . . . If the babies elicit awe, adults spark full-blown terror." Andrew Buncombe of the United Kingdom's *Independent* opined, "What a waste," after telling his readers how the man who had purchased the snakeheads had dumped them into the pond. Not only are the fish held in awe by some cultures—the Karen people of Burma, for instance — they are also considered something of a delicacy. To prove the point, Buncombe quoted Paul Shafland as saying, "I have eaten quite a few snakeheads since we started our research and can attest to their excellent taste."

Francis X. Clines, of the *New York Times*, noting that for weeks nobody knew from whence the snakeheads of Crofton came, called the story "an environmental mystery that had been titillating people with visions of alien, snaggle-toothed fish intent on a voracious land march up the East Coast." Clines also highlighted the possibility that the hype surrounding the fish might not match the reality of the threat. "Is this pond," he wrote, "only a resting spot to launch devastating schools farther north by way of the Little Patuxent River, a mere 75-yard flop away? Or might these fish flop in more ways than one, like the walking catfish that never lived up to the killer-bees–style warnings of headlines in slow-news times past?"

The comparison to the walking catfish was most appropriate. In many ways, the story of the northern snakehead thus far roughly paralleled that of the introduction of walking catfish in Florida in the 1960s. A native of Southeast Asia, the walking catfish (*Clarias batrachus*) is not a pretty fish. It was legally imported into the United States, but unintentionally introduced into the wild. The walking catfish can breathe air, but its modified lungs are much more developed and efficient than the northern snakehead's, enabling the catfish to stay out of the water, as long as it is kept moist, for periods far greater than three days. Unlike the northern snakehead, the walking catfish actually can "walk" after a fashion, propping itself up on it spine-stiffened pectoral fins and ambulating over the ground, even dry ground, with surprising alacrity, for a fish that is. And when it became known that the walking catfish had established a breeding population in Florida, there was a great hue and cry, and stories on the "invasion" of this new species and the impeding ecological doom that was sure to follow reached a fever pitch.

The story of the walking catfish's introduction is a family affair. The normal coloration of this species ranges from slate-gray to brown or black. In the early 1960s, someone found an amelanic

Walking catfish emerging from the water to take a stroll. Courtesy
Florida Fish and Wildlife Conservation Commission.

form of the walking catfish that was pale pink in color. According
to Walter Courtenay, Walter Rudy, who owned an aquarium fish
farm in southern Florida, thought that these unusually colored specimens would find a ready market with hobbyists, and he imported
and raised them for that purpose. Walter Rudy never denied the
claim made by some that a few of the walking catfish managed to
crawl out of his containment ponds into one of the numerous canals
that dot Florida's landscape. But when Walter's brother Richard
heard this story from Courtenay he got upset and sought to set the
record straight. According to Courtenay, Richard said, "Did my
brother tell you that he introduced walking catfish?" When
Courtenay said yes, Richard said, "He's a God damned liar. I introduced them." Richard said that Walter had asked him to transport

a load of walking catfish from Miami, and as he drove back to Walter's farm the catfish were flopping and jumping out of the boxes on the truck, and a few of them landed on the road, which was located next to a drainage canal. Richard didn't stop to collect the escapees. Indeed, the only time he did stop was to remove an errant catfish that had become lodged under the accelerator pedal. Richard was sure, he told Courtenay, that the loss of most of his cargo is what led to the establishment of waking catfish in Florida.

In a June 1969 article in *National Geographic* on the walking catfish, Vernon Ogilvie, a biologist with the state of Florida, expressed a level of alarm that was indicative of much of the feeling at the time. The author of the article quoted him as saying, "*Clarias* has already gotten into Lake Okeechobee, and I'm holding my breath for what will happen when it reaches Everglades National Park. It may have disastrous consequences." Both Courtenay and Paul Shafland are very familiar with the story of the walking catfish and they agreed that the press's coverage of this fish during the late 1960s and early 1970s was every bit, if not more, dramatic than the coverage accorded the northern snakehead in Crofton, Maryland, during the summer of 2002. In some instances the coverage was so similar that one could insert "northern snakehead" for "walking catfish," or vice-versa, and the story would remain essentially the same.

But what of the walking catfish and the fate of Florida's native freshwater fish? Although this species is broadly established in Florida, it hasn't resulted in ecological ruin. According to Shafland, while walking catfish have created some problems for the tropical fish industry, by slithering into containment ponds and eating their way through swordtails, mollies, and other fish destined for aquaria, "if there is an overall effect on the fish community in Florida, it certainly isn't quantifiable and I would say it falls within the realm of dynamic equilibrium." Courtenay noted that the initial population explosion of walking catfish has dissipated and their presence hasn't caused a collapse of native fisheries. Whether the northern snakehead would, if established in Maryland, follow the same trajectory as the walking catfish did in Florida was, of course, unknowable, but it was a reasonable question to ask.

When the television show, the "McLaughlin Group" took up the snakehead, the conversation was characteristically entertaining and prescriptive. The segment began with the *Jaws* theme playing in the background while Mark Gillespie told of his famous and nerve-wracking encounter with the snakehead, that, he said, "looked like a little shark." The moderator, John McLaughlin, solemnly informed his listeners that the fish that had such a dramatic impact on young Mark was none other than the Chinese snakehead, "a rapacious predator with razor-sharp teeth that can devour all the fish, reptiles, insects and amphibians in an entire pond." He added that "if this alien species is not contained, it could threaten all freshwater fish and ecosystems in its path." Turning to his trusted and trenchant panel for their input, McLaughlin elicited surprising information and insights. Tony Blakely mentioned that then–majority leader of the U.S. House of Representatives Dick Armey "said that he would be prepared to kill those fish even though the bass fish he always catches he throws back." Eleanor Clift wondered how the guy who dumped the fish ever got them into the country, noting that when she enters the United States, "They won't even let me bring a piece of fruit." Lawrence Kudlow added, "We need to harness these fish, get them on land and have them either attack the al Qaedas living in this country, or possibly the members of the Senate appropriations committee." Realizing that his panel was hopelessly offtrack and had failed to appreciate the seriousness of the situation, McLaughlin got to the part of the show he clearly relishes the most—telling his panel and the audience what should be done. He had no doubts. "The solution is you poison the whole pond and get rid of these fish," then restock it with less objectionable species.

One of the most interesting and dramatic news stories to appear in the week after the discovery of the baby snakeheads was in the *New York Daily News*. On July 13, the front page of the paper was almost completely devoted to a full-color image of baby snakeheads in water, with a massive headline that read "The Fish From Hell." A box offered a brief and chilling bio of the northern snakehead, stating that "they've got big teeth, can live on land, eat everything in sight—and they're on sale live for $9-a-pound in Chinatown." Given that the front page of the *New York Daily News* is used primarily for pulse-pounding stories that are sure to sell papers, the appearance of the snakehead was quite complimentary to the species and the story it had generated. And lest one think that the snakehead made the front page only because there was little else newsworthy to report that day, at the top of the cover ran a banner that read, "Worst Stox Week Since 9/11." What's a billion here, a billion there, when Satan's offspring could be found not only in a small Maryland pond, but also right in the fish markets of New York?

The headline on the story inside the *New York Daily News* read, "Fierce Fish Dragnet, Chinatown Monster Loose," and the story began, "A predatory, saw-toothed monster fish that can walk on land has migrated from New York's Chinatown to a Maryland pond, and authorities fear its ravenous spawn will invade the Chesapeake Bay." To gain more perspective on the snakehead threat, the reporters interviewed Dr. Paul Loiselle, curator of Freshwater Fishes for the New York Aquarium, who recommended that the officials in Maryland "dynamite the pond." Loiselle has a lot of experience with snakeheads, particularly *Channa striata*, the chevron snakehead. Loiselle's extensive research and efforts to save native fish in Madagascar led him to confront the chevron snakehead head-on so to speak, because that species has had a dramatic and negative impact on native fish populations in that African country. (Some ichthyologists contend that the snakehead species in Madagascar is not *Channa striata*, but *Channa maculata* [the blotched snakehead].) "If you had to carry out a job interview," Loiselle told me, "for the worst imaginable fish to introduce to a place like Madagascar where you have a highly endemic and highly endangered fish fauna, there is no question that the snakehead would wind up winning the job hands down. . . . What they simply do is eat everything they can fit in their mouths, and since they can get to be about three feet long, there isn't a whole lot native to Madagascar that they can't fit in their mouths." That is why, when the *New York Daily News* caught up with him, Loiselle urged decisive action to eradicate the snakeheads. "My recommendation," he told me, "was nail that population while you still have a chance. While it is still in one isolated body of water do what you have to do to get rid of it. Because if it ever gets out of that quarry into a major river system, it's Katie bar the door, there is nothing you can do at that point."

Madagascar's experience with snakeheads illustrates, yet again, the unintended and at times devastating impacts of introducing nonindigenous species. Loiselle's account of the introduction of the chevron snakehead to Madagascar during the early 1970s is as interesting as it is alarming.

This was the personal project of the ex-president of the country during his phase as military dictator. He saw these fish on a visit to North Korea where they are used as a predator in tilapia ponds to control reproduction. He was very impressed by this for much the same reason that many men are impressed by pit bulls. He felt that he had to have these fish in Madagascar. He came back and contacted the head of the fisheries service and that guy said that is not a good idea, everywhere they have been introduced they have invariably had a very negative impact on the fish fauna. The president seemed to agree with this. A couple of months later a plane arrives from Beijing with two boxes of these things, a gift to the president of the Malagasy Republic from the People's Republic of China. He split the fingerlings into two lots. One bunch was set up at the pond at the presidential summer house just outside of the capital and that is in the headwaters of a westward draining river, and the other batch was sent down to his personal home on the East Coast, so they got in on the East Coast as well. Within a very short space of time the snakeheads did what snakeheads do, which is reproduced and climbed out of the ponds and started wiggling overland to other bodies of water. There have subsequently been translocations to other areas. . . . I'll talk to local people and I'll be looking for members of a particular group of fish, and the answer is oh, yes, such and such used to be very common and it has become very scarce since the fibata, or else we haven't seen it since the fibata came. [Fibata is the acronym for the bus company that was used to transport snakehead fingerlings down the coast and is how locals often refer to the fish.]

The Internet provided one of the surest signs that the snakeheads of Crofton were big news. The search engine Lycos prepares a daily report, called the Lycos 50, which tracks the terms its users query the most. For the week following the capture of the baby snakeheads, Lycos 50 noted that a large number of users were plugging "snakehead fish" into the search field. The Lycos 50 said that, "snakehead fish got as many searches as popular actresses Catherine Bell or Sarah Michelle Gellar," and received "three times as many as salmon and ten times as many as trout." This volume wasn't enough for the snakehead to crack the top fifty list, but it was a very respectable showing, especially when one considers that virtually no one had searched for information on snakeheads just three weeks earlier. To rank with Hollywood celebrities and to put traditionally newsworthy fish to shame was heady stuff, even for a snakehead. And it wasn't only the snakehead whose star had risen in the web-based universe where the number of hits one collects is a widely accepted surrogate measure of fame, or at least notoriety. When the DNR's Heather Lynch plugged her name into various search engines, she was surprised to see it appear in a large number of articles written not only in English, but also in German and French. Joe Gillespie, too, played the search-engine game. At his peak, he got eight hundred hits on Google.

Dealing with the media and reading the rapidly expanding press coverage of the snakehead story was frustrating for the staff at the DNR. Schwaab said the story "was very quickly spinning into these fish were going to be walking into your yard type of thing. Our credibility dictated that we keep to the facts, saying this is what we know, here's what we believe the risks to be, here's what we believe to be the possible remedies. All of this rampant speculation, you know, the awfulizing, the worst-casing could be left to others. We didn't want to contribute to that." Nevertheless, the DNR's ability to control the flow and accuracy of information and to make sure that the press didn't blow things out of proportion was, to some extent, compromised by comments made by DNR staff to the press in the earliest days of the story, which did portray the northern snakehead as, well, a little larger than life. "There is a tendency when somebody is sticking a microphone in your face to become part of the show, to fulfill their expectations," said Schwaab. "Some media folks wanted to make it a bigger story than it was, and there were some people here who were willing to play that part in a way that, ultimately, might have contributed to the hysteria or hyperbole that frankly wasn't accurate."

Surrick pointed to Lunsford's original quotes as being "slightly inflammatory," and he made it clear that his use of the word "slightly" was facetious. According to Early, "A few initial statements just overwhelmed any ability to react to it. You could try and turn the tide, try to get information out, but in the absence of information . . . something will fill that vacuum."

The DNR's ability to provide accurate information was often compromised by the lack of hard facts. "It was frustrating," said Early, "not being able to have all the information. People were saying, you're a fisheries biologist, you're the expert, what's the scoop." Although there was a range of scientific and anecdotal data on snakeheads, one would be hard-pressed to characterize the amount of information as extensive, especially as compared to what one might find when researching better known species of fish, such as bass and trout. Much of the information on snakeheads was in Chinese, Russian, or one of the other languages spoken in the region where snakeheads are normally found, making the data far less accessible than if it had been in English. Even Courtenay and his colleagues, who, in preparing the risk assessment, had been intensively studying snakeheads for nearly a year still had questions about their behavior and their potential to cause harm. As the snakehead story progressed, more of what *was* known about the fish came out, in some cases overturning earlier misconceptions or mistaken assumptions. But this, too, added to the difficulty of providing accurate and nonconfusing information to the public. According to Thomson, "It was like building a train while rolling down the tracks. This wasn't like picking up the specs on a Ford Mustang. The truth about the fish was always moving." In her search for information on snakeheads, Thomson saw firsthand the difficulties the experts were having in coming up with firm answers to her many questions. "You would call them," Thomson recalled, "and they would say, 'What, wait a minute,' and you could hear them going through papers, you could hear them getting online. It's like don't even bother going online, I've been there, you know, I've got my library here pulling stuff. Either you know something or you don't, and if you got to look it up you can't help me."

When the DNR staff tried to provide more accurate and qualified information, they often felt they had limited success. "People would call me," said Lynch, "and say why don't you tell me about this Frankenfish, and I'd say, Actually it's not, it's called a snakehead fish. Why don't you talk to me about how it walks on land, and I'd say, Well it doesn't. And they'd say, oh, I know, I know, but, and then you'd read their story and it would say that it did. People kept perpetuating it. It was like they couldn't stop. They wanted to write that story and maybe their editors wanted to play it up." According to Surrick, "It is the first time I've ever been involved in a situation where the story, the exaggerations to reality were so present. Usually, you can get a little bit wrong here and a little bit wrong there. But in this case the story was so out of control and the reporters reported it anyway. I watched people say in practicing for standup [on-air interviews] that they are voracious fish that are going to eat everything in the pond. And I would say, Look, they are not going to eat everything in the pond; that is something that is hype. And they say, Okay, and would go back and do their standup and say, They're voracious fish that are going to eat everything in the pond."

Another frustrating element of the DNR's interactions with the press was the sheer volume of requests. The fisheries people at the DNR had never experienced anything like the avalanche of press coverage that attended the snakehead. Representatives from virtually every segment of the Fourth Estate—television, radio, newspapers, magazines—wanted to interview Schwaab or some other agency staff to gain insights into the story. Traditionally, one of the most newsworthy items on the Fisheries Service's agenda is the announcement of the annual estimates for the number of blue crabs in the Chesapeake Bay. Maryland is famous for its blue crabs, and those estimates were watched closely not only by crabbers, but also by the legions of people who loved to eat the tasty crustaceans. The announcement of the blue crab numbers is always good for widespread local, and to a much lesser extent, regional and national coverage. In 2001, when *Newsweek* called to do a story on the blue crab numbers the people at the Fisheries Service got very excited. Their small piece of the world had hit the big time. Then the snakehead, figuratively, blew the blue crabs right out of the water. Now, the big time was on the phone and at the door begging for interviews. At first, the people at the DNR were nonselective. If a media outlet wanted to talk, the DNR folks would talk. That strategy, however, soon proved too unwieldy to sustain. DNR staff was spending so much time talking about the snakeheads, that it was getting increasingly hard to do all the other things they were hired to do, including devising and implementing a strategy to deal with snakeheads. As Schwaab recalls, "Fairly early on I stopped doing the local stuff from Wisconsin or wherever . . . I knew it wouldn't be a good use of my time." Then, "It got to the point, where we were saying, Do I really have to get on CNN. Literally, we began to filter. [All of the press coverage] was very distracting for the whole agency."

The DNR's perspective on the snakehead story and how to handle it was evolving as well. According to Thomson, initially the people at the DNR "didn't see the two-headed baby, four-headed calf, kind of gruesome jaws-like fascination the public would have with this." At the "beginning of the snakehead saga you couldn't have pulled a knitting needle out of Schwaab's butt," added Thomson, "he was so tight about it. He said everyone was making too much of a story out of it." That perspective was shared by many of the biologists in the Fisheries Service. The biologists were also, not surprisingly, wary of talking to the press. Scientists are often reluctant to interact with the press for fear that they will not be able to explain complex issues with sound bites and that the comments they do offer will be misunderstood, taken out of context, or misreported. The trajectory of the snakehead story thus far compounded rather than allayed such concerns for the biologists in the Fisheries Service. Another reason for the DNR biologist's wariness of the press had to do with disposition. Thomson remembers Early saying at one point during the summer, "I became a fish biologist so I wouldn't have to deal with a lot of people." While some scientists seek the media attention, most are much more comfortable doing their work and letting others deal with the press.

Now, however, the DNR was becoming more strategic in its thinking. Not only were they filtering contacts with the media, but they were also making greater efforts to control and structure the message. The DNR focused on two goals. First, maintaining the appropriate level of concern. The presence of snakeheads in Maryland was a serious issue, certainly, but it was no cause for panic. The DNR had a responsibility to provide accurate and appropriately qualified information to the public, but it didn't have to add to the hype. Second, the DNR wanted to take advantage of the press coverage to educate the public more about the threats posed by invasive species. "We figured," said Schwaab, "we've got this opportunity. We've got people's attention focused on this fish because of the mythology that had grown up around it. It had captured people's attention in a way that many of the other nonnative species we deal with hadn't. There was clearly a desire on our part to use the snakehead experience to symbolize the broader issue of nonnative invasive species. We began to add into the conversation, couch the snakehead experience in the context of the broader threat of nonnative species introduction."

The DNR folks were also learning how to deliver the message more effectively. Realizing that a large number of media outlets were interested in covering every change in the story, Lynch began, early on, taking names, contact information, and business cards so she could develop an e-mail database. Whenever something newsworthy was about to happen, Lynch fired off a mass e-mail. This saved her the effort of contacting numerous people individually, while at the same time ensuring that everyone who wanted to be was in the loop. To further increase efficiency, the DNR began opting for press conferences whenever possible. That way, the same message could be delivered once instead of numerous times.

Another part of message control focused on the messenger. Schwaab became the go-to guy. In part, the high profile of the story demanded that, but there were other reasons as well. The DNR wanted to stick to the facts, as much as possible, and avoid further "inflammatory" statements, which would likely serve only to make its job harder. Schwaab was used to dealing with the press and was skilled in staying on-message. According to Thomson, Schwaab's "got a Jack Webb, sort of just-the-facts-ma'am kind of style." Practice makes perfect, and Schwaab was getting loads of practice in speaking to the press about the snakehead. He became very adept at saying the same thing numerous times and still managing to sound fresh. Schwaab also mastered one of the most important skills necessary for effectively interacting with the press—knowing when to say nothing or, to put it into fisheries terminology, when not to rise to the bait. For example, a number of interviewers wanted Schwaab to compare the snakehead to

Osama bin Laden, keying in on the snakehead's apparently elusive and secretive habits, and even the notion that the dumping of the snakeheads in Crofton might be part of a terrorist plot. "They would always pose the question tongue in cheek, but they wanted you to respond on camera. . . . I just said I wasn't going to go there."

Not only were the DNR people becoming more strategic, they were also beginning to relax a bit and even laugh at some of the coverage the snakehead was receiving. And with each passing day, there was more to laugh about. On July 12, CNN's "News Night with Aaron Brown" presented "three tales about what lurks in the deep"—a so-called "creature triple feature." There, alongside stories about killer sharks and an orphaned killer whale was one about the snakehead, titled "Snakehead: The Fish That Ate Crofton, Maryland," and subtitled, "Doomsday Fish." While introducing the piece, which he called "the really scary part of our creature triple feature," Brown laughed in anticipation of what he knew would follow.

Anderson Cooper, CNN Anchor: Our tawdry tale begins innocently enough in this murky Maryland pond. Hidden by the still water lurks an alien terror.

All right, so maybe alien terror is a little too Geraldo.

Hidden by the still water lurks something kind of creepy. It's a fish, a northern snakehead, indigenous to China. For the purposes of ratings, however, we'll call it demon spawn, a monster, a Frankenfish.

[Cooper on camera with images of Godzilla in the background]: Krikey! Snakeheads are predators. They grow up to three feet in length and feast on fish and insects. They're not content to stay in the water, so they creep ashore using the creepily—did I say "creep" twice—using their eerily strong pectoralis fins. I didn't even know fish had pecs, but that's beside the point.

They survive for days on land moving from pond to pond, destroying all God's creatures in their path. Krikey!

[Voice over]: The trail of terror began a few weeks ago when the first fish was found, oddly enough, by a fisherman.

Unidentified male [Paul DiMauro]: I grabbed his mouth. He opened me some mean looking teeth.

Cooper: Okay, I didn't really understand any of that, but I'm assuming he's saying he was surprised by the fish. Authorities didn't like the smell of it. It was fishy, damn fishy. How did a Chinese fish get in a Maryland pond? Were there more? Had they bred like slimy, scaly rabbits? Had they moved to other ponds, other lakes? Would Washington itself be threatened?

Local media, not wanting to blow the danger out of proportion, tried to play down the story.

Unidentified female [newscaster]: Their focus now is to make sure these land-walking eating machines don't try to make a break for it.

Cooper: Local villagers mobilized [a clip from the Universal Pictures movie *Frankenstein* plays in the background, showing people, with torches in hand, running to face the monster. One of the actors in the clip says, "You search there! The rest, come with me!"].

Not since Frankenstein have they been so determined. They sent their bravest and not-so-brightest out to hunt the tiny tadpoles.

Unidentified male [one of the teenagers at the pond who wanted to catch the snakehead and sell it]: If they're not going to do the job, we will.

Cooper: But the kids failed to find all the fish, so federal officials called in the big guns, just as they had when Godzilla battled Geigen (ph), only this time they used much smaller guns, electric prods, actually, to stun the fish. They have killed about a hundred so far, and they're trying to figure out how to get the rest.

Eric Schwaab, Maryland Department of Natural Resources: We have put together a scientific panel of experts to recommend eradication options to us, from electroshocking on a large-scale basis, which is a temporary stunning of the fish in the pond, to large-scale netting. Other options we might consider would include draining of the pond, possibly a limited use of poison.

Cooper: The problem is snakeheads have no natural enemies, so right now, it seems, the only thing standing between them and us is a man named Reserve Officer Fisher.

Unidentified female: So if you see one coming up here, what are you going to do?

Reserve Officer Fisher: Stomp on it.

Cooper: Anderson Cooper, CNN, New York.

Brown: Okay. If you thought the mystery was good, here come the facts: how the snakehead fish got into Maryland. According to the *Washington Post* it all began with a local man who wanted to make soup for his sister who was sick. Two years ago the man called an Asian fish market here in New York City and ordered some live snakehead fish. Because, and who would have ever thought it, they make great soup. By the time the fish arrived the sister was already well. The snakeheads grew too big for the house, so he tossed them into the pond, where they did what snakeheads do. They mated and spawned and on it goes. Well, actually it stops right now. (Courtesy CNN)

On July 13, Kevin Cowherd of the *Baltimore Sun* took his own satirical turn on the story. "We got northern snakeheads," wrote Cowherd, "Chinese thug fish, in our pond. And who knows how big these monsters are? One fisherman said he saw one as big as a golf bag. But what if he's wrong? What if the sun was in his eyes or he's got a cornea problems and he only saw half the damn fish? What if these northern snakeheads are as big as a sleeper sofa?" Cowherd labeled Gillespie as the "Steve 'Crocodile Hunter' Irwin of northern snakeheads," and said he heard that the snakeheads "can walk on land and close in on you from 50 yards like a cheetah," and that the "only way to kill 'em is with a silver crucifix through the heart. And you gotta be reciting the Lord's prayer—backwards."

On the same day Cowherd's article appeared, the snakehead had a cameo on National Public Radio's weekly news quiz program, "Wait, Wait . . . Don't Tell Me!" Peter Segal, the show's host posed a limerick challenge, asking the contestants to fill in the blank at the end of this verse:

> *It lurks in the deep water with a ranklin' swish.*
>> *With razor-sharp teeth and strong shanks that squish.*
> *The Asian-born snakehead*
>> *Will eat the whole lake dead.*
> *They're calling this horror a _____.*

Of course the answer was "Frankenfish."

Gene Mueller, outdoor writer for the *Washington Times*, decided that it was about time that someone set the record straight about the fearsome snakehead. So many people were worrying about what snakeheads would do to other fish that nobody stopped to think what those other fish might do to the snakeheads. In a burst of piscine patriotism, Mueller threw his support behind the home team. "Can we talk a little common sense?" wrote Mueller. "Are you tired of hearing about the northern snakehead fish that some clever desk jockey at a newspaper dubbed 'Frankenfish'? Franken, Shmanken." People wrote that snakeheads ate baby ducks and geese. Big deal, huffed Mueller, "largemouth bass will eat them; so

will pike, rockfish, and others—all of them good old Americans."
If northern snakeheads did escape the confines of the Crofton pond,
they would be in a heap of trouble argued Mueller. Simply put, they
wouldn't stand a chance against some of America's home-grown
predator fish species, some of which "are veritable Godzillas. . . . The
tiger muskie is a lean, mean, feeding machine. It'll have a northern
snakehead for breakfast and not even burp." If a bowfin or garfish
caught up with a snakehead, "Gulp! Gone."

The people of Crofton, too, were having a good time with the
story. On the village green, at local eateries and the post office, and
in living rooms and kitchens throughout Crofton the number-one
topic of conversation was the snakehead, which was quickly giving
Crofton a peculiar claim to fame. The *Baltimore Sun* reporter Rona
Kobell learned that instead of playing Marco Polo in the pool at the
Crofton Swim and Tennis Club, they were playing "snakehead." A
few people urged the local swim team, the Crofton Cats, to change
their name to the Crofton Snakeheads, but they were voted down.
Chefs at Rick's American Grill thought it might be good to name
a dish after the snakehead, using the tag line, "Try the snakehead,
it'll walk off your plate." A short distance away from the pond, on
Route 3, William Berkshire's Uncle Nicky's Fish'n Hole restaurant
had already turned that notion from an idea into a reality. There one
could order Frankenfish Nuggets, which, according to a sign on the
door, were "select catfish fillets with secret spices and cooked in
imported snake oil. Melts in your mouth, walks to your tummy."

Before the snakehead story hit the press, it is likely that few people outside of Crofton's borders had ever heard of the place. Now,
it was famous, or more accurately, infamous. It is hard to imagine a
more unlikely location to find an alien species of fish than Crofton.
Turning off of the heavily traveled Route 3 and driving in through

The sign in front of Uncle Nicky's Fish'n Hole advertising Frankenfish Nuggets. Courtesy Eric Jay Dolin.

one of the gates of Crofton forces you to slow down, literally and figuratively. Within the confines of the original boundaries of the community the speed limit is twenty-five miles per hour, and that feels right. The roads are well paved, the sidewalks and yards are neat and attractively landscaped, and the houses are beautifully maintained. During the warmer months, the main road in town, Crofton Parkway, is the site of a patriotic display of American and Maryland state flags, hung to either side of the many light posts that line the way. The town hall, located in a converted house, and the village green also contribute to Crofton's small-town, thoroughly American image. And all around are trees, some quite large, adding to Crofton's character and sense of seclusion.

The pace of life seems slower in Crofton, and that is the way it was intended to be. Located about halfway between Washington, D.C., and Baltimore, Crofton was created in 1964 as a bedroom community and it remains steadfastly so today, in the face of creeping urbanization. The gates of Crofton are symbolic now, and always open, but in the early years they were a means of setting Crofton apart; residents had to use a key to gain entry.

Crofton is not a town, but a special community benefits district, which means that it has the ability to raise taxes to pay for local amenities such as its own police force. The 27,000-plus residents of Crofton are predominantly white collar and middle to upper-middle class, with a large contingent of federal government workers. They live in apartments, condominiums, townhouses, and detached homes that range in style from colonials and ranches to Cape Cods and split-levels. As local real estate agent Glenna Kidd observed, "The people who move in, often move up instead of moving out." The seven hundred or so, mostly small, businesses peppered throughout Crofton are concentrated outside of the residential core, thereby helping Crofton maintain its charm.

A story of this magnitude had never visited Crofton before. After all, this was a community where a battle over a white picket fence built in a resident's front yard in contravention of a local covenant ignited an intense and heated multiyear debate and scores of stories in local newspapers. Now, Crofton residents were getting calls and e-mails from all over the country and the world, from friends and colleagues inquiring whether they had been to the pond and seen the fish. And many Crofton residents, who formerly didn't even know there was a pond behind the mall off Route 3, took time to visit and stare, and they were joined by other people from near and far who wanted to see what all the fuss was about. The lucky ones were there when babies were being caught or when Gillespie was showing off his catch. Then there was some drama, something exciting to see. Most visitors,

One of the gates of Crofton, Maryland, off Route 3. Courtesy Eric Jay Dolin.

however, witnessed only a small, weed-infested pond; other bystanders, a few of whom might have had a line in the water, hoping to catch a snakehead; and media types, lots of them. The snakehead story was hot and reporters, photographers, and camera crews wanted to be on hand in case anything exciting happened or a good interview opportunity arose. Even when the media was not in sight, they could materialize quickly; Mike Slattery was convinced that there was a mole tipping them off. "We suspected," he said, "that there was someone in the bank building, that every time one of our trucks showed up must have called a TV station. Because we'd be down there doing our work and within minutes there would be a TV crew stumbling over the bank coming down toward the pond." Mike Thomas, an insurance agent with an office in the bank building abutting the pond observed that "the reporters spent more time in the parking lot than we did, and we work here." More than once, when Thomas showed up for work at 7 A.M., every single parking space was taken.

With such a large media presence and not much action, reporters and camera crews were eager to interview anybody who stopped by, in the hope of adding an interesting quote or perspective to liven up their stories. But one of the people the media wanted to interview most was very hard to find. Danny MacQuilliam, the vice president of the MacQuilliam Organization, which owned the pond and the adjacent mall, had little use for or interest in the media event taking place on his property. MacQuilliam didn't want to do interviews or share his thoughts on the snakehead. What he did want was for the DNR to do what they had to do to deal with the problem, and then have the story die so that he and his tenants, who were his primary concern, could focus on what they wanted to do, namely, running their businesses without the distractions posed by the snakeheads and their entourage. The media knew where MacQuilliam worked. His office was on the second floor of the bank building. But he was still hard to find because he didn't want to be found. Making the search for MacQuilliam more difficult was the fact that few in the media knew what he looked like. As a result, when anybody got out of a car in front of our building, said Thomas, the media would rush over and say, "Are you Mr. MacQuilliam?" The media wasn't only pursuing MacQuilliam at the office, they were also calling him at home, early in the morning and late at night. When one persistent reporter told Mrs. MacQuilliam that her husband had to get back to him, she said, "No, he doesn't." Huslin, one of the few reporters who caught up with MacQuilliam face-to-face, remembers him as being "very reluctant to dish about where he was coming from."

While many Maryland residents followed the snakehead story with varying mixtures of concern and amusement, some were already fed up. One person going by the name of Gman, who posted a message on the *Baltimore Sun*'s website, wrote, "What's wrong with the people of our state? . . . The way the DNR and the people of Maryland are acting, you would think that the fricking 'Loch Ness Monster' was living in that pond!!!" Despite the varying perspectives on the snakehead story, there was one thing everyone wanted to know—what was the DNR going to do? Everyone was about to find out.

The first known drawing of *Channa argus* in the scientific literature. It was published in 1855, in a book by Stephan Basilewsiky, *Ichthyographia Chinae borealis, Nouveaux Mémoirs de la Société impériale des naturalistes de Moscou* (vol. 10). Basilewsiky identified the species as *Ophicephalus pekinensis*, a name that is now recognized as what fish taxonomists call a "senior synonym" of *Channa argus*. Courtesy Christian Kanele and www.snakeheads.org.

Japanese angler holding a northern snakehead. The color of northern snakeheads is variable. Walter Courtenay reports seeing adults, like this one, that are totally black as well as others that have a light background and tan bars and splotches. Courtenay has even watched captive northern snakeheads dramatically alter their color, going from pale, with bars and splotches, to very dark brown (nearly black). Courtesy Jean-Francois Helias Pictures.

The triumphant trio of anglers show off their trophy, with Joe Gillespie holding the fish and Mark Gillespie holding the Sunday edition of the *Capital*. Jake Harkey is on the right. Courtesy Cait Gillespie.

Front page of the *New York Daily News* on July 13, 2002. © New York
Daily News, L.P. Reprinted with permission.

A worker at the Khaiseng Fish Farm displays a snakehead that has been harvested and is on its way to a Singaporean dinner table. This image accompanied many of the articles on the northern snakeheads that appeared during the summer, which is ironic because it shows what is likely a giant snakehead, and definitely not a northern. Nevertheless, there is little doubt that the nasty demeanor of this fish contributed to the general alarm about snakeheads. Courtesy AP Photo/Ed Wray.

Eric Schwaab faces part of the media contingent on the day of the herbi-cide application. Notice the yellow police tape demarcating the area beyond which the media was not to go. Courtesy Tom Darden.

This illustration by David Goldin accompanied the Dave Barry column on snakeheads when it appeared in the September 1, 2002, issue the *Washington Post Magazine*. Courtesy David Goldin.

The back of one of the Berkshires' T-shirts. Courtesy Eric Jay Dolin.

Spraying rotenone from one of the johnboats. Courtesy Tom Darden.

FIVE

POISON 'EM

On July 16, DNR Secretary Chuck Fox announced the thirteen members of Snakehead Fish Scientific Advisory Panel. In addition to its chair, Donald Boesch, panelists included Courtenay and Shafland as well as representatives from the U.S. Fish and Wildlife Service, the U.S. Customs Service, the DNR, the University of Maryland, a few nonprofit organizations, including the Chesapeake Bay Foundation, and one private environmental consultant. The panel's task was to evaluate eradication options and recommend actions related to the broader policy issues surrounding the introduction of nonnative species.

Boesch, a marine ecologist by training, was an excellent choice to head the panel. He was well respected in the region for his analytical and management capabilities. More importantly, he had proven particularly adept at chairing scientific panels on controversial issues and helping those panels go beyond simply debating and calling for more study to offering practical policy advice. For example, in 1997, Boesch chaired a scientific panel charged with the task of recommending actions for addressing the problems caused by blooms of the marine dinoflagellates in tributaries to the Chesapeake Bay. The dinoflagellates, in the genus *pfiesteria*, were linked not only to large-scale die-offs of fish, but also to possible human health impacts such as memory loss and nausea. The public and media attention focused on this problem, both local and national, was extremely intense, leading many to label it the "*pfiesteria* hysteria." The panel explored the connections between nutrient-rich agricultural runoff and the blooms of *pfiesteria*, and recommended policy actions that were ultimately incorporated into a law aimed at improving nutrient management.

In Boesch's experience scientific panels charged with evaluating and recommending management options usually met in private, with the head of the panel briefing the press afterward. Initially, Boesch wondered whether that might be an appropriate model for the snakehead panel and broached that subject with Secretary Fox. For two reasons, however, they decided to open the meeting to the public. Given the great media interest in the snakehead story, the press would likely raise a stink were they excluded from the meeting. Additionally, the DNR knew that if it wanted to educate the public on what was being considered and ultimately what course of action was chosen, an open meeting was the best choice. While the press and the public were welcome, there was one condition. Questions would not be entertained during the meeting while the panel members were debating eradication options. Instead, panel members would be available for comment after the meeting.

This eerie drawing by Alison Elizabeth Taylor appeared in an article titled "A Breath of Fresh Air: The Beauty of the Snakehead," by Tom Scocca, which ran in the July 19, 2002, edition of the *Washington City Paper*. Scocca had a unique take on the snakehead story. Although he discounted the snakeheads' supposed ability to destroy "everything that swims," Scocca argued that it was the exaggerated image of the snakehead that troubled us most. "The general public is caught up in the bigger danger: This alien fish can scour a pond clean of life! It can spawn uncontrollably! When it's done, it can crawl up the bank and march off to conquer new territory! Could we be more transparent? We're talking about *us*. We're mad at the snakehead because the snakehead is playing our game." Courtesy Alison Elizabeth Taylor.

The panel met on July 19 at the conference room in the Tawes State Office Building, where the DNR was located. That morning the readers of the *Baltimore Sun* were greeted with a front-page story by Rona Kobell titled, "Florida's Dr. Snakehead Is Making a House Call." When Kobell contacted Walter Courtenay for the article and told him that some people in Maryland were calling him Dr. Snakehead, he loved the moniker and laughed about it. Not only did his new nickname appear in the article, his picture did too. This being the first time Courtenay had been in Maryland since the snakehead story broke, he wanted to see where the snakeheads had been caught. He met Bob Lunsford for lunch at the Friendly's on Route 3 and then they headed over to the pond. As they pulled into the parking lot, Courtenay noticed that there were reporters and camera crews in the area, but he didn't think much about it. He got out of the car and walked down to the edge of the pond, intent on taking a bunch of pictures. "I got one photograph taken," remembers Courtenay, "and when I turned around there was an entire bank of TV cameras, other cameras, and news reporters right smack behind me." Courtenay is convinced that they knew he was coming, whether due to Kobell's article, which conveniently offered a visual ID, or because they were tipped off by an alert patron or worker at Friendly's. Courtenay lowered his camera and faced the phalanx of media. Many of their questions focused on whether the fish could walk on land and attack people. Courtenay said he felt that "the press was trying to make it more spectacular than it was."

Kobell's article chronicled Courtenay's background with snakeheads and his thoughts on the situation in Crofton. She also interviewed Paul Shafland, and in so doing hinted that the two Floridians came at the issue of invasive species from different perspectives. Courtenay and Shafland have dedicated their professional lives to studying and managing nonnative fish. Both are extremely knowledgeable and committed, both believe that the issue of invasive species is very important, and both would argue that if you find an exotic species that could be a problem in an isolated situation, you should go in and kill it as fast as you can. Or as Courtenay said, "shoot first, ask questions later." However, their approach to the issue is not the same. Early in his career, Shafland thought that the introduction of exotic fishes "was a very serious if not catastrophic event." But over time his level of concern has been "muted," because, he says, "there was relatively little, if any, hard data to support the suppositions" that introduced species would actually have such dramatic impacts. Pointing to the situation in his own state, Shafland claims that "none of the species of fish introduced into Florida have had horrific type of effects." He added, "Why is it that simply because man has moved a fish [which is desirable in its original location] from one place to another it instantly becomes a catastrophic event, if not satanic? Why can a native largemouth bass not pose as big a threat to biodiversity as an introduced peacock bass [a species that Shafland helped to introduce into Florida]? Why is it that way, they are both predators." In light of this it is not surprising that Shafland told Kobell that "these stories tend to get exaggerated and take on a life of their own. You hear the fish have teeth, they breathe air. Pretty soon you hear they climb trees, they eat dogs, they tap-dance, whatever."

Courtenay, on the other hand, has a stronger and more negative view of the potential for nonnatives to cause ecological harm. In an article in 1979, he wrote, "The introduction of exotic organisms for *nonagricultural* purposes . . . is a game of ecological roulette where the gains have been few and the mistakes many. And, as in any game of roulette, there have been great losses." Reflecting on their differences, Courtenay said of Shafland, "his philosophy seems to be there's no such thing as a 'bad fish' if it can be caught and enjoyed by anglers. . . . Paul seems to think that ecologists predict possible consequences of introductions from a strictly theoretical basis. . . . He feels that those of us who have raised concerns about introductions don't live in what folks like Paul would term a 'real world,' whereas my gut feelings based on research tell me that we need to extremely vigilant about any kind of introduction."

Boesch was well aware of the philosophical divisions between Courtenay and Shafland, and he said he was led to believe by some of those who helped to set up the panel that there might also be "some sort of a personal" disagreements, or a "history" between the two. As a result, Boesch was a little apprehensive about the meeting. "We had knowledge beforehand," said Boesch, "of some of the difference of opinions of the two Floridians. I was concerned that Courtenay and Shafland would get into a little bit of a debate or discussion over the things that might, based upon their issues in Florida, detract from the proceedings."

While Courtenay and Shafland would certainly concur that their philosophies on invasive species differ, and that they have disagreed professionally on many occasions, the notion that there was something personal between the two came as a surprise to both. "Socially and one-on-one," Courtenay contends, "Paul and I get along very well." Shafland's take is similar: "Walt is one of the most likable and entertaining individuals I've ever met. . . . I can only assume that because of our similar professional interests, close associations, and obvious differences, some erroneously conclude I must have a personal grudge rather than substantive scientific and philosophical differences with Walt. In fact, much of who I am and how I think about introduced species is due to Professor Courtenay's influence. As is sometimes the case, those who influence us the most positively can be those that we professionally disagree with the most. Of course, from Walt's perspective, he may see having me as a colleague eliminates any need for enemies!"

At the meeting the panel members sat at the head of the conference room. The tables were arranged in a U-shape pattern to facili-
tate dialogue. The conference room, which can hold fifty-two people, seated, was standing-room-only, with most in attendance being
from the media. Four or five television cameras were trained on the
panel. According to Boesch, the capacity crowd, and especially the
presence of so many media outlets, was a bit intimidating. "I had to
break the ice a bit," Boesch recalls, "nobody wanted to start at first."
Soon, however, the discussion took off and the panelists relaxed.
Rather than fearing that the debate would go on and on, Boesch
found himself worried that there wouldn't be much debate at all.
Despite the concerns of some, Courtenay and Shafland reached general agreement quickly, as did the other panelists. "There was a tendency to cut to the chase and pick rotenone [a fish poison]," Boesch
said, "but I forced them to discuss other options." Those included
doing nothing; draining the pond; physically removing fish through
trapping, angling, electroshocking, introducing new predators, or
using dynamite; and applying other piscicides besides rotenone.

The panelists discussed each option and the related pros and cons.
A wait-and-see approach with the hope that this population of snakeheads in the pond would die out made no sense because they had
already proven their ability to survive and procreate. And because
there was great confidence that all of the fish were still contained in
the pond, the DNR had available the best option of all, eradicating
the fish rather than trying to manage them once they invaded a larger
area. While all of the physical removal options under consideration
would likely result in the capture of some percentage of the snakeheads in the pond, none of them offered 100 percent confidence that
all the snakeheads would be killed. Dewatering might be an effective method of eliminating the snakeheads, but it posed a range of
complex technical challenges. For example, where would the water be

drained to? If it were drained to the Little Patuxent River or some other body of water, a filtration system would likely have to be used to ensure that very small fish or even smaller eggs were not inadvertently spread. The water could be sprayed onto land, but what land? One person raised the possibility of injecting the water into the ground, where any entrapped snakeheads could not survive, but this seemed to be even more complex of a solution than the others. And, no matter which method of dewatering were used, it might not be possible to actually get all the water out, if, as many observers believed, the pond was spring fed.

As for piscicides, others were available, but rotenone was clearly the preferred choice for fish biologists, who have been using it for decades as a means of eradicating unwanted aquatic species. Rotenone comes from the roots of tropical and subtropical plants, and the natives of Central and South America have used it for centuries to catch fish. First they would smash the roots to a pulp, then throw them in the water, and before long, dinner would be bobbing at the surface, ready for collection. An article by Huslin, appearing on the day of the panel meeting, made clear how the two Floridians felt about the use of rotenone. Shafland was quoted as saying, "We have a standing policy of eliminating [alien] fish. Rotenone is the only fish toxin I use." Courtenay confirmed the poison's value. "The water turns milky, the fish suffocate, and an air-breathing fish like the snakehead will come to the surface. If you've got enough people out there with dip nets, you can just capture these little guys on the spot." Anita Huslin noted, however, that rotenone didn't have a spotless record. She dredged up information about a test application of rotenone in Maryland, thirty years earlier, which did kill thousands of fish, but it also left a mess that still lingered in the memory of a retired state biologist. "It was a good idea, but the execution failed," said Nick Carter, who supervised the test and was quoted by Huslin. He and his colleagues spent days cleaning rotting fish carcasses off the beach. He added, "Everybody remembers it and laughs at me. It got pretty smelly." Huslin also briefly touched upon the most infamous case of rotenone poisoning, an effort to eliminate northern pike from Lake Davis in California, a human-made reservoir and a popular destination for anglers in search of rainbow trout.

There were some parallels between the situation in Lake Davis and that confronting the DNR. Northern pike, which was found in Lake Davis for the first time in 1994, is an introduced species. Its normal range is to the east of the Rocky Mountains. Like the northern snakehead, the northern pike has an impressive set of sharp teeth and is a top-of-the line predator with a wide-ranging palate that includes fish, crayfish, frogs, and even juvenile waterfowl. It had proven its predatory prowess in other locations to which it had been introduced, dramatically impacting sport fish populations and altering the local food chain. Local wildlife officials, the media, and the public viewed the northern pike as vicious invader that would likely soon snack its way through the lake's fish population and that, if not stopped, might get into the Sacramento–San Joaquin Delta and then move downstream where it could threaten other species of fish. And like the northern snakehead, the northern pike generated some unusual nicknames, including "saw-tooth Satan spawns."

The California Department of Fish and Game declared war on the northern pike in Lake Davis and selected rotenone as the weapon of choice. To allay local concerns, the state handed out information packets that discussed rotenone, why it was chosen, and how it would be used. The application occurred in early October 1997, and it was an unmitigated disaster. The rotenone killed more than twenty tons of fish, but the poison migrated well beyond the intended area of application, killing large numbers of fish downstream and devastating the local tourist economy, which depended heavily on fishing. There were also claims that rotenone had poisoned local water supplies. Over the next two years, roughly $20 million in fines and fees were handed out as a result of the rotenone application, including over $9 million that was awarded by a court to compensate citizens for having to use alternative drinking water sources and to compensate businesses for lost income. Worst of all, the pike returned to Lake Davis in 1999; it is not known whether a few hardy fish survived the poisoning or someone reintroduced pike into the lake. Since then, the pike have reasserted their supremacy in the food chain, and the state has tried eliminating them through various means, including electrocution, netting, and the introduction of potential predator species—all to no avail. The most recent entry into the state's armamentarium is dynamite. Despite the Lake Davis experience, the panelists expressed little concern about the application of rotenone going awry in Crofton. There were many more examples of where rotenone, properly applied, had worked exceedingly well, and that was the expected outcome in this case.

A couple of hours after it began, the panel meeting ended. Selecting Boesch to head the group proved to be a wise choice. Watching the proceedings from the audience, Steve Early commented, "He got 'em in, got 'em the facts, and whipped them into shape and they came out with a recommendation, *boom, boom, boom*, it was amazing." Shafland labeled his experience with the panel as outstanding and said he was "very impressed with the expeditiousness." The panel recommended that the DNR use rotenone to kill the fish in the pond where the snakeheads were captured, as well as in the two adjacent ponds owned by William Berkshire. The panel also recommended that, prior to the use of rotenone, herbicides be applied to the pond to clear away the vegetation, a move that would likely improve the effectiveness of the poisoning.

After the meeting, Boesch talked to a reporter about the snakehead's exaggerated ability to walk, possibly to other bodies of water. Boesch wondered out loud, "Even if the fish got out of the pond, how would it know which way to go?" The reporter had no idea, but when Boesch got back to his office the following week, one of the women there told him that "if it was a female fish it would ask for directions."

The panel was confident that rotenone was capable of killing snakeheads, but there was still a question about dosage. Nobody had experience using the piscicide on northern snakeheads and some wondered whether the fish's air-breathing capabilities and modified lung might affect how it reacted to the poison. On July 24, and at the urging of the panel, biologists from the University of Maryland Center for Environmental Science's Horn Point Laboratory set out to determine the lethal dose. Using some of the captured juveniles, the biologists conducted a bioassay at the DNR's laboratory in Oxford, Maryland. They subjected the juveniles to different doses of rotenone and evaluated the fish over time. Within an hour, the treated snakeheads were dead. Based on the concentrations used in the test, and then building in a margin of safety, the biologists recommended that the pond be laced with rotenone at a concentration level of three parts per million.

The press knew about the bioassay and many reporters showed up at the laboratory hoping to witness the procedure. They were turned away, however, due to concerns about them possibly distracting the biologists or inadvertently interfering with the experiment. A DNR representative promised, however, that the results would soon be released. Rather than leave, veteran snakehead reporter Huslin lingered and chatted with one of the biologists. Her lingering turned into entrée and she soon found herself inside the lab, with the fish, watching them die. When Huslin and one of her colleagues wrote about her exclusive the next day, Boesch caught hell from other reporters. Why was Huslin allowed in, and not them? "They were livid," said Boesch, "and complained to me at great length about the unfairness of this."

When the panel's official report was delivered to Secretary Chuck Fox on July 26, it was well received, and Fox said he would soon decide on a course of action. In between the time the panel met and when it issued its report, the broader universe of the snakehead and its future in the United States was rocked to the core. On July 23, U.S. Secretary of the Interior Gale Norton strode to a press conference podium in Washington, D.C. Next to her, on a table, lay a preserved snakehead in a bag, serving as exhibit A and offering silent witness to the pronouncement to come. Norton told the assembled throng that the federal government was proposing to ban the importation and interstate transportation of live snakeheads, and not just the northern snakehead, but all twenty-eight species. She didn't mince words.

> These fish are like something from a bad horror movie. A number of these species can survive in the wild in freshwater almost anywhere in the United States. They can eat virtually any small animal in their path. They can travel across land and live out of water for at least three days. They reproduce quickly. They have the potential to cause enormous damage to our valuable recreational and commercial fisheries. We simply must do everything we can to prevent them from entering our waters, either accidentally or intentionally.

The U.S. Department of the Interior press release for the event noted that "three species of the fish have been found in open water in California, Florida, Hawaii, Maine, Maryland, Massachusetts, and Rhode Island, and at least two have been established as reproducing populations (Florida and Hawaii)."

One of the interesting things about the press conference is how Norton's comments added to the generic snakehead branding that was already in full flower. Although there were twenty-eight different species, many with unique characteristics, the term "snakehead" was quickly becoming a catchall phrase, shorthand for an entire family of fish. For example, consider Norton's statement above, that "they [snakeheads] can travel across land." When Norton made this statement she should have known that not all snakeheads perambulated. Indeed, a U.S. Fish and Wildlife Service fact sheet titled, "'Frankenfish': The Facts," which was distributed with the press release for Norton's announcement informed reporters that "scientists do not know how many species of snakehead are capable of overland migration, but several are known to do so." And the proposed rule Norton's agency would publish three days hence would indicate only that "many" snakeheads could perform "overland migrations." While "many" was a big step up from "several," it still wasn't all. Perhaps the image of the walking snakehead was too compelling to merit qualification. A snakehead was a snakehead was a snakehead.

Another interesting thing about the press conference was the fish, which traveled to Washington via a circuitous route. Earlier in the summer, Courtenay and his colleague, Jim Williams, asked Karsten Hartel, a curatorial associate in ichthyology at Harvard's Museum of Comparative Zoology, to buy a few live snakeheads from a Boston fish market and send them to Florida. Hartel sent two fish in an overnight package, but by the time it arrived one of the fish had died. The dead one, which was promptly preserved, was the one that was sent to the U.S. Fish and Wildlife Service for use at the press conference. When Courtenay and Williams first got the fish, they thought they were northern snakeheads. And indeed, at the press conference the preserved specimen was identified by U.S. Fish and Wildlife Service staff as a northern. But when the preserved snakehead was later brought to the Smithsonian's National Museum of Natural History, Dr. Ralf Britz, a German ichthyologist on sabbatical there, determined that it was not a northern, but a blotched snakehead, *Channa maculata*. The mistaken identity is not surprising because the northern and the blotched are what Courtenay referred to as "look-alike" species, which are often quite difficult to tell apart short of doing a detailed anatomical evaluation.

The proposed ban would place the family of snakeheads on the federal list of "injurious wildlife" under the Lacey Act, through which the secretary identifies nonindigenous wild animals deemed to be "injurious, or potentially injurious, to the health and welfare of people as well as to the interests of agriculture, forestry, and horticulture, or to the welfare or survival of wildlife or wildlife resources of the United States." Norton broadened the issue beyond snakeheads, commenting, "We talk a lot about endangered species, but, at the other end of the scale, invasive species pose at least as great a danger." Schwaab was there to lend his support. "I would like to thank the Department of Interior for taking this action today," he said. "Across this country, nonnative species invasions pose a great threat to our natural landscape." According to Elizabeth Shogren, of the *Los Angeles Times*, during the question-and-answer period, Schwaab was asked if Maryland officials had thought about importing a natural predator (a "counterpest") to eat the snakeheads into history, to which Schwaab replied, "We don't want to go down that road."

If adopted, the new regulations would empower U.S. Fish and Wildlife Service and U.S. Customs inspectors to seize shipments into the country or across state lines of live snakeheads or their viable eggs. Anyone caught moving snakeheads in this manner would be subject to penalties of up to six months in prison and fines of as much as $5,000 for individuals and $10,000 for organizations. The only exceptions allowed would be for those holding permits allowing them to import or transport live snakeheads or their eggs for scientific, medical, educational, or zoological purposes, as long as such activities didn't conflict with state laws. The proposed regulations were federal in nature and as such would not make it illegal for people to own snakeheads as long as the state in which they resided didn't ban them.

The proposed ban was based on the information gathered from the risk assessment headed by Courtenay and Williams, as well as supplemental information collected by the U.S. Fish and Wildlife Service. Many observers, including more than a few reporters, believed that there was a cause and effect connection between the appearance of the snakeheads in Crofton and the proposed rule, but there wasn't. As mentioned earlier, the risk assessment began almost a year before the world knew about the snakeheads in Crofton. And even before the first story broke in late June 2002, the U.S. Fish and Wildlife Service had a draft of the proposed rule and was preparing to send it out for review to all the people who needed to sign-off on the text before it could be made public in the *Federal Register*. According to Sharon Gross, the head of the U.S. Fish and Wildlife Service's Invasive Species Branch, the situation in Crofton forced us "to pick up the pace of the review." When Secretary Norton decided she wanted to hold a press conference announcing the ban, that focused everyone's concentration and the required signatures came in faster than would have otherwise been the case. In late

November 2002, Gross commented that had they begun the process of evaluating the snakehead family after the Crofton discovery, they "would still be working on the risk assessment now."

Three days after Secretary Norton's announcement, the proposed rule appeared in the *Federal Register*. It went into great detail about the fecundity and development of snakeheads, their range, feeding habits, the history of introductions in the United States, and their physiology. It was pointed out that most snakeheads guard their young "vigorously," and that one species, the giant snakehead, "reportedly attacked and in some instances killed humans who approached the mass of young." On the topic of movement, the proposed rule read, "many [snakeheads] are capable of overland migration by wriggling motions." Also offered were statistics on imports. According to U.S. Fish and Wildlife Service Law Enforcement data, between 1997 and 2000, 16,554 individual snakeheads or 20,567 kilograms of all species were imported into the country, with a declared value of $85,425 (import records list weight *or* the number of fish). And imports were trending upward.

In arguing for the ban, the proposed rule cited a range of factors, which were briefly listed in a concluding paragraph.

Because snakeheads are likely to escape or be released into the wild; are likely to survive or become established if they escape or are released; are likely to spread since there are no known limiting factors; are likely to compete with native species for food; may transmit parasites to native species; are likely to feed on native species [including threatened and endangered species], which will negatively affect native fishes, amphibians, crustaceans, birds, small reptiles, and small mammals; and because it will be difficult to prevent, eradicate, manage, or control the spread of snakeheads; and because it will be difficult to

Titled, "Something Fishy," this cartoon by Sage Stossel appeared in the July 25, 2002, issue of *Atlantic Unbound* on *The Atlantic* Online. According to Stossel, "The whole idea of a walking fish—and the fact that it could pose such a big menace—struck me as refreshingly absurd. As threats go, it was a nice break from the relentless talk about terrorism and a plummeting economy. The cartoon tries to makes light of the snakehead hysteria by taking everyone's dire predictions [about the fish walking all over the place and taking over whole ecosystems] to an extreme." Courtesy Sage Stossel.

rehabilitate or recover ecosystems disturbed by the species; the Service finds snakeheads to be injurious to the wildlife and wildlife resources of the United States.

Although the normal comment period for proposed rules is sixty days, the public would get only thirty days for the snakehead rule.

Sped-up regulatory action was justified, said the proposed rule, because the fish were so predacious and difficult to control.

The establishment of Maryland's Snakehead Fish Scientific Advisory Panel, its first meeting and report, and the federal proposal to ban snakeheads kept the media fires stoked. Many of the stories simply chronicled the new events. And more than a few of these continued the short-lived, but potent tradition of leading with a dramatic headline. For example, the *Scotsman* ran a story titled, "U.S. Declares War on Aggressive Invader," and the *Providence Journal* led with "Gracious! It's Voracious!—U.S. Bans Importation of Fearsome Snakehead." The *Los Angeles Times* chose, "Fish and Game's Enemy No. 1: The Snakehead," and a Fox News banner read, "Sniggling Snakehead Ousted from U.S." Many adjectives had heretofore been coupled with the snakehead, but "sniggling" was a first. According to *Webster's II New Collegiate Dictionary*, it's not even a word. Perhaps they meant to use "sniggering," which is defined as "to snicker," meaning to "utter a stifled laugh." Maybe that was it, for if snakeheads could read, there is little doubt that their own press would amuse them.

One of Huslin's articles in the *Washington Post*, which came out on the day of Secretary Norton's press conference, was particularly interesting. After Huslin told her readers about the proposed ban, she referred to the snakehead as a "voracious air-breathing, ground-slithering fish," and said that it had been found in at least seven states where it had "upset the natural order by eating virtually everything—plant and animal—within its reach." That news no doubt came as a surprise to the residents of those states, for in none of them had snakeheads led to any sort of ecological disaster. Indeed, only two of those states had reproducing populations of snakeheads (Hawaii and Florida); as for the other states, the very few fish that were found in their waters were caught well before they could do much of anything, much less turn the local environment upside down. The article's characterization of the snakeheads' dietary desires was also off the mark. While snakeheads are carnivorous and will eat many different types of animals, not just fish, they do not eat plants according to Courtenay. But it wasn't just Huslin's portrayal of the fish that was somewhat alarming. She quoted Ken Burton, a spokesman for the U.S. Department of Interior, as saying that snakeheads "eat literally anything that's living, including cannibalizing themselves. They'll eat ducklings. They will eat amphibians. So if you leave them in a body of water for any given time, there'll be nothing left. They're a bad actor."

Early in the summer there had been a smattering of articles that talked about the problem of invasive species, using the snakehead as a lead-in and then adding information about other species. Now, such articles were coming out at a rapid clip. An editorial in the *Boston Globe* titled, "Snakeheads in the Grass," began with, "The scariest creature in the water and woodland is man, and people coming to a pond in Crofton, MD, to gawk at the 'monster'—a.k.a. 'Frankenfish,' 'freaky fish,' and 'X-Files fish'—should take a look in the mirror for some real thrills." After noting that one man's decision to release the snakeheads lay at the root of the problem, the editorial offered evidence of how other shortsighted human decisions to move species around had "created many a monster out of plants and animals that simply do what comes naturally in the wrong place." To wit, gypsy moths, zebra mussels, and nutria. Traci Watson in *USA Today*, under the headline, "Aquatic Aliens Spawn Trouble," pointed out that there were plenty of other fishy invaders, or "monster fishes" threatening America's waterways, including the lionfish, the Asian swamp eel, and the Asian carp. The last of this trio is a particularly scary brute. It can grow up to four feet and weigh over one hundred pounds. The Asian carp is so effective at eating vegetation, plankton, small mussels, and other fish that its massive appetite can greatly diminish or possibly eliminate the populations of native fish that share the same body of water. Biologists and others are particularly fearful that the carp, which is working its way up the Mississippi River, will soon enter the Great Lakes, leading to an ecological disaster. Watson quoted Dianna Padilla, of the State University of New York–Stony Brook, as saying, "On a monthly basis, we get reports of new invasive species we haven't known about before. Not all species will cause huge damage, be we can't really predict ahead of time which ones will." A commentary piece in *USA Today* by Alcestis Cooky Oberg, titled, "Exotics Chomp Up U.S. Wildlife," tapped a similar vein. Oberg began, "When someone supposedly tried to save the lives of two monstrous snakehead fish by dumping them into a Maryland pond—and threatened every fish, frog, aquatic bird and small mammal on the East Coast in the process—I thought it was an isolated case of monumental stupidity. I was wrong." Oberg then noted that 185 alien fish have been found in U.S. waters, and nearly half of them have settled in and are breeding. John Biemer, of the Associated Press, wrote a story on invasive species that featured the snakehead, but also gave equal billing to other invaders ranging from the West Nile virus to the wild boar. Numerous media outlets picked up this story, including CNN and the *Independent*, in South Africa, the latter of which ran it with the headline, "Flesh-eating Fish Leads Alien Invasion." The article quoted Notre Dame biologist David Lodge as saying that invasive species are the "most irreversible form of pollution." Jeff Lampe, outdoor columnist for the *Peoria Journal Star*, in Illinois, penned a piece titled, "Latest Scourge of Nature Is the Snakehead," in which he asked readers to reflect with him on a basic question, namely, "How many of us have introduced exotic species without considering the long-term implications?" He added, "What is certain when it comes to exotic species is that we usually identify the most troublesome imports after it's too late to halt their spread." One of the most wide-ranging articles of this type to appear was written by Bob Dart and distributed by the Cox News Service. In it, Dart offered brief profiles of some of the worst invasive species to land on America's shores, including the following, most of which were already on the Lacey Act's list of "injurious wildlife"—walking catfish, zebra mussels, fruit bats, raccoon dogs, brown tree snakes, Asian longhorn beetles, round gobies, and the red-whiskered bulbul, a small bird that has become established in Florida and which threatens fruit crops.

Part of the reason that more reporters were writing about the broader issue of invasive species was because government officials and others interested in this topic were raising it with increasing frequency. People like Secretary Norton, Eric Schwaab, and others whose job involves managing invasive species realized that the snakehead story offered a golden opportunity to get the word out about this important issue. For a couple of weeks now that notion had been part of the DNR's outreach strategy. Reflecting on the increased media coverage, Schwaab said, "You suddenly saw the carp issue on the Mississippi making it into the news, which is a much bigger threat than the snakehead is or ever will be. As an issue it had never gotten any traction. Now, suddenly, in the midst of all of this you actually saw some spin-off stories that tied that back to the snakehead. Our counterparts in the Midwest said we can take advantage of this [snakehead] story and piggyback." This is not to say that reporters were unaware of the invasive species issue prior to the appearance of the snakeheads in Crofton. On the contrary, many of them had been covering the issue for years and were very knowledgeable. But news stories don't get published simply because they tell an interesting story, there needs to be a news peg to hang them on. The snakehead provided that peg, and a hell of a peg it was.

The most germane example of this involves the nuclear worm, which played a minor but key role in breaking the snakehead story in late June. Once Candy Thomson began writing about the snakehead, the nuclear worm story was placed temporarily on hold. After all, there were literally and figuratively bigger fish to fry. Ironically, while the snakehead initially shunted the nuclear worm aside, it was the snakehead's notoriety that ultimately made the nuclear worm much more newsworthy. That is why, on July 15, the *Baltimore Sun* ran Thomson's nuclear worm story on page one. According to Thomson, the story "probably wouldn't have made page one if it had not been for the snakehead." A similar story could be told for the *Washington Post*'s article on the nuclear worm, titled, "Gone Fission: The 'Nuclear Worm,'" which ran on the first page of the style section on July 27. Nuclear worms are a brilliant shade of red and are kind of creepy, but in normal times they wouldn't rank up there with the celebrity profiles and culture-heavy stories that usually grace the front page of that section.

It was not only government officials who were beaming out the broader message on invasive species. Environmental and conservation groups, too, some of which have been sounding the alarm on this issue for decades were eager to use the interest in the snakehead as a lever for coverage. For example, on July 26, the World Wildlife Fund issued a press release titled, "Snakehead Is One of Many Invasive Species Damaging U.S. Crops and Native Wildlife." The lead paragraph set the tone. "The air-breathing snakehead fish found in suburban Maryland has received national attention, but it's only one of more than 30,000 invasive species that now call the

United States home and are making life difficult for the species that were there first." The following text offered a brief region-by-region tour of the United States, profiling some of the worst invasive species along the way. John Morrison, of the World Wildlife Fund's Conservation Program, said, "The threat from invasive species like the snakehead is nothing new. They're everywhere. In fact, just looking outside my office window right now, the only birds I see are pigeons, house sparrows and starlings, all natives of Europe. . . . While it's probably too late to address starlings in our environment, we should actively try to prevent other non-native species from becoming established here."

Another vein of the snakehead story that was increasingly being tapped could be called the "us too" angle. Many of the early press reports briefly mentioned that northern snakeheads had turned up in the wild in other states. Then, there was the Department of Interior's press release on the ban, which listed the seven states where the fish had been found. As a result, reporters from those states smelled a story. For example, Dianne Chun, of the *Gainesville Sun,* wrote an article on July 20 that not only covered the Crofton situation but also brought it home, informing readers that northern snakeheads had been found virtually in their backyard. Courtenay told her, "In 2000, two northern snakeheads were caught by anglers in the St. Johns River near Lake Harney, east-southeast of Orlando. To make it worse, we have unverified reports that anglers had caught three more the week before. So there could be as many as five caught out of the St. Johns River. But this has been the whole history with introduced species worldwide. Once they get out and start to spread, you cannot eliminate them. You can't poison the St. Johns River." Way north, in Massachusetts, there were also stories to be told. On July 24,

Beth Daley of the *Boston Globe* informed Bay Staters about their own encounters with snakeheads. In October 2001, biologists from the Massachusetts Department of Fisheries, Wildlife, and Environmental Law Enforcement pulled a northern snakehead from a pond in Shrewsbury, Massachusetts, during a routine sampling effort with electrofishing gear. Daley quoted state biologist Todd Richards as saying, "This one we caught . . . smacks of it simply [growing] too big for the aquarium as opposed to one of a litter of thousands." And it wasn't the first time a northern had surfaced in Massachusetts; in 1990 an angler caught one in Andover. The day the *Boston Globe* article ran, the *Providence Journal* reported on a giant snakehead that was hooked in the state back in 1968. A few days after the *Providence Journal* article appeared, the Rhode Island Department of Environmental Management, wanting to avoid another appearance of a snakehead in its jurisdiction, issued emergency regulations prohibiting the importation, transfer, or release of snakeheads within the state.

People around the country began asking whether the snakehead problem could come to their state, and those questions generated a raft of "what about us" stories. On July 25, Joe Rankin, writing for Blethen Maine Newspapers, Inc., noted that after Maine was mentioned in the Department of Interior press release on snakeheads, some alert readers in the state called the state's Department of Inland Fisheries for more information. At first, the department had nothing to say because nobody could recall when or where the snakeheads were found. A search of files finally uncovered that way back in 1975 a giant snakehead had been captured in one of Maine's rivers. There was also an unverified report of another snakehead being caught later that decade. Rankin allayed residents concerns only partially, telling them that although the northern snakehead had been found in

Maine, it likely could not survive the state's harsh winters. According an article written by Brad Morin for *Foster's Online*, out of neighboring New Hampshire, a few Maine residents had expressed mortal fear of the snakehead. Morin quoted Don Kleiner, of the Maine Fish and Wildlife Service, saying that "people called about whether or not they should let their kids go swimming."

Just two days after Secretary Norton held her press conference on the ban, one of her lieutenants, Steven Williams, the director of U.S. Fish and Wildlife Service, gave a speech at the CITGO Bass Masters Classic in Birmingham, Alabama. In his remarks he spoke about many of the challenges to effectively managing fish, including dealing with the growing problem of invasive species. On that point, Williams touched on the northern snakehead, saying that it is "an omnivorous critter that can eat everything in a small pond, then waddle off across land on its belly to find new waters and new prey." Although most of Williams's talk focused on issues other than invasive species and northern snakeheads were mentioned only briefly, when it came time for questions from the audience, it seemed as if only one thing was on people's minds. Thomson was in attendance and she recalls that the first four questions were about snakeheads. People wanted to know how the government was going to keep their states from being invaded by the fearsome fish.

Many who were concerned that snakeheads might show up where they lived looked to the DNR for assistance, perhaps thinking that it was best to go to the source of the story for information. Steve Early remembers being "flooded" with calls from around the country from people wanting to know if they had caught a snakehead. One of the funniest was from a woman who was fixing up a house she had recently bought. When she looked in the toilet she found a dead fish floating in the bowl. In a turn reminiscent of the urban legends about alligators in New York's sewers, the woman asked Early if snakeheads could swim through the pipes into toilets. Whether the answer, which was no, pleased her or just deepened the mystery and increased her fear of the house's plumbing is unknown. The people at the DNR also received numerous e-mails, many with attached images of fish and the basic question—snakehead?

In Chicago, Alderman Jesse Granato was unwilling to sit around and fret about the possibility of snakeheads visiting the windy city. Instead, on July 31, he took a bold, decisive action and introduced an ordinance to ban snakeheads. According to published reports, Granato nicknamed the snakehead *Chamuco,* which is Spanish for Satan. He was particularly concerned about the fish's ravenous appetite, and he told Gary Wisby of the *Chicago Sun Times* that a snakehead he had purchased at a local fish market for $10 and that he kept in an aquarium in his office, had eaten six small tropical fish within ten minutes. And Granato wasn't the first in his city to step up to the plate. Two Chicago city council committees had already passed resolutions urging the state legislature to ban snakeheads in Illinois.

Surprisingly, the proposed rule's reference to giant snakeheads and their apparent propensity to attack and sometimes kill humans who ventured too close to their babies surfaced in only a few press accounts. Given the dramatic nature of much of the media coverage thus far, one would have thought that reports of possible snakehead maulings, albeit not by the northern snakehead, would have merited more ink and airtime. But it is just as well that this nugget of information remained largely buried because the evidence for such attacks is purely anecdotal. The proposed rule cites a 1993 paper by Kottelat et al., titled *Freshwater Fishes of Western Indonesia and Sulawesi,* as support for its comment that such attacks have occurred.

"It is not unknown," notes the paper, "for fisherman or swimmers who have accidentally gone too close to the fry of the largest species, *C. micropeltes* [the giant snakehead], to be attacked, sometimes with grievous or fatal results." Case studies or specific examples did not bolster this statement, nor, apparently, are there documented reports of attacks elsewhere in the literature. Of course, that doesn't mean that giant snakeheads have never attacked humans, just that there is no hard evidence of this having happened. But some of the anecdotal evidence is quite chilling. For example, when Courtenay wrote to Singaporean snakehead expert Peter Ng, asking about giant snakehead attacks, Ng responded that he knew of a man who was almost castrated by one. Ng added that although he had not heard of a giant snakehead killing a human, "it is of course very possible— a meter-long fish ramming a man in midriff is no joke!"

Thus far, most of the stories about snakeheads concentrated on the negative characteristics of the fish. There might have been a sentence or two about the snakehead's medicinal value or its culinary attributes, but that was the extent of it. Now, with a ban on snakeheads in the offing, those who preferred to look on the brighter side of the snakehead's curriculum vitae became more vocal. The *Malaysian Star* ran an article by Farid Jamaludin, which began, "The snakehead, a fish that is causing a scare in the United States as a 'predatory killer,' had a much kinder reputation in Malaysia—it is recognized by all ethnic communities as a 'healer fish.'" The article noted that the most common species in Malaysia were the striped and the giant snakeheads, and it said that, "The three major communities in the country—Malays, Chinese, and Indians—believe that the fish can help those who undergo surgery to recover quickly." Jamaludin added that some viewed an herbed preparation of snakeheads as aiding in the recovery from childbirth. Sharmilpal Kaur, of

Singapore's the *Straits Times,* wrote that Singaporeans love eating snakeheads and use them for medicinal purposes as well. Fox News and the *Seattle Post Intelligencer* were among a number of outlets that ran an Associated Press story by Edward Harris that echoed the themes of the stories written by his Asian colleagues. Harris interviewed Koh Boon Wah, the manager of the Khaiseng Trading and Fish Farm, which sells large quantities of snakeheads. Koh offered a range of juicy sound bites. "We've been eating snakeheads for centuries. They're tasty and the flesh is so tender. . . . If you cook them with green apples, it's also very good for the complexion. . . . It's no monster, it's good with noodles. . . . The best way to get rid of them is to just eat them." As for the snakehead's purported use as an aphrodisiac, Koh was equally direct. "Yes, eating the snakehead will make you healthy and strong, but not like Viagra."

Reading the Asian coverage of the snakehead story at this time one couldn't help but get the distinct impression that the people of that continent were laughing at us. And who could blame them? A fish that they had known for hundreds, if not thousands, of years as a culinary delight with healing powers, was being portrayed in the U.S. press as an embodiment of evil, a beast bent on destruction. The revered and tasty snakehead had Americans on the run.

In late July, if you had asked an average American consumer of news what was so bad about snakeheads, it is good bet that the response would be something like, "Snakeheads can breathe air and survive out of water for three days, walk on land, and eat anything in sight." This would not be surprising given that these alarming characteristics—at least when present in a fish—had become almost a mantra, repeated in one form or another in numerous reports. The problems associated with such statements, especially when offered without appropriate qualifications, were first raised in early July, and, in some cases, subsequent reporting recast the snakehead's profile to accommodate the new and admittedly less alarming information. Toward the end of July, however, the number of media reports questioning pieces of the mantra and the actual scope of the snakehead problem grew.

An Associated Press piece by John Biemer, published in the *Capital* on July 26 and titled, "Snakehead Facts, Misconceptions," argued that "information continues coming out to dispel . . . the beast's reputation." Courtenay told Biemer that the northern snakehead doesn't really walk, rather it wiggles forward. Shafland was reported as having said, "I'm just a country boy, but if you ain't got legs, you can't walk." Courtenay clarified that the snakehead's ability to survive out of water depended on conditions being very wet. Direct sun, he said, would kill the fish quickly. When some local Asian experts were interviewed they offered a much different perspective on the snakehead attributes than what people in the United States were used to hearing. For example, Koh told reporter Kaur that "the U.S. report is a bit exaggerated. The fish doesn't die immediately after leaving the water, but it certainly can't survive for three days without water. It can survive only several hours on wet ground." Kaur's interview with Goh Shih Yong, the corporate communications manager of the Agri-Food and Veterinary Authority in Singapore, elicited a similar response. "It's a hardy creature," said Goh, "and it's true that it can wriggle its way on the ground, but only during the rainy season." In the August 5 issue of *Time*, which hit the streets at the end of July, Jeffrey Kluger wrote a story appropriately titled, "Fish Tale." In it, he wondered whether all the fuss about the snakehead was justified. Paul Shafland was quoted as saying, "This has been more Hollywood than science," and Kluger labeled the snakehead as "nothing more than a common swamp fish," whose form of "clumsy locomotion does not lend itself to wanderlust." As for air breathing and surviving on land, Kluger contended that "the best they usually seem to manage is several hours under wet burlap in open markets where they're sold for their flesh. On dry land under a sunny sky, they fricassee fast." The article concluded that "all the hand wringing . . . might just be a too little, too late effort to do something about the larger problem of non-native species."

Meanwhile, the satirists were continuing to have a field day with the snakehead story. On July 17, Comedy Central's "The Daily Show with Jon Stewart" offered the following take on how to handle the snakeheads of Crofton.

> Jon Stewart: If you thought the northern snakehead was just an exotic sexual position, well, please teach it to me. But in the meantime, environmental officials in Maryland are battling an invasion of a different kind of northern snakehead. Yes, in Crofton, Maryland, environmental officials are combating an exotic species of Chinese fish that is extremely aggressive, always hungry, and has a pair of primitive lungs that allows it to wiggle across land for up to three days.
>
> [In the background is a caricature image of a snakehead with sharp teeth eating a frog. Under the image are the words, "Death Fish."]
>
> The fishes' mobility has caused them to spread like wildfish through the county ponds where their razor sharp teeth quickly devour everything their path. As a result, state officials have posted these wanted signs asking residents to find and kill this deadly creature. It's been a frustrating search though. Interviews have turned up very little.
>
> [Image in the background of a snakehead wearing shades and a hat.]
>
> "What's that officer, no, no I haven't seen him, sure is an ugly sucker

though, yep, yep. Yes, if I do see him, I will call right away officer. You take care now. You fools."

According to Maryland's Department of Natural Resources the snakeheads are being fruitful and multiplying.

[Eric Schwaab on camera]: This was a fish that was turned in this morning. It appears to be a young snakehead. If in fact it is confirmed to be a young snakehead that does suggest that reproduction has occurred or is occurring here in the pond.

[Back to Stewart]: Other signs that reproduction is occurring included the discovery of a Luther Vandross CD floating on a lily pad [image of CD floating on a lilypad]. The problem began two years ago when a local man released two Chinese snakeheads into a pond. He ordered the fish, known for their curative properties, to make a soup for his ailing sister. But by the time the fish arrived, the woman had recovered, having turned instead to Campbell's new chunky rhinoceros gallbladder and noodles. With more on the northern snakehead, we take you out live to Stephen Colbert, who joins us now, our dangerous animal control expert.

Stephen Colbert [reporting live from Crofton, Md.]: Yes, John.

Stewart: Stephen, has there been any progress in finding a solution to the environmental devastation being caused by these Chinese snakeheads?

Colbert: John, officials here are really grasping at straws. They're talking about administering electrical shocks to the water. They're toying with the idea of poisoning the waterways to flush the snakehead out. But they'll probably just kick those proposals back to some subcommittee that'll issue a report and by next Friday snakeheads will be swimming in your toilet bowl and snapping at your produce.

Stewart: So, in your mind you're not hopeful about these government efforts.

Colbert: John, all I know is that the fat cats at the Maryland Department of Natural Resources are up in their swanky penthouse suites counting their money and doing the Charleston, while real frogs and real trout down here with real families are really suffering. Sorry John, I just get so emotional when I talk about trout.

Stewart: But these government agencies, they know what they're doing. They face this kind of environmental issue—

Colbert: John, listen, I may not have a detailed environmental impact report, or a fancy degree, or knowledge, but I do have something those bureaucrats don't—horse sense. That is why I have taken the liberty of solving the problem myself, free of charge, no questions asked.

Stewart: Well, that's wonderful, how did you do that Steve?

Colbert: Well, the snakehead doesn't have any natural predators in the ponds and streams. It's at the top of the food chain. Not anymore, thanks to the piranhas.

Stewart: I'm sorry, piranhas?

Colbert: Yes, John, I've just dropped a few from my personal collection in the pond to rid these waterways of the snakehead once and for all. No need to thank me.

Stewart: But you know that may not do it, because as you know the snakehead can crawl up onto the land. That's the problem with them, they can survive outside of that pond and infest new waterways. The piranhas may not get to them all.

Colbert: Well, John, that's where the scorpions come in. I've covered the entire area here in Tunisian black-back widowmakers. Thousands of them, probably too many, but I got them on the cheap. Anyway, it's a full snakehead-containment zone with scorpions surrounding the pond all the way over to the playground by the elementary school.

Stewart: I don't mean to be a naysayer, Stephen, how are you going to contain the scorpions?

Colbert: Owls. A few well-placed spotted and great-horned owls could easily handle the scorpions.

Stewart: What, what about the—

Colbert: African condors, John. I know they're not indigenous to the region, but just a couple African condors will hunt down and kill the fiercely breeding swarms of owls once they've taken care of the scorpions who've done in the snakeheads, the ones who aren't killed by the piranhas. It's a circle of life John. It's a beautiful thing to behold.

Stewart: Stephen, this is kind of the whole problem though with this kind of environmental management. Aren't you worried that introducing these new species to an area might have some dire consequences?

Colbert: Not when I'm standing next to a couple of canisters of napalm, John. If we have any problems, we'll turn this area in to the surface of the moon.

Stewart: Thank you very much Stephen. You keep on the case.
(Comedy Central © 2002)

On July 24, on the "Late Show with David Letterman," the host ticked off the Top Ten Little-Known Facts About the Snakehead Fish, with number one being, "It's the result of a drunken genetic engineer and a dare." Lewis Grossberger, of *Mediaweek,* in an article on July 29, took on a lonely job: "It's about time someone in the media had the guts to stand up for an innocent victim who's been smeared, vilified, stereotyped and all but given a pre-emptive death sentence," he said, referring to the snakehead. Grossberger proceeded to dispel the nasty rumors that had been circulated about the fish he said had "replaced al Qaeda and Martha Stewart as most terrifying specters threatening the American public." As for the snakehead being identified as a big-toothed predator, Grossberger responded, "So what? We're predatory, and we have lots of big teeth. Did you ever look closely at a photo of Julia Roberts?" About the same time, *The Onion* published an infographic titled "The Snakehead Menace" that listed

VOLUME 38 ISSUE 27   AMERICA'S FINEST NEWS SOURCE™   1-7 AUGUST 2002

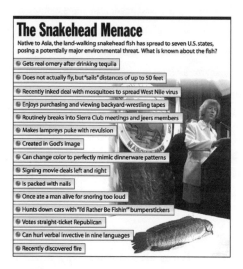

The Snakehead Menace

Native to Asia, the land-walking snakehead fish has spread to seven U.S. states, posing a potentially major environmental threat. What is known about the fish?

- Gets real ornery after drinking tequila
- Does not actually fly, but "sails" distances of up to 50 feet
- Recently inked deal with mosquitoes to spread West Nile virus
- Enjoys purchasing and viewing backyard-wrestling tapes
- Routinely breaks into Sierra Club meetings and jeers members
- Makes lampreys puke with revulsion
- Created in God's image
- Can change color to perfectly mimic dinnerware patterns
- Signing movie deals left and right
- Is packed with nails
- Once ate a man alive for snoring too loud
- Hunts down cars with "I'd Rather Be Fishin'" bumperstickers
- Votes straight-ticket Republican
- Can hurl verbal invective in nine languages
- Recently discovered fire

Infographic on the snakehead from *The Onion*. The woman at the podium is Secretary of the Interior Gale Norton. Reprinted with permission of THE ONION. Copyright 2002, by ONION, INC., www.theonion.com.

what was known about the fish. Among the items included was that the snakehead "gets real ornery after drinking tequila," and it "hunts down cars with 'I'd Rather Be Fishin' bumperstickers." Conan O'Brien, of NBC's "Late Night with Conan O'Brien," did a brief piece on the snakehead in which he told his viewers that he had recently learned "some more really frightening characteristics" of the snakehead that hadn't been publicized, one of which was that "the snakehead fish can fly over people's heads and memorize their credit card numbers."

On July 30, Froma Harrop, of the *Asheville (North Carolina)*

Top Ten Little-Known Facts about the Snakehead Fish

10. The fish is 50 percent snake, 50 percent head

9. Mortal enemy is the fishhead snake

8. High-protein diet of fish and frogs means slim look for summer

7. They love kids

6. Bush promised to find and catch them … of course we've heard that before

5. Fans of the snakehead fish are known as snakehead-heads

4. Available for a limited time at participating Red Lobsters

3. It's very popular with lawyers, am I right people?

2. Developed by the government to distract people from the whole Cheney-Halliburton thing

1. It's the result of a drunken genetic engineer and a dare

Citizen-Times, argued with tongue firmly in cheek that we should let the free market resolve the snakehead problem. She noted that many fish with unappealing names had been made more palatable to diners through semantic conversions. For example, hake being sold as "butterfish." Why not a similar turn for the snakehead, she wondered? Her nomination—"honeyfish." With a name like that, diners might come running and soon the snakehead problem would be under control, at a profit. A "honeyfish" cookbook, Harrop continued, might serve to further increase sales and, thereby, decrease the population of snakeheads. And why stop with the culinary? Perhaps, Harrop wondered, snakehead oil might help with heart problems, and "Scalp Massage Cream with Snakehead and Green Tea" could be a strong seller.

Of all the humorous articles and skits about the snakehead, none had a greater impact on the DNR than the piece on Comedy Central. "When this episode made 'The Daily Show,'" Schwaab said, with a smile, "I knew we had really made the big time." When asked why, Schwaab responded, " 'The Daily Show' is how I get the real news." In the days and weeks that followed, Schwaab not only told many people about the skit, he also made sure they got one of the tapes of it that Lynch had made at his request. For the remainder of the summer, the skit served as a tension breaker. "When things got hectic around here," said Lynch, "John [Surrick] and I would watch 'The Daily Show' and laugh and laugh and laugh."

On August 6, Secretary Chuck Fox agreed with the snakehead panel's recommendation and decided to forge ahead with the eradication plan. "We are ready to act," he said, first applying the herbicides, then two weeks later, the poison. Fox added, "I feel confident that this is the most effective and efficient course of action." The DNR was ready to go almost immediately because when the potential use of herbicides and poisons was floated in late June, Steve Early began planning for this eventuality. For example, the DNR needed environmental permits for these applications. Obtaining most of these was straightforward, but one proved quite interesting. In applying herbicides to the entire pond it was DNR's hope that the resultant die-off of plants would cause the oxygen levels in the water to plummet, thereby causing many of the fish to suffocate and die. But the manufacturer of Diquat, one of the herbicides being used, placed a label restriction on the product that said it could only be used on one-third to one-half of a body of water at a time. Ironically, the reason for this restriction was that if Diquat were used on the entire body of water at once, it would depress oxygen levels and kill fish. Being that killing fish was one of the main goals of the herbicide application, the DNR had to get exemptions from the manufacturer and from the U.S. Environmental Protection Agency to apply Diquat to the entire pond. The DNR also had to make sure it had people on hand who could carry out the poisoning. Applying rotenone is not as simple as going to the pond and dumping it in. One needs to wear special protective suits, use respirators, receive health certifications, and complete special training. Early knew it would take time to get the permits and certifications, and train DNR staff, so, in July, well before the panel met, Early had begun the process. Now, because of that forward thinking, the DNR was ready. The only hurdle left was getting permission from the pond owners to do the applications. Getting that permission, however, proved more difficult than the DNR had expected.

SIX

GOING IN FOR THE KILL

William Berkshire and Danny MacQuilliam had been very supportive of the DNR's efforts thus far and both of them wanted to cooperate with the DNR now, but they had concerns about liability. What if something went wrong during the DNR's operation at the ponds? What if someone got hurt or there was an environmental disaster? Berkshire and MacQuilliam wanted assurances that the state, not they, would be held responsible. In talking with a Jon Ward of the *Washington Times*, Berkshire's lawyer said that his client "was waiting for a statement that the state will protect them from any damage that might result from this chemical operation." An article by the *Baltimore Sun*'s Rona Kobell quoted a letter MacQuilliam wrote to Secretary Fox: "I hope you understand that we have, and want to continue to cooperate with the DNR, but we need to protect ourselves from any liability and financial burden. We have allowed the DNR to work on our property without any restrictions. We have tolerated the media frenzy and the circus surroundings without many demands and complaints."

The state and the pond owners discussed their differences in the hope of coming to a mutually acceptable solution. Berkshire found the first draft agreement offered by the state unacceptable because he didn't feel that the issue of liability had been solved.

> We were totally cooperative [said Berkshire]. The only condition we had is that they be responsible. Right before this agreement was to be signed, when they delivered it, they withdrew their commitment to be responsible for this. In a letter they gave us they said, we'll be responsible and we'll do this and we'll do that, comma, subject to available appropriations, but that takes it away. So, this agreement of being responsible for any accident, liability for any trouble, and responsible for defending any legal action was taken away. . . . Essentially that is when we both said, no, we can't do this under those circumstances because why should the property owner be responsible. And the state said, well we don't have the money. Well, if you don't have the money to defend that how do you think we possibly could?

In the midst of the negotiations, MacQuilliam took a short vacation to Ocean City, Maryland. Although he wanted to resolve the issue quickly, MacQuilliam didn't feel that his trip would delay the matter, especially because his father, and the president of the MacQuilliam Organization, was out of the country at the same time and would have to return and be consulted before any final agreement was reached. If MacQuilliam thought he was going to escape the snakehead story in Ocean City, he was sorely mistaken. One day on the beach, his friends were ribbing him about the snakehead when a woman walked over, holding out a copy of a newspaper. She wanted to know if MacQuilliam was the owner of the pond mentioned in an article on snakeheads she'd been reading and was quite excited to find out that the answer was yes. After all, it's not every day that you get to share a beach with the owner of the most famous pond with the most famous fish in America.

The DNR was becoming increasingly agitated about the delay in following through with its eradication plan. Some with the state hinted at the possibility of taking unilateral legal action to gain access, without the permission of the owners, but that was clearly an option of last resort, assuming it could be done at all. Part of the reason for the DNR's sense of urgency involved the weather. It had been hot and sunny, the best conditions for herbicides to do their job, and there was no telling how long that weather would hold.

Although no deal had been inked, the merchants whose stores backed up to the pond knew the day of reckoning for the snakehead was coming, and that sooner or later herbicides then poison would be applied just yards from their businesses. According to the *Baltimore Sun* reporters Jackie Powder and Rona Kobell, merchants were not worried. Craig Wharton, a worker at the Family Bike Shop, said, "We trust the government." A stylist at the Miracles Salon, Mark Goldsborough, wondered, less than seriously, "Is it Agent Orange? Are we going to grow another ear?" Alex Yeung, owner of the Fortune Cookie Express Restaurant said of the pond, "It's very far away, over there," but he did have some lingering concerns about the smell.

It's surprising that the concerns about the smell were not more pronounced, given some of the recent reporting on the subject. At the end of July, Anita Huslin wrote an article on the impending "war" on the snakehead, in which she asked Bob Lunsford what might be expected in the wake of the "two-step snakehead eradication process." Contemplating the cleanup, Lunsford said, "I know all the tricks— rubbing lemon juice, Lava soap, just to get the smell off your hands. My guess is I won't have many friends for a while." As for how bad the smell could get, Lunsford added, "Use your imagination. How bad do you think it could be and then double it." Lunsford noted that MacQuilliam was "worried about his tenants, who are going to have this reeking pond in their back yard." That Huslin quoted Lunsford was a bit of a journalistic coup. Largely as a result of his earlier statements to the press, Lunsford was, from the DNR's perspective, no longer available for comment. Nevertheless, Huslin got him on the line. Lunsford's comments did not sit well with Eric Schwaab, who later said, "I think frankly [Lunsford's comments] created some problems for us when there wasn't any factual basis on which to project what the smell would be like. We could all speculate, but to be quoted in the paper as saying that it was going to be bad when there is no factual basis for that, didn't help anybody, including us."

On Thursday, August 15, MacQuilliam agreed to allow the DNR to proceed after the state offered to lease his pond and the adjoining land for the remainder of the year, thereby assuming all liability for anything that occurred during or after the herbicide and poison applications. That night the DNR set Sunday, August 18, as the date for the herbicide application. In making that announcement, Secretary Fox noted that Berkshire had yet to accept the state's lease offer. In an interview with Kobell, Fox said he found the negotiations with Berkshire "very frustrating. We have tried to address every single legitimate issue. We have tried to do so forthrightly. We have tried to do so expeditiously. I do not begin to understand their motivations for what has happened so far."

Berkshire's attorney, when reached by Kobell for comment, expressed surprise that the DNR had set a date for the application and vowed that he and his client would continue working with the state to resolve the outstanding issues, which they did the next day.

On Friday, the DNR issued a news release announcing the herbicide application. The media was invited to observe, with restrictions. In recent weeks, a few television stations had used aircraft to get aerial images of the ponds, and there was reason to believe that the same might happen now. So, no helicopters or airplanes would be allowed overhead on Sunday, at least within one thousand feet of the ponds' surface. The media was also instructed to dress appropriately. The manufacturer of the herbicides Diquat and Glyphosate required those in the treatment area to wear long-sleeve shirts and pants, socks, and closed shoes (no sandals). Although the media would be corralled in along the edge of the pond and away from the immediate treatment area, they too would have to abide by the dress code.

While the DNR and the landowners wrangled over who would be responsible for what and when, the snakehead story continued to swirl through the media. Sheila Jackson and Faith Hayden, of the *Baltimore Sun*, wrote an article titled, "Fish Has a Grip on Our Attention: Headlines about Snakehead Just Keep Hooking Us In." They observed that, "Apparently, the American media has never had a houseguest like the amazing eco-invader from China, the northern snakehead fish. . . . [It] has merited more fish wrap, er, newsprint, it seems, than any run-of-the-mill corporate scandal." The article was essentially a compilation of many of the more memorable headlines and press quotes generated by the snakehead story thus far, offering the ultimate proof that the snakehead story itself had become the story. Clarence Page, of the *Chicago Tribune*, delivered a "fishy story" to the viewers of PBS's "NewsHour with Jim

Lehrer," in which he said, "The Frankenfish speaks to the dark side of our progress. Like an urban legend come to life, it evokes a primal fear that maybe globalization is shrinking the world too much and letting in too much of what we don't want." The capture of two northern snakeheads in North Carolina generated alarm in that state and contributed to a CBS news story titled, "Freak Fish Found in Two More States," in which viewers not only heard about the North Carolina snakeheads, but also four that had been seized by authorities in West Virginia after a raid on a local pet shop. An article in the *Lancaster New Era*, by Ad Crable, noted that Pennsylvania had decided to add its name to the list of states banning possession of snakeheads, and he quoted Guy Bowersox, of the Pennsylvania Fish and Boat Commission as saying of the snakeheads, "The potential is there to destroy ecosystems in waterways throughout the United States, as well as in Pennsylvania." Tom Doggett, from Reuters, in an article titled, "Snakeheads Put Small Maryland Pond on World Map," opined that the fish "appear to have no friends. Even . . . People for the Ethical Treatment of Animals (PETA) said it favors killing the snakeheads, though it prefers a more humane method instead of the state's broad poison plan."

Corey Ross, of the *Omaha World-Herald*, interviewed pet store owners to find out what they thought of snakeheads and the proposed ban. One called the snakehead "a pit bull with fins," and added, the "type of person who's going to have a pit bull is the same type of person who's going to have a snakehead. They like to watch fish eat other things." As for the ban, there were doubts as to how effective it would be. Not only did a lot of people already own snakeheads, in Omaha and elsewhere, but the impact of the ban, it was argued, would only to increase demand. When Ross asked a local zoo director whether the zoo would ever keep snakeheads, the director said no, they're too much trouble. Commenting on the situation in Crofton, the director added, "I would've poisoned that pond a long time ago."

William Wineke, of the *Wisconsin State Journal*, saw in the snakehead story a reprieve of sorts. He wrote that he was "truly relieved" when he heard about the snakehead threat because it had given him "something tangible to worry about," as opposed to all the intangible things that strike fear in people's hearts but that one can often do "very little to change," such as coping with terrorists or the dramatic fluctuations in one's stock-based retirement account. Perhaps, Wineke mused, the city of Madison could follow in Chicago's footsteps and attempt to ban the snakeheads within the city limits? As for his own efforts, he said, "I can even do my part. If I find a snakehead slithering across my lawn, I can hit it with a club and stop it from eating my cat." Joe Julavits, of the *Florida Times Union* had a different take. "I'm reading the headlines, and I'm on edge. As if the stock market scandal, the war on terrorism and the global warming crisis weren't enough, now the news media are reporting that certain species of fish [including the snakehead] are out of control and poised to take over the planet."

With all the bad press and the impending ban, *Baltimore Sun* reporter Rona Kobell wondered how food sales of live snakeheads were faring. In New York fish markets and restaurants she learned that the answer was not too well. Although it was still legal to sell snakeheads in the Empire State, many merchants were washing their hands of the species. Some, mistakenly, thought the ban had already gone into effect and didn't want to risk breaking the law. For others, the fish had just become too hot to handle. Spencer Chan, the owner of a Mott Street restaurant, was quoted in Kobell's article as saying, "We did serve it. No more now. As soon as we saw the newspaper, we had to stop." But the snakehead well was not completely dry. There were still some hardy souls willing to sell them, and, more importantly, there were those willing to buy.

According to an article by Max Gross, a writer for the *Forward*, a weekly newspaper covering Jewish life, one would-be purchaser was Dick Horne, the co-owner of the American Dime Museum, a quirky establishment in Baltimore that bills itself as "the world's only exhibition, research, and performance space dedicated exclusively to variety and novelty entertainment, perhaps the oldest form of entertainment and one identified as the country's most treasured forms of Americana." There, visitors can see Fiji mermaids, replicas of shrunken heads, the "only surviving Nelson Supply Co. giantess mummies," and a great variety of sideshow paraphernalia. Upon reading about the northern snakehead, the ultimate, up-to-the-minute novelty and quintessential slice of Americana, Horne knew he had to have one. But when he went to buy a snakehead he couldn't find a willing seller. Not one to give up easily, Horne turned to a friend for help, Amanda Topaz, a contortionist whose stage name is "Ula the Pain-Proof Rubbergirl." As Gross relayed it, when Horne asked Ula to buy a snakehead, she responded, "What am I gonna say?" Horne's reply, "Tell them you're an Orthodox Jew." Ula concocted a story about needing to buy a live snakehead and have a rabbi "slaughter it according to Jewish law," notwithstanding the fact that there apparently is no such thing as a kosher method of killing a fish. Despite the dubious foundation of Ula's story, it worked. She returned from her foray to New York's Chinatown with not one, but three live snakeheads, which were promptly named Oedipus, Fluffy, and Bartholomew, and placed on display at the museum. Shortly after the fishes' arrival, Horne told *Washington Post* reporter Michael O'Sullivan, "They're here, and they're evil as expected," but then added, "actually, they're not. They're kind of nice, but they're supposed to be evil." Horne placed the snakeheads right next to a pair of nuclear worms, in a larger exhibit he calls, "Dangerous Animals in the News."

When writer Nick Paumgarten read about the snakehead he saw a race. "To the list of dream matchups . . . Wilt vs. Shaq . . . grizzly vs. crocodile," wrote Paumgarten in the August 5 issue of the *New Yorker*, "add one more: turtle vs. snakehead." Zeroing in on the snakehead's most vaunted talent, its purported ability to "walk," Paumgarten wanted to put the fish "to the test." In a Chinatown fish store, he and a few friends found what were labeled as northern snakeheads. The owner of the store had made good use of the *Daily News* front page on "The Fish From Hell," preparing a sign beneath it that read, "Eat the fish from hell. Live Longer. Most of them are well train, they do not eat and bite now. $4 each." Fearing that these snakeheads were too "listless and uncompetitive," Paumgarten and company moved on to another fish store where they purchased a livelier snakehead. Although he had wanted to match the snakehead with a turtle, Paumgarten couldn't find one, so he settled for a blue crab. The next stop, Sara D. Roosevelt Park. The snakehead and the crab were placed side-by-side in a muddy area. A bag of water was dumped on the competitors and someone yelled, "Go." Nothing happened, even after some prodding with a back-scratcher. Then, Paumgarten wrote, the fish "writhed forward . . . like a snake with really short arms," covering three feet in short order, leaving the crab in the, well, mud. The race over, the fish was returned to the market from whence it came, alive and victorious.

Satirists continued preying on the story. Dan Rodricks, of the *Baltimore Sun*, bemoaned the weather that was gripping the region, noting that the "drought has rendered things so dry around here I saw a snakehead at BWI [Baltimore Washington International Airport] looking for a flight back to China." Rodricks's colleague, Kevin

Cowherd, wrote that only a gubernatorial grant of clemency could keep the snakehead from meeting its maker. "[DNR] hopes to call in a massive air strike," he said, "and a large thermonuclear device will be dropped on the pond, wiping out . . . [the snakeheads] that have terrorized the other decent, God-fearing species who want nothing more than to live in peace and . . . oh, wait, they're going with poison, aren't they?" Once the herbicides cleared away the vegetation, Cowherd argued, the snakeheads will have no place to hide, and "they'll stand out like Anna Nicole Smith at a convent." But there was a wistful element to Cowherd's joking. After the snakeheads were gone, he said, there might be little else to talk about. "Me, I miss the toothy killers already."

In the *Pittsburgh Post-Gazette*, L. Wayne Moss and Donna and Eve Shavatt used the snakehead drama as the subject of their "He Said–She Said" column. The women offered a few alternatives to doing away with the snakeheads. The Shavatts wrote, "Why not . . . put up 'snakehead crossing' signs and charge admission. . . . Men can wear T-shirts that say 'Want to see my Snakehead?'" If the fish had to be killed, they suggested, then send them to Saddam Hussein, with a note telling him that adult snakeheads like "it when humans tease and interact with their babies. Then let nature take its course." Moss would have none of that. "Women are so gullible," he wrote. "Apparently, with very little effort you can convince them there is a fish built like a linebacker that can run up out of the water, take a Mike Tyson–sized chomp out of your keister, then dive back in. Oh really?"

There was one totally new element to the story that surfaced in the early weeks of August. The snakehead was put to music. David Cotton lives in Fairfax, Virginia, and teaches language arts to seventh-graders in nearby Prince William County. In early July, Cotton began following the snakehead story, and quickly became, he said, "consumed" by it, especially after seeing pictures of the fish. His snakehead infatuation might have remained a personal thing, but Cotton was also half of the rock band, BrainFang, which was formed in 1999 when Cotton and his partner, Patrick Williams, now a computer software developer in Gaithersburg, Maryland, were in high school in Northern Virginia. According to the official BrainFang website (www.brainfang.com) Cotton and Williams "write songs, play music, and, in our free time, develop our plans for global domination with our legion of long-phalanged associates." BrainFang had recorded one CD ("We Right the Songs") and were at work on another when the snakehead story erupted. "I just had to write something about it," said Cotton, "and I wrote the first draft of the song in probably ten minutes and then went back later and did some major revisions." The song was titled, "Spawn of Snakehead," and subtitled, "A Story of Love, Loss, and the Frankenfish."

Cotton sent the lyrics to Williams in late July, and Williams laid down the tune within twenty-four hours. After they got together to record the track, they submitted it to the WashingtonPost.com's MP3 site, an electronic portal where bands upload new songs and people can download and listen to them. "Spawn of Snakehead" became the "Editor's Pick" for the week of August 7, and it was the most downloaded song the following week, with 143 people making copies. For a track that was recorded in a "patchwork, guerrilla recording style," as Cotton calls it, "Spawn of Snakehead" sounds good and it's got a great beat, and the lyrics, well, they speak for themselves.

The northern Chinese snakehead
　The next red scare
Half fish, all monster
　Aqualife beware.

Belly to the pavement
　Pectorals working hard

He'll eat your goldfish
    Then scamper thru your yard.

The killer fish
    The jutting jaw
The killer fish
    The toothy maw.

Frankenfish Frankenfish
    Get the hell out
Snakehead spawning.

Spawn of Snakehead
    That we fear
The Spawn of Snakehead
    Get 'em outta here!

Spawn of Snakehead
    That we fear
The Spawn of Snakehead
    Get 'em outta here!

Hide the housecat
    Bring the babies inside.
Snakehead on the loose
    How long can we hide?

He's the red-neck Chinafish
    With indiscriminate gullet
Twenty pounds of fury
    With the aquamatic mullet.

(*guitar solo*)

It's the Spawn of Snakehead
    That we fear
The Spawn of Snakehead
    Get them outta here!

It's a nasty nasty fish.
    Forty inches of Chinese dynomite.

While the song is certainly out there, it might have gone even further down the line in terms of creativity and zaniness had Cotton been aware of the most lurid information floating about on the snakehead. "I never heard the bit about snakeheads attacking people and potential fatalities," he said. "That would have sent me over the edge, I can tell you. I would have just gone nuts."

Two days after "Spawn of Snakehead" made its debut, another song about snakeheads was launched. The "Kirk, Mark & Lopez Morning Show" on 98 Rock, a radio station out of Baltimore, has a regular feature called Twisted Tunes, in which the words of well-known songs are stripped away and replaced by new, more topical lyrics. On August 9, the Twisted Tune was "Snakehead," which married the tune of "Mack the Knife" with lyrical commentary on that "old snakehead" who "is back in town."

Oh the Snakehead
    Has sharp teeth, dear
And he's really
    An ugly sight
Oh that snakehead
    Likes to eat meat, yeah
So beware of his nasty bite.

And when that snakehead
    Bites with his teeth, babe
All the small fish
    They end up dead
And they can walk
    Up on the beach, yeah
And they start
    Oh how they start to spread.

Up on the sidewalk
    Woo they are walking
They're from China
    Just like fried rice
You could end up
    At the coroner
If you sample
    That snakehead's bite.

They're sending out divers
    And some poison
Look out there's a lot
    Of them in old Maryland.

There's no life forms
    In the lake there
Now that snakehead
    Is back in town.

Look out old snakehead is back.
(Courtesy "Kirk, Mark, and Lopez Show," 98 Rock, Baltimore)

As the day of the herbicide application approached, anticipation rose. The DNR was itching to proceed now that access had been granted and the weather was still hot and sunny. Editors at media outlets saw the event as a perfect news peg for generating another story in the ongoing snakehead saga, and so the call went out to their reporters: Be at the pond by dawn. And they were there, dozens of them, trooping down to the pond's edge, bleary-eyed, juggling notepads, pens, cameras, and sustenance from the nearby Dunkin' Donuts. As it turns out, they could have left the doughnuts behind. DNR Secretary Chuck Fox had brought along a bunch for them to share, as "sort of as a joke," according to Huslin. The media dutifully settled in behind the yellow tape strung between trees, which had emblazoned on it the words, "Police line, do not cross." Although it was very early, the temperature was in the mid-seventies, and it was humid. Many of the reporters, decked out in the required long-sleeved shirts and pants, were already sweating.

One reporter who wasn't sweating was Liane Hansen, a correspondent for National Public Radio's "Weekend Edition" program. While her colleagues were settling in at the pond, she spoke to Schwaab on the phone from her office. "As film lovers know," Hansen began, "Frankenstein's monster met his fate in a fiery blaze. The Frankenfish won't go out quite so cinematically." After describing the northern snakehead as a "predatory fish that can crawl on land and survive for days out of water," and calling it a "savage swimmer" and the "dreaded snakehead," Hansen spoke with Schwaab about the eradication plan.

Back at the pond the DNR, with the aid of a host of state and federal officials from across the region, readied for the day's assault. The location, between MacQuilliam's pond and one of Berkshire's, was chosen for practicality. It provided a relatively broad expanse of flat and open land for use as a staging area, and it was accessible by

The airboat making the rounds at the herbicide application. Courtesy
Tom Darden.

a dirt road. These features were particularly important, given the
size of the operation. Besides the people, the expeditionary force
included an airboat and two johnboats from which the herbicides
would be sprayed, an ambulance, a food truck to feed the masses, a
water tank to dilute the herbicides in case of a spill, and a pickup
truck serving as a utility infielder, moving about supplies and running errands if need be.

The herbicide sprayers were filled and the boats loaded. Each
person with responsibility for spraying the herbicides wore protective clothing. As dawn broke, the boats shoved off from the shore
and began their deadly rounds. "This is the beginning of the end for
the snakehead fish," said the DNR's Lynch. "Time is up." Back and
forth went the boats, spraying every square inch of the pond's surface. At twenty-minute intervals, the boats returned to the staging
area so that fresh crews could take over and the herbicide tanks
could be refilled. Occasionally the airboat grounded itself in shal-

low areas from which it had to be dislodged. The media passed the time watching the less-than-enthralling spectacle, telling jokes, eating, scribbling down story outlines, just sitting on the ground, or daydreaming. Globules of herbicides wafted through the air, enveloping all in the general vicinity in an invisible mist that had a subtle, chemical smell that dissipated quickly.

There were a couple of exciting moments, however. At one point, a camera crew appeared in the staging area, to the consternation of the press, which was relegated to the media pen across the way. According to Candy Thomson, "We are all sitting behind police tape like some crime scene, and I'm looking through my binoculars and all of the sudden over where they are actually mixing the herbicides I see this camera crew. Of course, handling it really, really well at that hour, I go running up to [John] Surrick and scream, Who the @#$% is that over there? He's like 'What's a matter, what's a matter?' And I go, There's a crew over there, who is that, CNN or Fox, did you cut some exclusive deals?" Surrick assured Thomson and her colleagues that no deals were cut. The crew was hired by Berkshire to videotape the event. Berkshire was hoping to prepare a documentary on the snakehead and its eradication to sell to the Discovery Channel. The other bit of excitement came awhile later, when a few overeager camera operators flouted the rules and crept beyond the yellow warning tape to the edge of the pond, and then a few feet beyond into the shallow water. When one of the boats came close to the shore, the camera operators, realizing that they would soon be in the line of fire, jumped back, but not before their feet were doused in herbicides, making them the unintended victims of a drive-by spraying.

As the morning progressed, the mercury rose rapidly, into the eighties and then the nineties, on its way to a high for the day of ninety-six. Assorted tourists, Crofton residents, and gawkers who just happened to be in the area milled about on the outskirts of the pond or in the nearby parking lots, adding to the "event." Gillespie was there. He gave a few interviews and watched the pond carefully, hoping to see if the "golf bag"–sized snakehead he claimed to have seen the year before would rise to the surface, belly up.

Another person who showed up was Steve Koorey, an investment-banking manager who lived in Crofton and was between jobs. On a camping trip in July, Koorey and a couple of his friends were sitting around a fire chatting when he started talking about how people are always saying they have an idea for an invention and want to go into business for themselves. Koorey, who has a self-proclaimed "entrepreneurial streak," told his friends that he, too, had an idea, namely selling T-shirts with the snakehead on them. The more he thought about it, the more he liked the idea, especially since it would be a good way of teaching his three boys about business. Although he would love to get rich off this venture, he said his main "goal was not to lose any money." So Koorey found a snakehead image on the Internet and took it to one of his neighbors, a graphic artist, who doctored it to the point where Koorey was confident that he could use it without having to worry about trademark or copyright infringements. The T-shirt had a fairly simple design. The front sported a large snakehead head rising out of the water, toothy jaws open wide. The words above the image read, "Crofton, Maryland"; underneath, it said, "Home of the Snakehead." With the design in hand, Koorey went to Maryland Apparel Graphics, Inc., in Crofton, to place an order for 288 T-shirts.

Earlier in the summer, just after the story broke, Mike Smith, the manager of the graphics store, had thought about making his own snakehead T-shirts. He certainly knew about the business of producing high quality T-shirts, having thirteen years of experience under his belt, but he didn't have a distribution network, and as he told Koorey when he walked in the door, such a network is the "key" to success. Koorey's appearance, however, didn't cause Smith to think wistfully about a lost opportunity. He wasn't convinced that snakehead T-shirts would be a hit, and anyway, with it being early August already, Smith thought that the snakehead hysteria had crested and was likely now on the slide toward disappearing. If you want to sell something, Smith knew, it's best to strike while interest is high, not when it is waning.

Smith gave Koorey a crash course in producing and selling T-shirts. He was particularly concerned that Koorey not get in over his head by ordering more product than he could unload, leaving him not only with unwanted inventory, but also debt. But Koorey, wanting to avoid that outcome, had already developed a small market for the T-shirts. Before he visited Smith, he brought a picture of his design to a dozen local shops, offering to supply them with shirts on consignment. Most of the shop owners said yes to the deal. Thus, 288, although a fairly ambitious number, seemed within reach.

A few days later, Smith called Koorey to tell him that someone else had come in and placed an even larger order for snakehead T-shirts using a number of different designs. Koorey recalls saying, "That's fine, that's what competition is all about," and he thought that was that, but it wasn't. Smith called again, and according to Koorey, told him that the person making the big order was William Berkshire and that he had raised a fuss and warned him against printing Koorey's shirts. As Smith recalls, Berkshire told him he had applied for a copyright on the images and if Smith wanted to, "he could talk to . . . [Berkshire's] lawyer." Indeed, on July 24, Berkshire, through the Lancer Corporation, had filed four trademark applications with the U.S. Patent and Trademark Office. He was attempting not only to trademark the words "Frankenfish," "Crofton Snakehead," "Northern Snakehead," and "Snakehead," but also related designs, including one that showed a northern snakehead with boots on its outstretched pectoral fins. The trademarks, if approved, would cover clothing, apparel, and accessories as well as toys and playthings. The approval process, however, was lengthy and it would be at least a year before Berkshire would know if he had been awarded any of these trademarks. Although Smith didn't know the particulars of Berkshire's applications, he was sure he didn't want to get in the middle of this dispute. For one thing, Smith worried that it might be a conflict of interest to produce shirts for two customers competing for the same market. More importantly, Smith was concerned about the reference to Berkshire's lawyer. "I'm not going to get into a pissing match," Smith said sharply, "with someone who can stay in court forever."

The circumstances led Smith to inform Koorey and Berkshire that he wasn't printing either order, and he asked the two of them to talk to each other to see if they could work things out. Smith was also a bit angered by Berkshire's approach to dealing with Koorey's nascent entrepreneurial efforts, and he told him so. "This is a little guy," Smith remembers saying to Berkshire, "who is unemployed, trying to make a couple of hundred bucks to cover his mortgage, cut him a break."

Koorey called Berkshire and told him he was just trying to have a good time with this and teach his boys about business. The two of them spoke cordially for a while and then Berkshire asked him to call his lawyer. Koorey and Berkshire's lawyer spoke soon thereafter, whereupon she asked Koorey to fax over the artwork for his shirt. When she called him back, Koorey remembers her saying, "Your artwork looks nothing like his. Go ahead and set up your stand with your kids. I'm going to tell him [Berkshire] not to worry about it." With this understanding worked out, Smith printed Koorey's T-shirts.

A day or two later, Smith printed Berkshire's shirts. If things had worked out the way Berkshire had hoped, back in late June when he and his daughters first hatched their plans, the shirts would have already have been on the street for weeks, perhaps even a month; not just going into production, as was now the case. Berkshire, like Smith, knew you must ride the wave of a fad as it is cresting to reap the most benefits. But that wasn't to be. The process "took too long," Berkshire reflected. While getting the domain name for their erstwhile site on the web took five minutes, everything else dragged on. Berkshire said the he did the initial designs for all the T-shirts, then his daughters and one of his sons-in-law finished them. That took two weeks. When Berkshire brought the designs to Smith to discuss printing them, Smith told him that although they looked good on paper, there was still work to be done, e.g., color selection, to ensure that they would not only transfer well onto T-shirts, but would also look professional. Smith's in-house designers worked with the Berkshires to refine the designs, and that too took time. Yet another delay revolved around the Internet portal for selling the products. The company hired by the Berkshires to create the website took three weeks to deliver.

The lack of products and a fully operational website during July and much of August didn't deter the Berkshires from forging ahead. They advertised in local publications and were able to post a single opening page to their slowly developing website, which informed visitors that soon there would be a range of snakehead T-shirts and other items to purchase; in the meantime, the page invited the curious to send an e-mail signaling their interest in one or more of the planned products. In short order, e-mails poured in from all over the United States and other countries, including Canada, Australia, England, and Israel.

Koorey had a two-pronged strategy for selling his T-shirts, the first part of which, bringing the design to local businesses, had already borne fruit, and now with the T-shirts in hand Koorey delivered them to the store owners, who promptly displayed them. Koorey also had been carefully monitoring the snakehead story and he knew that there would likely be a mob of potential buyers at the herbicide application. But to get to them, he needed a place to set up shop. So he asked the owner of the Dunkin' Donuts near the pond if he could sell T-shirts in his parking lot the day of the application. The owner consented and Koorey rented two parking spots for $50.

The Sunday of the herbicide application, Koorey and one of his sons and his son's friend, Andy Bieler, drove to the Dunkin' Donuts with a small table and a supply of snakehead T-shirts, one of which Koorey was wearing. He went into the store to tell the manager they were there, and as soon as he walked out of the store a reporter ran up to him and said, "I love your T-shirt, where did you get it?" Koorey told her it was his design and that he was just about to set up a stand to sell the shirts. The reporter, who turned out to be from Fox Television, called to her cameraman and asked Koorey if she could film him setting up. Sure, Koorey said, and soon he and his boys were surrounded by a growing number of reporters and film crews all jockeying to hear his story and get a good shot of his stand.

In the midst of all this media attention, Koorey remembers someone tapping him on the shoulder and pointing to a man standing across the way, who was intently watching the proceedings. The anonymous bystander told Koorey, "That's Mr. Berkshire and he doesn't look too happy." Berkshire then walked over and introduced himself. Koorey thinks that Berkshire "had gotten a little bit of a thorn in his craw" because of all the attention lavished on Koorey's stand, especially considering that Berkshire's daughters had a stand a little ways down Route 3, in front Uncle Nicky's Fish'n Hole restaurant, where they were selling their own snakehead T-shirts.

This picture was taken on the day of the herbicide application, near Steve Koorey's T-shirt stand in the parking lot of the Dunkin' Donuts. Koorey is at the upper left, with his hand on his son Tyler's shoulder, and is accompanied by Walter Courtenay (a.k.a. Dr. Snakehead), Tyler's friend, Andy Bieler, and Koorey's daughter, Kimberly. The three kids are wearing the T-shirt that Koorey designed. The image upon which Koorey's design is based is shown in the color section. Courtesy Patricia M. Courtenay.

Koorey remembers Berkshire saying, "As long as this is it, we'll be fine, because I know you talked to my lawyer, but I'm more aggressive than she is." From Koorey's perspective, the message was clear — "I'm not having any competition here," and if you push this matter, I'll sue. From Berkshire's perspective, he was just doing what any prudent businessman would—defending his financial interests. Berkshire believed that he and his daughters had "first priority" on the use of terms such as "snakehead" by virtue of their registrations for trademark protection earlier in the summer. "We had the best position," said Berkshire, and we were concerned about Koorey's activities "impeding that." By the end of their short conversation, Berkshire felt he had made it clear that he wouldn't take any further action as long as Koorey printed no more shirts after selling out of the ones he had. Berkshire and Koorey then said good-bye to each other, but it wouldn't be the last time these two crossed paths.

Sales at both T-shirt stands were brisk. Koorey, who sold fifty T-shirts, folded up his stand around one in the afternoon. By that time the herbicide application was over and the assembled throng was packing up and heading out. Candy Thomson interviewed Steve Early, who seemed pleased with the way things went, noting that "it pretty much came off as planned." Berkshire told Thomson, "We're happy that the state has taken these steps. This is what's best for the people of Maryland." Anyone who expected to see any real drama at the pond that day was disappointed. After being doused with herbicides, the plants didn't die back immediately, nor did any snakeheads, or any other fish for that matter, surrender their lives. It would be a while before the DNR would know the impacts of the herbicide application.

For two weeks, state biologists from the DNR came to the pond to check its status and haul away any rotting vegetation or fish. The herbicide did kill many, though far from all the plants in the pond, and as expected that caused the dissolved oxygen levels to drop, falling to below one part per million for more than a week, which is well below the four parts per million ordinarily needed for fish to thrive. But the fish in this pond were not ordinary. Before the herbicide application,

William Berkshire and his daughters, Chris Ramsey (*left*) and Erin
Berkshire, standing behind some of their products at the sales tent
erected in front of Uncle Nicky's Fish'n Hole restaurant (November
2002). Courtesy Linda Berkshire.

the dissolved oxygen levels in this pond were unusually low, reaching
down to a couple of parts per million at night and rising only slightly
during the day. Given such numbers, the DNR biologists knew they
were dealing with a fish population that was well-adapted to life in
an oxygen-deprived environment. That still didn't diminish the shock
the biologists felt after the herbicide application dramatically reduced
the oxygen levels and nothing happened. "To my surprise and everyone else's surprise," said Early, "we didn't kill a single fish by crashing
oxygen, and we crashed it." The fish in the pond, and not just the
snakeheads, which had the advantage of being able to make use of
atmospheric oxygen, were true survivors. This turn of events, while
puzzling, did not discourage the DNR. They had always planned for

a two-step eradication plan. And they chose September 4 as the day on which to apply the rotenone.

State officials, often with reporters in tow, weren't the only ones visiting the pond. People who had heard about the snakehead story continued to show up almost daily just to see the famous body of water. As Anita Huslin noted, "Joe Q. Public had this irresistible fascination with the place." For example, two days after the herbicide application, Huslin saw a man and two children ambling down to the pond. Curious, Huslin followed them. The man was a farmer from the next county, and the kids were his. To Huslin's surprise, this family unit walked right by all the signs that said "no trespassing—there has been a herbicide application," and the kids proceeded to play in the water, splashing around and picking up things near the pond's edge, including bottles. The father seemed only abstractly concerned. He told his kids not to get too close to the water, but took no action when they did. "And I'm looking at him," said Huslin, "and saying, Do you know they have chemicals in there. And he said, 'Yeah, you probably want to be careful about that, my brother-in-law died of cancer and he was a chemical applicator.'"

In between the use of herbicides and rotenone, the snakehead story continued to expand and morph in different directions. Dale McFeatters, a syndicated columnist with the Scripps Howard News Service, called the snakehead story the "best August scummy-pond story since a Georgia swamp rabbit attacked President Carter," and he predicted that the snakeheads and their story would die by Labor Day. When it became clear that snakeheads were doing just fine, thank you, despite having been exposed to an herbicide cocktail, a raft of "the snakeheads aren't dead yet" stories rippled through the media. The *New York Daily News* tapped into the growing vein of broad-brush invasive species stories with its own entry, replete with a characteristically subdued headline, "Eco-invaders Go Hog-wild, Foreign Species on Rampage in U.S." The *International Herald Tribune*, in contrast, chose a more subdued lead for the same type of story —"Hitchhiking Species a Threat Worldwide." In that article, which began with a brief recounting of the northern snakehead's bona fides as an invasive species, reporter Michael Richardson quoted Klaus Toepfer, executive director of the United Nations Environment Program. "Few people recognize," Toepfer said, "how profoundly invasive alien species have reshaped the natural landscape around them over the past decades and centuries. From tree-killing diseases to rats and other alien predators, invasives have traveled with traders, emigrants and now tourists to new lands where the native species have not had time to evolve adequate protections against these sudden threats. As globalization continues to accelerate, the risks can only grow."

Matt Bivens, the Washington correspondent for the *Moscow Times*, delivered "a report from the front line of America's most-watched military campaign." It was not Afghanistan, which was pretty much over, nor Iraq, which was still simmering. Rather, the "formidable foe" threatening American security was none other than the snakehead. James F. Sweeney, of the *Plain Dealer*, had a similar take. "While we've been bombing Toyota pickups in Afghanistan," he wrote, "and drawing big red circles around Iraqi palaces, an insidious threat has infiltrated our nation's waterways. It's not al Qaeda frogmen in the harbors or arsenic in the drinking supply. It's worse. It's giant ravenous fish from the Far East. Specifically, northern snakeheads and Asian carp." In its section on "Breaking U.S. News," the London-based *Guardian Unlimited* website passed along to its readers an Associated Press story reporting that North Carolina's

Wildlife Resources Commission, still reeling from its brush with snakeheads earlier in the summer, had enacted emergency regulations outlawing the purchase, sale, transport, or ownership of snakeheads within the state. In Louisiana, Doug MacCash, a writer for the *Times-Picayune*, lamented his state's relatively unsuccessful battle with nutria or "poodle-sized muskrats" as he called them. The nutria's proclivities toward procreating with reckless abandon and their preference for the roots of plants that serve to keep soil in place, was, MacCash opined, "exacerbating the erosion of the Bayou state, which is melting into the Gulf like a Hershey bar on the seat of a parked car in August." MacCash was hopeful about the state's recent decision to place a bounty on the nutria's head, or, actually, its tail—bring in a tail, get $4. But he thought there might be other ways to keep the noxious nutrias under control. Noting that Maryland had been having its own problems with invaders from far-off lands, MacCash mused that it might not be too long before snakeheads migrated all the way down to Louisiana. MacCash didn't view this possibility with fear. Instead, he saw an opportunity, and he asked his readers to ponder whether the snakehead might be just the species to put the nutrias in their place, a super counterpest of Asian origin. MacCash ended his piece wondering, "Does it [the snakehead] eat Nutria?," no doubt hoping that the answer would be yes.

Surprisingly, one angle on the snakehead story that had largely gone untapped up to this point was the fish's recreational potential. In Asia, the sporting virtues of snakeheads had long been noticed and promoted. For example, a Georgia-based company called Quest! Global Angling Adventures, offered a ten-day-long "Giant Snakehead Exotic Asian Angling Adventure," in Thailand, from $2,995, and all you have to do is get there. Calling the giant snakehead "a terrific topwater fighter," Quest!'s website enticed

Jean-Francois Helias holding a very large giant snakehead. Helias is well-known to the Southeast Asian sports fishing world and beyond, being recognized as a premier angler and as a snakehead master due to his skill, his fishing record, and his knowledge of how to catch trophy fish. Originally from France, Helias has lived in Thailand since 1986, where he founded the very successful Fishing Adventures Thailand (www.anglingthailand.com). Visiting this website, one is offered an amazing introduction to the wonder of fishing in Thailand. Helias and his customers combined have captured dozens of International Game and Fish Association World Records. Helias is especially passionate about fishing for snakeheads, which he calls "not any kind of fish, but THE FISH!" In December 2002, reporter Robert Davis accompanied Helias on a fishing trip in search of the giant snakehead and wrote an article about the adventure in the *Bangkok Post*. The subtitle of an article captured the excitement of the trip: "The massive fish are so aggressive that anglers use the term 'hunting,' rather than 'fishing,' when pursuing the prey that roam a picturesque lake in Kanchanaburi." Courtesy Jean-Francois Helias Pictures.

Jean-Francois Helias with emperor snakehead (*Channa maruloides*).
Courtesy Jean-Francois Helias Pictures.

adventuresome anglers with a simple question, "How much more
exotic can you get?"

Although most of the Asian fishing trip outfitters focus on giant
snakeheads, northern snakeheads are not exactly chopped liver. Many
anglers in Asia love to get a fighting northern on the line. The website Koreanflyfishing.com features the northern on a list of nine freshwater species sought-after by anglers. On its snakehead information
page, the website gives the northern's Korean name, *Ga mul chi*, and
notes that the fish's nickname is "'Fresh-water tyrant' because of its
outrageous behavior and flesh-eating habits." For the best results, the
website recommends a fishing strategy that is the aquatic version of
home wrecking. Just cast your line when the fish are spawning, the text
continues, and "fishers can easily catch a couple back to back as a male
tries to attack the trespasser after his female is caught."

While some observers urged that the northern snakeheads of

Crofton be welcomed as a new American sport fish, it was not an idea that had many adherents or much exposure. That is, of course, until satirist, Dave Barry took up the cause. Mere days before the DNR was slated to deliver the Crofton snakeheads their final meal, Barry's syndicated column appeared in hundreds of newspapers across the country, offering his perspective on the supposed snakehead menace.

We are about to blow a golden opportunity, here.

I'm talking about the Northern Snakeheads, which sounds like the name of a rock band that eats live hamsters on stage, but is actually a type of fish.

But this is not just any fish. The Northern Snakehead is a very special fish—what marine biologists refer to, technically, as "an X-Files type of fish." Here are some true Northern Snakehead facts that I am not making up:

FACT: It has a snakelike head filled with sharp teeth, is an extremely aggressive eater, and can grow to be three feet long.

FACT: It can use its fins to crawl on land.

FACT: It can breathe air, and survive out of water for three days—nearly two days longer than Michael Jackson!

FACT: Its home stomping grounds are northern Thailand and Myanmar, where, according to an article from Reuters, people believe that "a Snakehead fish is a reincarnated sinner."

FACT: A lot of us seriously question whether there is any such place as "Myanmar."

FACT: Likewise "Reuters."

But there is no question that the Northern Snakehead exists, because it has invaded the United States. You may have seen the news reports about the discovery of juvenile Northern Snakeheads (we know they are juveniles, because they wear their hats backward) in a pond in Maryland.

DISCUSSION QUESTION: What is the deal with Maryland? Wasn't Maryland also the location of the "The Blair Witch Project" tragedy, in which a group of annoying, yet somehow irritating, young filmmakers got lost in the woods and filmed themselves wandering around getting whacked by an evil supernatural hag who soon had the complete support of the movie audience?

But be that as it may—and, like you, I have NO idea what that phrase actually means—the fact remains that the Northern Snakehead is on the loose in this country. This has wildlife officials very concerned, because the Northern Snakehead is sometimes called "the male college student of the marine community"—eating everything in its path and then moving on to the next food source, leaving only devastation behind. As the *Washington Post* put it, the Northern Snakehead "can make short work of a pondful of sunfish, crappies and pickerel—and then shimmy on to other ponds on its belly and fins."

DISCUSSION QUESTION: "Crappies?"

So anyway, Maryland wildlife officials are desperately trying to kill off the Northern Snakeheads. The Bush administration has also gotten involved, issuing a ban that prohibits Northern Snakeheads from entering the country, or, if they are already here, from exercising stock options.

So it looks as though the wildlife authorities will eradicate this dangerous pest. On behalf of all Americans, I say to these officials: Are you CRAZY?? You're blowing the perfect chance to inject some excitement into the "sport" of fishing, which has degenerated into a pathetically unfair competition:

—ON THE ONE SIDE, you have the most advanced species on earth (humans), equipped with graphite rods, alloy reels, computer-designed lures, chemically-enhanced baits, copolymer line, sonar fish locators and vests with upwards of 50 Velcro-flapped pockets. —ON THE OTHER SIDE, you have: "crappies."

Is that fair? A guy with thousands of dollars worth of high-tech equipment against a worm-eating creature with the IQ of broccoli?

Listen, wildlife authorities: Instead of DESTROYING the Northern Snakehead, we should IMPROVE it. We need a Snakehead Enhancement Project, in which these fish are genetically mutated via exposure to radiation, toxic waste and Mountain Dew. We need to develop a Snakehead that is bigger, meaner, toothier, and—above all—faster.

Think what this would do for the sport of fishing! You know those TV fishing shows, the ones starring smug, chunky men who act as though it's a big exciting deal when they win a "fight" with a bass that weighs less than any given one of their tobacco wads?

Well, imagine tuning in to one of these shows and seeing one of these guys sprinting desperately away from the water, waders flapping, pursued by a hungry, ticked-off, amphibious eating machine with a mouth like a grand piano, the soul of a reincarnated sinner and a cruising speed, on land, of 45 miles per hour.

That's right: It's time to even the scales (har)! It's time these fishermen had to play some DEFENSE! If you agree with me, please gather up as much cash as you can humanly stuff into an envelope and send it to: Snakehead Enhancement Project, c/o me. I will personally see to it that all of the money, every single nickel of it, gets spent. Please act now, before somebody else has this idea. Do it for sportsmanship. Do it for conservation. And above all do it because, if you don't, the witch will get you.

Stephen Smith, an intrepid reporter for the *New Statesman* (United Kingdom) didn't want to let his counterparts in America have all the fun, so, casting himself in the role of Ishmael, Smith went to London's Chinatown in search of a quarry decidedly smaller in stature than Moby Dick—a live snakehead. His quest was a bust, but, trying to keep that English upper lip very stiff, Smith ended on an optimistic note, claiming that "the quest is everything."

On the streets of New York's Chinatown Mr. Smith would likely have fared better. The already constricted commerce in snakeheads was getting tighter by the day, but if you knew the right people or where to go, there were still live snakeheads to be had. Around the middle of August, Kim Klopcic, the owner of the funky Asian-American Yin Yankee Café in Annapolis, and Chef Jerry Trice II were talking to one of their contacts at a restaurant supply company in the Bowery section of New York City. Jokingly, they asked their contact, who was Asian, if he could supply them with a few northern snakeheads, to which he replied, sure, how many do you want. Trice remembers thinking, "Oh %$#@, he called us on it. Let's get a half dozen [at $6 a pop] and see what happens." Klopcic soon took a train to New York to pick up the fish. There was only one problem. The fish were moving. "I didn't want them alive," Klopcic told the *Baltimore Sun* reporter, Rob Hiaasen. "Damn things would be walking down the aisle of the train." All the way back to Baltimore, the six snakeheads flopped around noisily in a watery container in the compartment above Klopcic's head.

This wasn't the first time this summer that Klopcic and Trice had thought about the snakehead. They had followed the story from the beginning, and on July 11 had even run a radio spot on WRNR, Radio Annapolis, using Trice's voice and the snakehead's growing fame as way to increase patronage at the café.

News Flash . . .

Announcer's Voice: And now this just in . . . Another Chinese snakehead fish has been caught! This big mamma was found sitting

The Yin Yankee Café, in downtown Annapolis, Maryland. Courtesy Eric Jay Dolin.

outside Yin Yankee Café wearing a robe and smoking a cigar. Eyewitnesses say it apparently showed up in a taxicab with two very attractive women under each fin. Head Chef Jerry Trice managed to reel him inside . . . but not without a fight. What did Yin Yankee do with the rare and dangerous fish?

Jerry's Voice [with funny hillbilly accent]: We're going to serve him Indonesian style . . . Wrapped in banana leaves rubbed down with house-made curry, tomatoes and basil served with Ancho Banana Jam. He may be ugly and able to live three days out of water but he tastes great!

Announcer's Voice: According to the DNR we haven't seen the last of what's being called "Frankenfish." . . . They are multiplying. So do your part and serve your community by stopping in the Yin Yankee Café at 105 Main Street this week to help devour this treacherous, but delicious, Chinese snakehead fish.

That ad was just a ploy. The curious who stopped by wouldn't be able the "devour" a snakehead because the café had none to offer.

But now, a little more than a month later, after Klopcic's trip to New York, there were six squirming northern snakeheads in Yin Yankee's kitchen. Trice had never prepared a snakehead, nor did he know how they would taste, but that didn't faze him. A self-proclaimed gastronaut, Trice decided to serve them Indonesian style, as promised in the radio spot. And he cooked them whole, he said, to "get the full effect and have the most impact." To launch the new dish, Trice taped another radio spot on WRNR.

> By now you've heard the commercial about the infamous Chinese snakehead fish that Head Chef Jerry Trice managed to reel inside Yin Yankee Café. [Sound byte from old ad.] Obviously we we're joking . . . But the joke's over. Yin Yankee Café has brought down from New York City several Chinese snakehead fish to serve as a special entrée this week. There's no telling how long they'll last but if you're interested to see how good these exotic fish taste just stop by Yin Yankee Café tonight and see what all the fuss is about. We must point again that these Chinese snakehead fish have been brought down from New York City and not taken from a pond in Crofton. And Yin Yankee Café only has a few, so you better hurry. That's the Yin Yankee Café right on Main St. in downtown Annapolis.

On Thursday, August 22, the Yin Yankee held a special taste-testing event. Customers were greeted by a sign in the window that read, "Snakeheads: Chicks Dig 'Em." The six servings of the Chinese Walking Banana Fish sold out quickly, for $20 each. The fish were between ten and fifteen inches long, and about a pound each; just the right size according to Trice because the smaller snakeheads are known to have the sweetest meat. Although there was some hesitation and even trepidation on the part of the diners, they soon were eating their way through the dreaded fish with gusto. The verdict? Bony, but delicious. Definitely nothing like chicken. Trying to characterize the snakehead's taste and texture, Trice says, it's "kind of a cross between halibut and eel. The meat is very sweet, more delicate than you think. It has quite a few bones in it, but still very savory." Only five of the fish were cooked at the restaurant that evening. The sixth fish left, raw, in a bag, purchased by Carolyn Watson the assistant secretary at the DNR. According to the *Baltimore Sun*'s Kobell, Watson was in a hurry and couldn't wait for that night's dish to be prepared. Watson said she planned to cook the fish herself and bring it in to lunch the next day, to share with the DNR staff, who had labored so hard for so long dealing with the snakeheads in Crofton. When Kobell asked Watson what readers should make of the purchase, she replied, "It's consumed us, so we're going to consume it."

Buoyed by this success, the Yin Yankee ordered four dozen more snakeheads from their source, and Trice drove to New York to fetch them. All the way back down Interstate 95, the fish were banging around in the cooler and occasionally knocking off the styrofoam top. Taking heed of customer complaints about the snakeheads being too boney, Trice decided to fillet most of the fish. This is when the snakehead really earned Trice's respect. "Honestly," Trice said in an effort to emphasize the absolute veracity of what came next, "I filleted one side and the thing still quivered and jumped. It scared the hell out of me. It was like they did not want to die." Trice said he made a point of telling this story to others who worked with fish, for they would appreciate the strangeness of this behavior. And it wasn't only the snakehead's apparent will to live that got Trice's attention. In order to keep the fish from escaping long enough to make it to their rendezvous with the filleting knife, Trice had to keep a brick on the lid of the cooler. "We caught one trying to make his way downhill," Trice said. "We were joking he was making his way to the back alley; he was trying to get out."

The Berkshires' most popular T-shirt design. Courtesy Eric Jay Dolin.

It took diners, including a liberal sprinkling of media and specially invited guests, fewer than three days to eat their way through the four dozen snakeheads. Klopcic told Michael Sanson, a reporter for *Restaurant Hospitality*, "on a day we would normally be slow, we had people fighting to get into the restaurant and taste the fish." In addition to the Chinese Walking Banana Fish, patrons had their choice of snakeheads served as seviche, in soup, or as yakatori, a dish in which the snakehead came skewered, marinated, and grilled. Many people came not to eat, but just to see the fish, a couple of which were given a temporary reprieve as residents of a small aquarium at the front to the restaurant. Once the last fish was eaten, the Yin Yankee's adventures in snakehead cuisine ended. It was already getting harder to obtain live fish and, as Trice observed, people's interest in eating the snakeheads, as opposed to watching them in the aquarium, had "kind of peaked."

The interest in snakehead T-shirts showed no signs of abating. In the weeks after the herbicide application, William Berkshire's daughters lured people to their location on Route 3 with an electrified sign that read "Snakehead T-shirts for sale" and had a flashing red arrow pointing people in the right direction. In an article in the *Bowie Star*, on August 22, Sarah Schaffer found that the sisters' enterprise was doing well. One especially enthusiastic customer had purchased eighteen T-shirts. Between the roadside stand and the snakeheadstuff.com website, which was being inundated with e-mail orders, the sisters had already sold out of their first run of nearly four hundred T-shirts, and they had just placed another order for three times as many. From Mr. Berkshire's perspective, things were turning out quite well indeed, as evidenced by comments he made to Huslin that were printed in an August 24, *Washington Post* article titled, "The Big One Doesn't Always Get Away." The snakehead was, as Berkshire had earlier predicted, "a textbook case for a good promoter." As for his daughters' success, Berkshire commented, "I'm glad to see them making this business effort and experiencing the thrill and the responsibility of being in business. That's exactly what this country is all about. That's what they're contributing to, and I'm really happy about that."

Steve Koorey, flush with his success on the day of the herbicide application and with sales through local shops, one of which had sold more than one hundred T-shirts, headed back to the Maryland Apparel Graphics to place another order with Mike Smith. In particular, Koorey needed more large and extra-large sizes, which had been the best sellers. Soon after placing the order, Koorey remembers getting a call from Berkshire, who was not happy that Koorey was printing more shirts, especially because Berkshire thought they had reached an agreement that Koorey's first printing would be his last. Koorey told Berkshire, "I don't appreciate you trying to strong arm me. I don't need this. I don't want to spend three grand to try to make five grand and then worry about you suing me and I got to spend seven grand to defend myself over something like this. Why don't you just buy me out." Berkshire thought that might work and asked Koorey to draw up a proposal. After some negotiations, described as cordial by Koorey and Berkshire, the two signed an agreement that transferred ownership of Koorey's design to Berkshire, effectively ending Koorey's days as a T-shirt salesman. When Berkshire recalled the competition between him and Koorey, as well as others who tried to cash in on the snakehead's fame through the sale of T-shirts, he said simply, "There were three or four other people who viewed this an opportunity and attempted the get in the business. We negotiated them out and in one case merged with one person and picked up a design we liked."

Koorey harbors no hard feelings. He and his sons had a great time selling T-shirts while it lasted. One of Koorey's fondest memories is of a phone call he received the day after the herbicide application. Koorey listened as the caller was leaving a message in which he said he was from St. Petersburg, Florida, and that he wanted to buy a snakehead T-shirt. Koorey grabbed the receiver, introduced himself, and said, with a hint of puzzlement, "How the heck did you know this all happened?" The caller replied that he had been reading the *St. Petersburg Times* that morning when he ran across an article about the snakeheads and, in particular, Koorey's stand next to the Dunkin' Donuts. The article even had a picture of Koorey and his son Tyler, resplendent in T-shirts of Koorey's design. The Floridian said he would send off a check that day. When the envelope arrived, it contained the check and the article too, which was happily placed in the unofficial Koorey family archives.

When the DNR convened the Snakehead Scientific Advisory Panel in July, it laid out two discrete tasks. The first was to devise a plan to rid the Crofton pond of snakeheads. With the plan now nearing its final stage of implementation, the panel turned to its second task, determining what Maryland should do to address the broader threat posed by nonnative fish species. Like the first panel meeting, this one, which was held on August 20, was public and was attended by a range of media. Predictably, however, this meeting was less of a news event. Compared to taking action against an invasion in progress, the job of planning for future invasions that might or might not happen was less glamorous, a distinction that was evidenced by the coverage of the second panel meeting, which was much less extensive and much more local than the coverage accorded the panel's first meeting.

Nevertheless, the panel members took their charge very seriously, no doubt realizing that advising on the course of state policies on invasive species would have a much greater impact on addressing this problem than solely dealing with the snakeheads in Crofton. The panel found that state law provided precious little in the way of legal restrictions on the introduction of nonnative species, and the restrictions that did exist were of questionable value; for example, levying a fine of as much as $500 for a purposeful introduction after the introduction had already taken place. Given that the panel's expertise lay primarily in the realm of biology, the panel members felt that it was "inappropriate" for them "to suggest specific language for statutes or regulations." Instead, they surveyed what other states and agencies had done and offered general principles and guidelines that Maryland might want to consider should it decide to develop its own comprehensive policies for nonnative fish. Among the panels' findings were that the risks of introductions would be reduced if the state were to prohibit the importation, possession, sale, or cultivation of those nonnative fish species that posed the greatest threat of establishing themselves in Maryland waters and harming native fish and wildlife. If an across-the-board prohibition were deemed too restrictive, the panel suggested that a two-tiered system, like Florida's, might work better, in which there was a list of prohibited species as well as one of restricted species, the latter of which being ones that might require special handling guidelines or the issuance of a permit. If any legal prohibitions were adopted, the panel argued that penalties for their violation must be such that they would serve as a real deterrent, not the equivalent of a slap on the wrist. Furthermore, the statute of limitations must be of great enough duration to take into account that it is often many years before the presence of an invasive species becomes known.

The panel recognized that a list of prohibited species would not solve the problem because it is often impossible to know which species are likely to become invasive, and therefore which ones should be placed on the list. To guard against "surprises"—situations in which either nonnative or cultured native species would cause problems later—the panel recommended a number of steps, including encouraging aquarium stores to educate their customers on how to be responsible pet owners, that is, ones that don't release their fish into local waterways. The panel also tackled the issue of stemming the spread of invasive species once introduced. With the access problems in Crofton still fresh on their minds, the panel recommended that the DNR be given the authority to take steps to eradicate or control the spread of prohibited species wherever those species are found, private property not excluded.

On the day that the panel met, Candy Thomson wrote an article in the *Baltimore Sun* pointing out how the state laws dealing with invasive species failed to adequately address the problem. To high-

Steve Early talks to the troops, shortly after dawn on the day of the rotenone application. Courtesy Tom Darden.

light the state's relative powerlessness, Thomson offered a timely example involving snakeheads. She pointed to a recent ad in a local paper on the Eastern Shore of Maryland offering an "aquarium sized" snakehead for $5. If the man had any doubts about the marketability of a live snakehead in Maryland, they were quickly erased. He told Thomson that the phone started ringing soon after the ad hit the streets, and in the end about a hundred people called about the fish. If the panel's recommendations were put into effect, perhaps such a transaction would be illegal, but for now it was perfectly okay.

In July when the snakehead advisory panel recommended the use of rotenone, a few people had expressed concerns about the disaster at Lake Davis, in California, wondering if it could happen here. As the day of the poisoning approached, those concerns were raised again, and the DNR acted quickly to allay them. In an article for the *Washington Times*, published on August 22, Eric Schwaab told

Eric Schwaab (*left*) listens as Steve Early discusses the rotenone application. Courtesy Tom Darden.

reporter S. A. Miller that he had spoken with California's director of Fish and Wildlife about the situation and that he was confident that, other than targeting an invasive fish, there were "no parallels at all" between Maryland's poisoning plans and what transpired in California. The brand of rotenone to be applied in Crofton was different, Schwaab said, than that used in California and it didn't contain the persistent chemical components that had caused problems in Lake Davis. The DNR would be using roughly fifteen gallons of rotenone; in Lake Davis, state officials had applied 64,000 pounds of powdered rotenone and another 16,000 gallons of a rotenone-chemical mixture. The Crofton ponds are tiny with no direct connection to other bodies of water, whereas Lake Davis was a massive 4,000-acre reservoir that fed into a river, had tributaries leading into it, and was linked to local water supplies. The Maryland Geological Survey and the local health department had evaluated the situation

Rotenone streams out of the nozzle and into the Crofton pond, leaving a visible trail. Courtesy Tom Darden.

at the Crofton ponds and were convinced that the poison would not migrate beyond the ponds' boundaries. In reflecting on these and other differences, Schwaab said, "The situation they had was infinitely more complex than the situation we are dealing with."

On Tuesday, September 3, the DNR issued a media advisory alerting the press to the rotenone application that would commence the following day at 7 A.M. As was the case with the herbicides, members of the media were instructed to dress properly and stay in the restricted area that the DNR had cordoned off. The media was also informed of a change in parking opportunities. Although reporters and camera crews could be dropped off in the shopping center parking lot, they could not park there, and would have to find alternative locations. This being the middle of the week, the local shop owners did not want their customers' spots to be consumed by the event. The media advisory also contained a morsel of information that undoubtedly delighted media types in search of dramatic footage. "Once the application of rotenone is complete," the advisory said, "fish mortality is expected within a few hours." In other words, the dreaded snakeheads might soon be floating to the surface or, if reality lived up to the sensationalized hype, all sizes of Frankenfish might be running for their lives right out of the water to escape the deadly poison. To temper media expectations, the advisory added that "reaction of the fish to the poison may or may not be visible."

With a few exceptions, the day of the poisoning looked much the same as the day of the herbicide application. Numerous reporters and camera crews showed up early, coffee and doughnuts in hand, and assembled expectantly behind the yellow police tape. Even at this early hour, there was excitement in the air. The DNR and other assorted government officials, backed up by a wide array of vehicles and vats, prepared for the day's activities in the staging

Two of the adult snakeheads pulled from the pond after the poisoning.
Courtesy William D. Berkshire.

area between MacQuilliam's and Berkshire's ponds. On went the
protective clothing, which this time was a little more extensive than
that used during the herbicide application, and included yellow
Tyvek suits, respirators, and nitrile gloves. Into the water went the
johnboats, whereupon they commenced their slow navigation of the
pond's murky, still somewhat weedy waters, all the while injecting
rotenone beneath the surface and turning the waters milky-white.
Every twenty minutes the boats returned to shore to rotate crews
and refill the rotenone tanks.

Berkshire's hired camera crew, free to roam, remained the envy
of the regular press, who stayed in their "pen." Onlookers, a greater
number than had showed up for the herbicides, milled around the
parking lots to see what they could see. For those wanting a memento,
the Berkshire girls had their stand again on Route 3. This time,
though, they were the only show in town.

A handful of the dead northern snakeheads, finished off by the rotenone. Courtesy Tom Darden.

By lunchtime, all of the rotenone was off the boats and in the ponds. Then the deathwatch began in earnest. It wasn't long before the suffocating solution of rotenone proved its mettle. The ponds' formerly calm surfaces were intermittently interrupted by ripples and splashes as fish rose to the top in search of oxygen. Mike Slattery, on hand to help out, said he witnessed a couple of five-inch long snakeheads "actually stick their head out of the water and swim. One must have come fifty yards with its head out of the water, and it scurried over a lily pad, and climbed over a little log and thought it was getting away, I guess." When the fish started dying, the DNR began taking them out. According to an account of the day's activities by CNN, Heather Lynch grabbed a juvenile snakehead and cut it open to highlight the species' predatory nature. Upon finding two smaller fish in the snakehead's stomach, Lynch said, "That was breakfast." At the end of the day, the DNR reported

One of the northern snakeheads taken out of the pond after the use of rotenone. Courtesy Tom Darden.

the grim but satisfying statistics. Biologists had recovered more than 120 juvenile snakeheads and one seventeen-inch adult, along with roughly sixty pounds of other fish. Although it wasn't exactly the Hollywood ending that some had hoped for, with choking snakeheads scampering out of the water, gasping for air and ready to march to better digs, it would have to do. The media took notes and pictures and left to file their stories, which shared the same basic story line that the poison appeared to be working. DNR officials promised to come back daily to check on the pond and cart away dead and dying fish to a local landfill.

One fish, however, that wouldn't be making that final trip was the seventeen-inch adult they had found that day. It was immediately sent to taxidermist Don Kemp, who was still working on mounting Joe Gillespie's fish. Kemp had done taxidermy work for the DNR before, and in advance of the poisoning they had asked him if he could prepare fiberglass snakehead mounts. Sure, said Kemp, all he needed was a recently deceased specimen to use as a model. The fish surfaced at 10 A.M., Sunday morning, and it was delivered to Kemp three hours later, whereupon he took it to the local camera shop to have its picture taken. That way, when it came time to paint the fiberglass mounts and Gillespie's skin mount, the picture could be used as a guide for mixing and applying the colors. The DNR asked Kemp to make four fiberglass mounts, two for the DNR and two for the U.S. Fish and Wildlife Service. Kemp normally got paid hundreds of dollars for such mounts, but he didn't want any money from the DNR. "I'm giving these to the DNR," he said. "This is not the first time I have done this for the DNR. The way I look at it is that they don't get paid enough for what they do. Every little bit helps. Because if it weren't for the DNR we wouldn't have the deer we have now, we would not have the rockfish we have now. And I don't think they get enough money from the state."

When the DNR biologists returned the day after the poisoning, the casualty list had grown considerably. Roughly 780 pounds of fish, including more snakeheads, were gathered and sent to the landfill. Just as the very end was in sight for the snakeheads of Crofton, the DNR was jolted by another snakehead story right in their backyard. While dead snakeheads were being scooped out of the pond, James Scritchfield was looking for crabs in Baltimore Harbor. When he saw an odd-looking fish struggling near the shore, Scritchfield netted it. Scritchfield said that the twenty-two-inch long fish put up a fight, so much so that he reportedly had to club the fish to subdue it. The DNR subsequently identified the fish as a giant snakehead. Baltimore's mayor, Martin O'Malley, told Foster Klug of the Associated Press that the capture of the giant snakehead in the har-

The giant snakehead that James Scritchfield caught in a crab net in Baltimore's inner harbor on Friday September 9, 2002. Courtesy AP Photo/Steve Ruark.

bor was "troubling. I hope it's an isolated incident, and someone's idea of a bad joke. The bay's a sensitive enough ecosystem without someone dumping 'Frankenfish' in it." To quell local fears that another snakehead infestation was underway, the DNR made it clear that the giant snakeheads, unlike their northern cousins, had too tropical of a disposition to survive in Maryland. As to the source of the rogue fish, the DNR was sure it was an aquarium discard. Thomson quoted John Surrick as saying, "It was in distress, which leads us to believe it was dumped within the last twenty-four hours. Whoever did it almost certainly knew what they were doing." When Walter Courtenay was asked to comment, he replied, "There's no need to panic. This is not a good thing, people dumping these fish indiscriminately, but they can't live long in water with high salinity and it couldn't possibly survive a Baltimore winter." As for Mr. Scritchfield, he planned to have his unique catch stuffed.

In subsequent days the death toll at the Crofton ponds rose and so too did the DNR's confidence that its eradication efforts were successful. On September 6, two more adult snakeheads were found, each one twenty-two inches long. The next day, a twenty-seven-inch adult was recovered. Two days later, two more adults appeared, one twenty-seven inches and the other seventeen. And throughout this time, additional snakehead juveniles and a great range of other fish were added to the growing pile at the landfill. As expected, no snakeheads were ever collected from either of Berkshire's ponds, just the usual suspects. And despite earlier concerns, smell was not an issue. State officials did a great job of taking away the dead fish before they started to rot.

More than a few people scratched their heads over the appearance of two twenty-seven-inch adult northern snakeheads, just an inch larger than the snakehead Gillespie had caught earlier in the summer. If two snakeheads were dumped two years earlier, shouldn't there only be two of the largest size in the pond? For Courtenay, the explanation is clear. He believes that the man who confessed to dumping the snakeheads in the pond, had to have dumped "at least three." Whether or not the number was two, three, or more, it didn't really matter. The goal was to get rid of all the snakeheads regardless of their origin, and by the third week in September it appeared that the invasion was over. At that point, more than twelve hundred northern snakeheads had been recovered from the pond, six of which were adults. Added to their ranks were eleven hundred pounds of other fish, including American eels, crappies, bluegills, chain pickerels, largemouth bass, and yellow perch. On September 17, the DNR applied potassium permanganate to the ponds to neutralize whatever rotenone remained. On November

20, the DNR revisited the ponds just to make sure that no rogue snakeheads had survived the poisoning. A thorough electroshocking turned up not a single fish of any species. "This is pretty much it as far as we're concerned," observed Surrick.

Every good tale has a beginning, a middle, and an end, and now that the stars of the Crofton snakehead saga were literally history, the media's fascination and obsession with the story quickly waned. For a while after the poisoning there was a steady stream of press accounts covering the snakeheads' final days, but these paled in comparison to the torrent of publicity the story had garnered through much of the summer, and, in any event, stories about the Crofton snakeheads virtually dried up once the DNR went in to neutralize the ponds. Headlines appearing the day after the neutralization summed up the endgame: "Voracious Snakehead Fish Killed; Maryland Starts Rehabilitating Ponds" (Fox News Channel) and "Voracious Fish Wiped Out in Md" (ABCNews.com). Maryland, the nation, and the world was ready to move on.

> • June 27, 2002: Wanted: Killer Fish That Walks
> • June 28, 2002: Killer Fish Can Move on Land
> • July 2, 2002: Bounty On Head of Predatory Fish
> • July 9, 2002: "Frankenfish" has spawned
> • July 10, 2002: More Predatory Fish Found in Crofton
> • July 11, 2002: Alien Fish Identity Confirmed
> • July 11, 2002: Police Identify Killer Fish Culprit
> • July 12, 2002: Source of "Frankenfish" Discovered
> • July 12, 2002: 100 More Young Killer Fish Found
> • July 19, 2002: Thousands of Killer Fish Could Be in Crofton Pond

- July 20, 2002: Snakeheads Not Maryland's Only Problem
- July 23, 2002: Killer Fish Gets Federal Attention
- July 23, 2002: Interior Secretary Calls for Fish Ban
- July 24, 2002: Poison Planned for Alien Fish
- August 16, 2002: Alien Fish Get Execution Date
- August 18, 2002: End Is Near for Alien Fish
- August 19, 2002: Days Numbered for Snakehead Fish
- August 22, 2002: Alien Fish Could Be Banned in Virginia
- August 23, 2002: Cashing In on Frankenfish?
- September 3, 2002: Poisoning to Begin in Crofton Pond
- September 4, 2002: Vicious Fish's Days Numbered
- September 5, 2002: Frankenfish Meet Their Match
- September 7, 2002: It's Back! Snakehead Found in Baltimore
- September 17, 2002: State Collects Dead Snakehead Fish
- November 20, 2002: DNR: Snakehead Fish Gone from Crofton Pond

Headlines from snakehead stories aired on NBC Channel 4 (Washington, D.C.) trace the trajectory of the summer of the snakehead.

SEVEN

AFTERMATH

At the DNR the relief was almost palpable. The summer of the snake-head was finally over. The men and women of the Fisheries Service had been alternately surprised, puzzled, amazed, angered, frustrated, excited, tired, and amused by the snakehead story. Most of all, though, they were proud of their success and overjoyed to be able to get back to all of the other work they didn't have time for because they were focusing so much attention on the snakeheads. As Steve Early commented, "It turned out to be a real big operation. Much bigger than I ever imagined." In the final accounting, the cost of the operation came to two human-years' worth of labor and another $30,000 to pay for chemicals, supplies, and the expense of twice bringing Walter Courtenay and Paul Shafland up to Maryland from Florida.

Although it is unlikely that the folks at the DNR will ever have to deal with another invasive species that generates as much media interest as the northern snakehead, they want to be prepared if they do. As Jill Stevenson, the deputy director of the Fisheries Service, commented, "From an administrative viewpoint, we're running a state agency where the state government has a million-dollar budget deficit, and we have twenty vacancies, and when you spend time dealing with this stuff it's time taken away from dealing with other things. It's not funny anymore. We want to spend time looking toward the future and how to address nonnatives . . . because we can't afford to repeat the same process over again." The DNR's soul searching on this issue will no doubt go on for some time and involve asking hard questions about how best to interact with the media and the public on the fly, in situations where the DNR doesn't have all the answers but still wants to relay accurate and useful information that will not cause unnecessary alarm.

A couple of months after things had settled down, Eric Schwaab sat in his office running through the events of the summer for my benefit when he leaned back in his chair and smiled. "That was another thing I always laughed about," he said, "when people told me, 'You're famous.' I would say, Yeah, I had hoped that I would become famous for something more substantial than the snakehead fish, but maybe there's still hope." If Schwaab or anyone else at the DNR needs a quick visual reminder of the summer and the fish that became an intimate part of their professional lives, they needn't go far. In Schwaab's and in Early's office, up on the wall, hangs one of the northern snakehead replicas so painstakingly created by Kemp. It's just under seventeen inches long with attractive markings and a small head. Not very menacing at all. Gazing at it, one marvels that the mere presence of northern snakeheads in a Crofton pond, even ones not much larger than the replica, unleashed a media tsunami.

One of Don Kemp's fiberglass mounts of a northern snakeheads taken
out of the Crofton pond on the day that the rotenone was applied. This
mount hangs in Steve Early's office. Courtesy Maryland Department of
Natural Resources.

Every year, the DNR's Fisheries Service gives a Team of the Year
award. For 2002, it was no surprise that the winner was the Snakehead Eradication Team, consisting of staff from not only the
Fisheries Service, but also from other parts of the DNR including
the Natural Resources Police, Office of the Secretary, Office of
the Attorney General, and the Public Communications Office. The
person who nominated the Snakehead Eradication Team for the
award remains anonymous, but the work for which the award was
given was clearly spelled out in an accompanying citation.

It is difficult to fully express our gratitude for the excellent job that the
Snakehead Eradication Team performed this summer. Staff showed
exceptional dedication to task at hand, but also quickly brought them-

selves up to speed collecting information about this non-native species, and represented Fisheries Service well in dealing with the media and other members of the public.

In addition they hosted two meetings of the Snakehead Fish Scientific Advisory Committee. The meetings were held professionally and provided important and productive discussion for the Department.

Once an eradication plan was developed, the members volunteered to complete duties in off-hours, often in trying circumstances of high heat and humidity. Despite their frustrations with environmental conditions and a plan that was perfectly executed but did not always result in expected outcome, team members proceeded to solve problems and move on. Their passion was inspiring, exactly what we hope to see in teams involving Fisheries Service staff.

It is difficult to describe the amount of staff time and energy that was involved in addressing this problem but there is no doubt in my mind that the team made it possible for the Director and Deputy Director to focus on all the other aspects of running the Fisheries Service.

Not ones to assume more than is their due, the people at the DNR were also quick to point out that other groups outside the agency played significant roles in making the eradication process a success, including the Anne Arundel County Fire and Police Departments and the Sanitary Landfill, the U.S. Fish and Wildlife Service, the University of Maryland, the Maryland Department of the Environment, the Maryland Department of Agriculture, and the U.S. Environmental Protection Agency.

Crofton, having regained its mantle as a peaceful slice of the good life, returned to normalcy. And more than a few residents were happy to be rid of the snakeheads. After all, it's one thing to be known as a beautiful place to settle down and raise a family, and quite another to be famous for harboring snakeheads. Nevertheless, wanting to make some use of its notorious fame, the leaders of Crofton decided to have a little fun. Each year, at the annual Crofton Banquet and Awards dinner, there is a raffle. At the 2001 dinner the prize was a Crofton quilt, but in 2002 the quilt was replaced with, what else, snakehead T-shirts.

One Crofton resident who had mixed emotions about the snakeheads' departure was Joe Gillespie. More than perhaps anyone else, he lived the summer of the snakehead. The story followed him, and he rode it for months. "If it wasn't for that snakehead," Gillespie said, wistfully, "it would have been a pretty dull summer. It really speeded things up." If Gillespie ever wants to travel down memory lane, he has plenty of signposts. There's the pile of newspaper clippings destined for a scrapbook, and the two hours of local and national news clips he recorded on videotape. Just pop it in the VCR and there's Gillespie and the fish, over and over again, interspersed among a few of the hilarious snakehead spoofs that aired during the summer. And then there are the two fish, one alive and one dead. As of this writing, Frank Jr., now eleven inches long, was lazily swimming in the ten-gallon tank in Gillespie's kitchen, watching the Gillespies eat their meals with perhaps a hint of longing, and growing bigger all the time. Keeping Frank Jr. sated requires eight to ten one-and-a-half-inch goldfish daily. Eventually, Gillespie will have get a new tank or get rid of the fish in some other way. He could have it mounted so it could join his other snakehead trophy, the twenty-six-incher that Kemp prepared. Gillespie plans on hanging the twenty-six-incher on the walls of Drop In Skateboarding, a Crofton establishment owned by his friend, Jim Brackett. Gillespie had been wearing a Drop In T-shirt when he

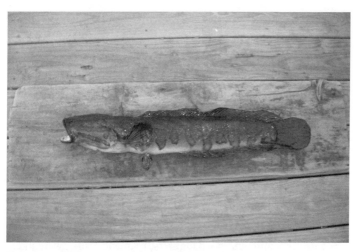

Don Kemp's skin mount of the twenty-six-inch northern snakehead Joe
Gillespie caught on June 30, 2002. Courtesy Joe Gillespie.

caught the baby snakeheads, and he thought it would be a good idea
to hang the mount in the store, rather than have it tucked away in his
house, so that locals and curious visitors could glimpse the fish that
placed Crofton on the world map.

Gillespie's memories of the summer are not all pleasant. Although
he was usually eager to share his story and thoughts with the media,
at times the intensity of the coverage annoyed him and his family.
Another sore point for Gillespie was a brief conversation he had in
early July when a photographer asked him if he had made money on
the photographs his daughter Caitlin had taken of the snakehead,
which had been reproduced in newspapers and magazines, and shown
on television the world over. When Gillespie said no, the photographer told him that if he had sold the rights to the pictures he could
have earned enough money to pay for his daughter's college education. That was, said Gillespie, the only time that he and his family felt

used. Overall, however, Gillespie will remember the summer of 2002 in a very positive light. "I guess this is my fifteen minutes of fame," he said, "but it lasted a lot longer than fifteen minutes for catching a fish. I hope I can tell my grandkids about it someday." Gillespie can already envision the scene. He'll be sitting in a room, surrounded by little ones, when someone will encourage one of them to ask Grandpa Joe about the snakehead fish. "Everybody else will leave the room," Gillsepie predicts with laugh, "and the poor kids will be stuck there for an hour while some old geezer tells them the story."

While Gillespie was daydreaming about how the story of the snakehead might reverberate through his life in the retelling, William Berkshire and his daughters, Erin and Chris, were planning to keep the snakehead story alive in a very different way—through sales. By late fall, the Berkshires had sold about five thousand T-shirts and earned roughly $12,000. Although interest in things snakehead has waned, the Berkshires have big plans for the future. In addition to snakehead T-shirts, sweatshirts, and caps, there might soon be other apparel in the snakehead line. Who knows, if the clothes take off, sporting equipment with snakehead logos could follow. When asked if he really thinks a snakehead putter might do well, Berkshire, ever the optimist when it comes to the powers of promotion, responded, "Yes, absolutely." And Berkshire is looking farther afield than that. He said he has been in contact with the company that makes "Big Mouth Billy Bass, the Singing Sensation," the wall-mounted, flexible rubber fish that belts out tunes such as "Don't Worry, Be Happy" when it detects motion or when its button is pressed. Berkshire hopes to interest the company in making a walking snakehead version of the product, one that would have boots on its pectoral fins. As for what the snakehead would say, one option is for the owner to record a personal message.

But a more intriguing option being considered by Berkshire is to have the snakehead deliver a rousing rendition of Nancy Sinatra's immortal hit, "These Boots Were Made for Walking."

If apparel, sporting equipment, and the walking snakehead wall plaque fail to perform, what about snakehead candy, snacks, or even a Maryland instant lottery ticket with a snakehead theme, all of which Berkshire has under consideration. There is one project, however, that in Berkshire's mind stands out from all the rest. "I think that the documentary is the biggest springboard to the future," Berkshire said. He is still hopeful that the Discovery Channel or another major outlet will team up with him to transform the video his hired camera crew made over the summer into a full-length show.

How the Berkshires' various enterprises fare over time depends on a number of factors. If Berkshire and his daughters are able to gain trademark protection for terms such as "Frankenfish," "northern snakehead," and "snakehead," marketing efforts could take off and someday the local grocery store might carry "Frankenfish nuggets." One wonders, though, what all those scientists who have been working on and talking about snakeheads and northern snakeheads would have to do if the terms they had been casually employing suddenly became private property. And if it turns out that a living creature's name, such as the snakeheads, can be trademarked, then the U.S. Patent and Trademark Office better prepare to be inundated with similarly based submissions. Imagine owning the rights to the word "panda" or "elephant"; you'd make a killing.

Another factor that will determine the fate of snakehead merchandise is the public's memory. Will the summer of the snakehead resonate with consumers to a degree that they will part with money for a snakehead-themed product? "I still believe," said Berkshire, "that a lot of people when you mention snakehead to this day will remember it instantaneously. Where it is going to go, I don't know." To help jog people's memories, Berkshire is mulling over the possibility of staging an annual Snakehead Ball in Crofton, most likely at his country club.

Unlike Berkshire, pond owner Danny MacQuilliam chose not to take advantage of the situation. He kept a low profile throughout the summer and focused his efforts on protecting his property and his tenants' businesses. "Because of all the liability issues," MacQuilliam said, "I could never get caught up in all of the hype. The property went from only being known to locals, to being broadcasted internationally. People were coming on the property all hours of the day and night. I learned that you're never really held blameless no matter what insurance or paperwork you have in place." The summer also further soured MacQuilliam's perspective on the media:

> I didn't have much respect for the media to start with and this ordeal just magnified my disrespect. They had no respect for someone's private property. The media constantly printed incorrect information without bothering to get the facts. Now it doesn't matter so much in something like this summer feel-good story. But if they can't get things right with this simple story, how can they get things right with more important stories. I learned to be more careful of what I say to those in the media and that the phrase 'off the record' only applies when they want it to. On the other hand, as I step back and look in, I realize that they have a job to do. Their job is to sell papers and stories. Whatever it takes to do their job, that's what they do.

Despite these frustrations, MacQuilliam does have some good memories of the summer of the snakehead. He especially enjoyed talking to people from the DNR, pond-side, early in the morning, before the press arrived. That's when he learned about the other fish in the pond and the animals in the woods beyond. It was like a private wildlife class. Early was particularly helpful in this regard and MacQuilliam credits him with making "the experience tolerable and interesting."

MacQuilliam could have done things differently. He could have made himself available for comment, or even sought out the press. He could have decided to cash in on the snakehead's fame, perhaps by making his own T-shirts. He could have ridden the media wave and, by virtue of being the owner of *the* pond, certainly gained a modicum of celebrity. But MacQuilliam chose not to play it that way. Reflecting on that decision he evinces only the slightest amount of regret. "I tell people that I hope this wasn't my fifteen minutes of fame because I didn't use it to my advantage. . . . I chose to stay out of the summer limelight."

Paul DiMauro didn't choose to stay out of the limelight, but circumstances and the flow of the story kept him there. His memories of the summer are mixed, but mostly negative. His initial excitement about catching the first snakehead quickly dimmed as his exploit, recorded only on film, receded into the shadows and then entirely disappeared in the glare of Gillespie's catches and subsequent twists and turns in the story. "I never heard of a fish getting more coverage," DiMauro said in the fall of 2002, "and I didn't get anything. I was like, damn."

Mike Slattery's memories of the Crofton snakehead saga are uniformly positive. "I found the summer fun and fascinating," he said. "Watching the sociobiological reaction to the issue was so interesting! . . . I could have fun with it because of the drought, the associated relative level of comfort that the potential invasion was apparently contained, and the knowledge that the solution was a straightforward one. . . . Otherwise I'd have been anxious as hell." Although, as evidenced by the aggressively worded e-mail he sent out in mid-June, Slattery would have rather had the DNR move more quickly and forcefully to confront the threat posed by the snakehead, the end result was just the same. And looking back Slattery admits that by waiting and taking a slower, more deliberate approach, the DNR was able to reap greater public relations benefits.

Slattery is still "amazed" by the phenomenal coverage of the snakehead story. "There is no other [invasive] species," he said, "that has generated as much excitement, period." Slattery heard from his colleagues in the U.S. Fish and Wildlife Service's Office of External Affairs that in the entire history of the Service there had never been an issue that had generated as much media exposure as the snakeheads. Slattery benefited from that exposure personally. "Fraternity brothers, family members, schoolmates and acquaintances from all over the country reconnected with me after seeing me on CNN, or reading a quote in their local papers. I loved it."

The reporters who worked most closely on the snakehead story will not soon forget it. As one of Candy Thomson's editors at the *Baltimore Sun* had predicted, the snakehead story did get them through the summer. And what a story it was. Thomson, who had been at the paper for fourteen years, put it in a class by itself. "I've covered presidential primaries," said Thomson, "I helped cover the *Challenger* explosion that took the life of Christa McAuliffe, [who was once] a local resident, but nothing I have ever covered has been like this. As far as a circus, this was a three-ring. It made my summer." Anita Huslin, of the *Washington Post*, was equally amazed. In terms of the number of press following the story, the only other events that she had witnessed that had generated as much coverage were, possibly, the announcement of the verdict at a big murder trial or the end of a congressional session where legislators are scrambling to reach a budget agreement. But she had never experienced anything, she said, "that attracted the breadth and interest from all over the world. It was really extraordinary." Huslin was glad to see the story end on a positive note, but it did create a slight problem. "Gee," she said jokingly, "what am I going to write about today? I don't have a snakehead story." For Scott Burke, at the *Capital*, the snakehead story was fun while it lasted. Whenever "something happened," Burke recalled, "we would blame it on the snakehead. It just became an inside joke." Looking back, he offered a summation that was short and to the point: "It was just a weird, weird summer."

In Florida, Courtenay and Shafland continued their work on various invasive species. By October, Courtenay and his colleague, Jim Williams, completed the major report on snakeheads for the U.S. Fish and Wildlife Service that they had been working on for more than a year. It is an impressive tome, covering all twenty-eight species of snakeheads in just over 160 pages. Virtually everything that is known about the taxonomy, characteristics, habitats, behaviors, uses, and the history of introductions for all the species is in this volume. It also includes a section that rates the species in terms of the risks they pose for colonization outside their normal range and the potential for economic and environmental impacts should introductions occur. Since completing that report, Courtenay has moved on to other studies of invasive species, including one that will explore the status of snakeheads in Hawaii, where one species has been present since before the turn of the nineteenth century.

Courtenay found the summer of 2002 exciting and frustrating. After working for decades on invasive species, it was gratifying to see so much attention focused on this issue. Ironically, that intense focus brought with it some displeasure as well. Courtenay felt that the press acted like sharks in a feeding frenzy and one of their favorite targets was himself. After all, if you want a good quote on what's happening in Crofton, it made sense to call "Dr. Snakehead." Dealing with the press "was not fun," Courtenay said, "because they ate a lot of my time when I should have been spending those many hours working on our final report to the U.S. Fish and Wildlife Service. The almost daily calls, some that lasted for an hour or more, from reporters was something I handled (and I hope well) because I feel that's a duty of a biologist, but it sure cut into my scientific productivity."

For Shafland, the summer of 2002 was not much different than other summers, the only exception being what he referred to as "the persistent interruptions afforded by the sensationalized media coverage" of the snakeheads. It might not have been so bad if the media's use of his comments had been different, but Shafland felt that all too often the media painted an inaccurate picture of his perspectives on invasive species in general and the situation in Crofton in particular. Just because Shafland believed that it was important not to overreact to the threat posed by invasive species that didn't mean he thought that such threats should be ignored, yet that is the way Shafland said he saw himself portrayed time and again. Now, with the Crofton snakeheads apparently vanquished, Shafland returned his full attention to the invasive fish species in his state, one of which was Florida's own snakehead, the bullseye. When Shafland first announced, in March 2001, that the bullseyes were breeding in Florida, he told the public that it was far too early to predict what might happen now that the fish were established. He also urged the public not to overreact, as had been the case when the walking catfish was introduced to the state more than three decades earlier. Now, nearly two years after breeding bullseyes were found in the state, their status hadn't changed, and in Shafland's eyes there is still no cause for alarm. Yet, given his experience with the

Crofton snakeheads, Shafland was not sanguine about potential future coverage of the bullseye snakeheads in his state:

> I'm guessing this snakehead story will remain on the back burner until we get hit by another media drought and a thunderstorm of ecological horror stories about invading aliens get concocted to quench the 'beast's' thirst. Then the Maryland scenario will repeat itself, and reporters will call and conclude, 'So, you don't think this is important?' To which, I will answer for the hundredth time: 'No, that is not what I think. What I think is that the illegal release and presence of numerous introduced fishes is important and needs to be dealt with, and *that* is why I have dedicated more than twenty-eight years of my life to their study. However, I also think grotesque exaggerating and sensationalizing of yet-to-be documented impacts leads to a diminution of effort to manage our natural resources responsibly. And I think such exaggerations and diminution could be counterproductive in the long term, like the boy who ended up losing his entire flock because he repeatedly cried wolf.' Of course, the reporter has long hung up by this point!

Still, Shafland is glad that for the time being snakeheads are no longer in the news. "All in all," he said, "the 'aftermath' is quieter, which is the way a country boy like me likes it."

As the snakeheads in Crofton were taking their last breath, the U.S. Fish and Wildlife Service was deciding what to do about all of their relatives. The deadline for comments on the proposed ban on snakeheads was August 26, and by that date, 453 people and organizations had responded. But that number was deceiving. Fully 386 of the comments had nothing to do with the snakeheads at all. The most interesting thing about that number is that it really is not surprising. In days not too long past, when people who wanted to comment on proposed regulations had to write something and mail it in, most of the comments submitted were, as they should be, relevant to the issue at hand. When one's own time and money are involved, wasted effort is something to avoid. With the advent of e-mail and the opportunity to submit comments electronically, however, the floodgates to spam mail were opened wide, and the irrelevant, annoying, and, at times, amusing junk has been flowing in ever since. It's not that spammers actually read the *Federal Register* to glean new e-mail addresses for their nefarious use; rather, there appear to be any number of computer programs that troll the depths of the Internet universe, scavenging any and all e-mail addresses they come across and, in that way, greatly increasing the scope of the spammers' reach. Since the *Federal Register* is on-line, all the e-mail addresses it contains are fair, or in this context, dishonorable game. Not all federal agencies or offices allow for e-mail submissions of comments, but for the proposed snakehead ban e-mail was an option, and judging by the numbers it was the option of choice.

The U.S. Fish and Wildlife Service received plenty of the infamous Nigerian e-mails from supposed residents of that country intent on sharing their riches with the addressees. In one variant, with the subject line marked "Personal and Confidential," the folks at the Service were offered an enticing opportunity, much more exciting than the traditional, thoughtful but often dull comments one gets in response to serious proposed regulations. In this e-mail, a man claiming to be the "former minister of petroleum to the late head of state" of Nigeria took altruism to a whole new level. By virtue of his formerly exalted position he came into—legally of course—the impressive sum of $28 million, all of which has been conveniently tucked away in an offshore bank account. Better yet, he wanted to share some of it with his newfound e-mail confidant. If you would only become his "honest, reputable and capable partner," the man implored, then you could share in the riches. Heck, he was even willing to let you invest his money and keep 30 percent of the entire amount, principal and earnings. All one needed to do to grasp the golden ring was contact the man's attorney and provide some particulars about yourself, after which point the money would be transferred to your account.

Other senders of spam mail were less giving than the man from Nigeria. There were solicitations from magazine vendors, including a couple from *Playboy*, a publication not normally seen in the offices of government bureaucrats and one that has, so far as is known, nothing to do with invasive species. Then there was the e-mail from a man from Bucharest in search of an engineering job. He was a perky fellow, writing "HELLO!" in the subject line and was apparently well versed in spam etiquette, if such an oxymoronic term has any meaning. At the end of his note he wrote that under U.S. law any e-mail "Cannot be considered spam as long as the sender includes contact information and a method of removal," both of which he did. Despite his perkiness, credentials, and desire to distance himself from spammers, the man from Bucharest turned up no job leads at the U.S. Fish and Wildlife Service.

It is almost appropriate that the proposed regulations elicited a large number of spam mailings, for in a figurative and arguably literal sense spam mail is the number-one invasive species on the Internet. It is nonnative, at least with respect to the recipients, little corner of the Internet ecosystem; it is unwanted; it often reproduces and spreads with amazing rapidity; it can cause considerable damage (wasting your time and, in some cases, wasting your computer); and it is hard to get rid off. Nevertheless, the potential symmetry between the spam they received and the actual task at hand, while possibly a curiosity, was of no real interest to the U.S. Fish and Wildlife Service. The purpose of notice-and-comment rule making is to hear from the affected public and thoughtfully respond to their concerns about the proposed action. And it was to that task that the staffers at the U.S. Fish and Wildlife Service now turned.

Of the sixty-seven comments considered relevant and significant, thirty-two were opposed to and thirty-four were in favor of adding snakeheads to the list of injurious wildlife, thereby banning them from import or interstate transport. On the con side of the ledger, the comments generally decried the vilification of snakeheads and spanned from those who would rather eat than ban snakeheads to people arguing that the ban would unfairly hurt fish hobbyists. A research associate at the Florida Institute of Technology wrote, "My point is very simple, introduce it [snakeheads] as a good food . . . to everyone in USA. Do not treat as a monster. Actually it is not. If consumers are up, the resources will be down or under control soon." Another person urged the government to avoid a blanket ban and instead ban snakeheads only from those states where they could possibly breed in the wild. "Do not turn this into a witch-hunt," he wrote, "study the fish, educate the public, do not cave into the ill spawned media frenzy! Most types of snakeheads would die in water as warm as 55F." A man from Dallas, Texas, wanted to set the record straight. "Many of the facts [that have been presented] were wrong and misleading or at best based on 'potential harm' that these fish can do to U.S. ecosystems. Enough already, politics has no place in the real works of protecting our environment."

Fish hobbyists were dismayed that they, who would never release a snakehead into the wild, were being punished because of the careless action of one individual who did. Why, they wondered, should responsible fish owners potentially be cut off from one of their favorite fishes? The owner/operator of the website, predatoryfish.net, an on-line community of people who love predatory fish, like snakeheads, urged the U.S. Fish and Wildlife Service to reconsider its proposed action, and "instead of making a terrible decision, that will anger many many people," just ban those species that survive in the colder parts of the country. He added that he encouraged the nearly two thousand members of predatoryfish.net to "voice their displeasure to you." And in a sentence that must have given the folks at the U.S. Fish and Wildlife Service pause, this person ended his e-mail stating, "If this ban goes through, I will devote my every effort into asking hobbyists that currently legally own *Channa*, to propagate the species in their home aquariums so that this incredibly interesting family is not lost forever to the hobby."

A pet store employee felt "obliged to speak up for the snakehead family," many of which, he said, are "beautiful fish." Among the alternatives this person offered to the ban were setting very large fines for dumping nonnative species and requiring people to get permits to own snakeheads. Then he turned the issue around. "The snakeheads are just doing what they need to survive. Before man arrived, there were thousands of buffalo all over the United States, from Pa. to California. Now, there are a few packs roaming the Midwest, but that's about all. *We* were responsible for their demise, but was anyone banning the import of humans (it sounds silly, but it helps prove my point)." The problem is not with the snakehead, the pet store employee argued, but with the "uninformed consumer." That's the way two other respondents saw it as well. "Why take down the hobbyists because of stupid people?" they argued, for there is much that is good about snakeheads. "They all are not as bad as the large species caught in Maryland. . . . All are not that way [voracious]. Some have cool personalities! They come to you when you are at the tank and some will eat right out of your hand. They are smart and learn who you are very quickly! . . . Adding the 'entire family of snakeheads' to the list would be like saying that a German shepherd is bad so let's ban all dogs." Another respondent ended her plea against the banning of snakeheads by invoking the almighty on their behalf—"God bless them!"

Some of the opposing voices cast the issue in racial terms. One person, who described himself "as an Asian who grew up in Asia," wrote an e-mail that had as its subject line, "snakehead fish ban—disdain for the Asian community—racism." The e-mail stated that instead of the ban, the U.S. government should consider another less absolute form of regulation on the importation and transportation of snakeheads. "By refusing any compromise about the snakehead fish," he continued, "some European Americans—including some in the U.S. government—have shown insensibility and intolerance to their Asian compatriots. Let us remind them that the U.S. is a tolerant country. Let them know that the U.S. government has a commitment to achieve equality of all races. Asian Americans also have the right to live their lives and to choose the foods they eat." He urged the U.S. government to consult more with the Asian community before taking any action, and added that if the measures in the ban were being enacted simply to protect "the sport activity [fishing] of European Americans," while depriving millions of Asian Americans of an important source of food, they "must be rejected by all of us. Since accepting them would be the equivalent to accept[ing] the racist point of view: White is more important than Non-White. . . . The U.S. is not a country where the rights of the minority could be sacrificed for the sake of the leisure of the majority."

The most extensively argued opposition to the ban came from Christian Kanele, a German representative of www.snakeheads.org, identified by him as "the world's largest website on snakeheads non-commercially." There is no reason to doubt this claim. The website offers a wealth of information about snakeheads, including images, recipes, taxonomic data, and fascinating firsthand accounts of encounters with snakeheads in the wild and in aquariums. The e-mail attachment he submitted to the U.S. Fish and Wildlife Service ran to four pages and was wide ranging. Like other commentors, Kanele distinguished between species. While he had no problem prohibiting five species, including the northern and the giant, which he believed could cause many of the problems identified in the proposed rule, assuming they could survive the "thermal environment," he argued that the other twenty-three species should not be tarred with the same brush and should therefore be excluded from the ban. Kanele felt that all the species of snakeheads were being unfairly lumped together. "You mention (mostly *C. argus*) a species, which has certain characteristics, and then you infer it to all other species implicitly . . . [whether] it makes sense or not. How else could you find supporting arguments to prohibit . . . *Channidae* in total? We disapprove this disproportional approach." He noted that most snakehead species do not pose a significant threat to other aquatic organisms. As for the northern's supposed tendancy to wander, Kanele said forget it —"one will not find a *C. argus* in Crofton walking on land!"

Those in favor of the proposed rule were equally vocal and, at times, dramatic. For example, one woman wrote, "Please do everything you can to keep these awful things out of our country." Another respondent urged the U.S. Fish and Wildlife Service to "act promptly and surely to protect us." Yet another chose to emphasize his position through capitalization—"WIPE OUT THE SNAKEHEAD FISH. THE ARGUMENT FOR ERADICATION IS SOUND." And two respondents thought that exclamation points might do the trick. One said, "Yes, go forward with this ban!!!!!!!!!!!!!" while the other weighed in with, "Down with the Snakeheads!!!!"

A "concerned citizen" wanted food and pet sales of snakeheads halted, and all other "precautionary" actions taken. As for the cause of the snakehead scare, the citizen thought that it might be much more sinister than what we had been led to believe. "Could the presence of Snakeheads in the U.S. waters be intentional," he mused, "and the result of a terrorist attack? . . . Wouldn't these fish be an easy way for terrorists to create a tremendous amount of damage? Could al Qaeda be out there at this very moment going from lake to river to lake around the country 'planting' these fish?" A respondent from Cross River, New York, whose comments were addressed to President George W. Bush, also had terrorism on his mind. "I would immediately ban the importation of this fish in any shape or form into the U.S. . . . But I would keep it quiet. I would not let the press in on it because they would play it up and perhaps give some sicko the idea to release some more as ecoterrorism. Why not?"

Twenty-nine state senators and representatives from Wisconsin signed a letter in support of the ban, in large part because they were concerned about protecting the state's $2.1 billion sport fishing industry from an invasion of snakeheads. The Pet Industry Joint Advisory Council, which is the largest trade association in the U.S. representing the pet industry as a whole, also supported the proposed rule. Aimee Delach, with the environmental group Defenders of Wildlife, encouraged the U.S. Fish and Wildlife Service to combine the ban with an outreach program aimed at teaching wildlife inspectors how to identify snakeheads and also educating those who might try to sell or buy live snakeheads about the need for the ban and alternatives to live specimens, for example, frozen fish. Representatives from a range of state wildlife agencies, including the Division of Wildlife at Ohio Department of Natural Resources, the Kentucky Department of Fish and Wildlife Resources, the Tennessee Wildlife Resources Agency, and the Illinois Department of Natural Resources all urged that the ban be implemented.

Shafland's employer, the Florida Fish and Wildlife Conservation Commission, came out in favor of the rule, but in its comments noted that some of the information included in the proposed rule was "of dubious authenticity (e.g., reports of human deaths, propensity for overland migrations)." These comments were from Scott B. Hardin, the chief of the Bureau of Fisheries, and they represented the commission's overall view, which incorporated a range of perspectives. Shafland contributed to and fully supported the comments, which he said were "clear and to the point." However, Shafland also sent an earlier e-mail to the U.S. Fish and Wildlife Service, which, while not part of his commission's formal response, did elaborate Shafland's perspective on the issues being considered, and in so doing, reflected his continued concern about the accuracy of some of the claims being made about snakeheads. On the issue of giant snakeheads attacking humans, Shafland noted that the authors of the cited paper offer "no personal testament nor any other verifiable evidence to support this statement. Furthermore, I have not seen any mention of snakeheads killing people elsewhere in the literature; something that would surely exist if this were indeed true." As for locomotion, Shafland said that snakeheads "can move through shallow swamp conditions, and even through semi-fluid mud that would otherwise immobilize most fishes; and, they can flop, wriggle, and squirm for short distances when placed on land, but these actions hardly qualify as 'overland migrations.' In Florida, we have never seen nor heard of a snakehead on land that was not physically placed there by a human."

The U.S. Fish and Wildlife Service issued its final rule on October 4, which officially added all snakeheads to the list of injurious species. As required, the service responded to the comments it received. On the possibility of selective banning, the answer was no. "Based on the aggressive, predatory nature of all species of snakehead fishes," the final rule read, "the fact that one or more species could become established in most waters of the United States, and the fact that it is very difficult to differentiate among the species of snakeheads, the U.S. Fish and Wildlife Service has determined that all twenty-eight of the currently recognized species of snakehead fishes in the *Channidae* family should be listed as injurious fishes under the Lacey Act." Although the agency had no interest in punishing hobbyists, it felt that the ban was necessary and noted that people who owned snakeheads prior to the ban taking effect could keep them as long as state law didn't forbid it and they didn't transport the fish across state lines. The U.S. Fish and Wildlife Service also credited responsible fish hobbyists as being the reason why over all these years of importing snakeheads into the country there had been only a precious few introductions into the wild. In an effort to help hobbyists maintain this good record, the U.S. Fish and Wildlife Service said it was considering joining forces with the Pet Industry Joint Advisory Council to launch an educational campaign aimed at teaching hobbyists and people in the aquarium trade more about invasive species and encouraging them to prevent unwanted fish from entering the environment.

To those who wanted to eat live snakeheads rather than ban them, the U.S. Fish and Wildlife Service said that although it recognized the culinary value of the fish, the ban was based on scientific data and environmental concerns, and, of course, consumers still had the option of purchasing frozen snakeheads as an alternative. As for the claims that the ban had racist motivations, the U.S. Fish and Wildlife Service said that was simply not true. The decision to list the species was "based solely on the biological characteristics of the fishes and the need to protect our native wildlife and wildlife resources." To those respondents who felt that the rule was more a knee-jerk reaction to media hype than a well-thought-out plan, the U.S. Fish and Wildlife Service noted that the evaluation of the family *Channidae* had begun well in advance of the recent media attention. Then, in an effort to distance itself from what had been reported in the press, the text continued, "Outside of what is published in our official press releases, the Service has no control over what is published in the media. We agree that some of the facts have been exaggerated."

Customarily, regulations go into effect thirty days after being published in the *Federal Register*, but in this case the U.S. Fish and Wildlife Service argued successfully that it had "good cause" under the Administrative Procedures Act to implement the regulations immediately upon publication. The U.S. Fish and Wildlife Service wanted to act fast to cut off the growing tide of snakeheads that were streaming into the country. Even before the secretary of the Interior announced the proposed ban, the law of supply and demand or, more accurately, potential supply and demand kicked in. Given the overwhelmingly negative press coverage that snakeheads were receiving, the importers of the fish and the consumers who fueled their trade could see the proverbial handwriting on the wall, and they decided to get while the getting was good. According to U.S. Fish and Wildlife Service estimates, 2.94 times as many snakeheads were imported into the country in July 2002 than had been the case in July 2001. And it didn't end there. In the following months, inspectors from ports around the country noted an increased interest in importing snakeheads before the regulatory ax fell. A few importers were quite forthright about their intentions, telling inspectors that they were trying to "beat the ban." If it didn't impose the ban immediately, the U.S. Fish and Wildlife Service feared there would be a last-minute rush of imports of snakeheads into the country as well as transports of fish

This cartoon by Tom Toles appeared in the *Washington Post* on October 6, 2002. Courtesy TOLES © 2002 Buffalo News. Reprinted with permission of UNIVERSAL PRESS SYNDICATE. All rights reserved.

across state lines. And that "could result in a significant potential for damage to the wildlife and wildlife resources of the United States." Case closed. Snakeheads were officially *pisces non grata*.

The implementation of the ban created a predictable blip in media coverage and then the news about snakeheads quickly faded again. In the months that followed, however, there were occasional stories that brought the snakeheads back out of media retirement. On November 28, Huslin penned a story for the *Washington Post* titled, "There's a Livelihood in That Dead Fish Yet." She noted that the Berkshire clan was still hard at work, squeezing dollars from the dear departed snakeheads. William Berkshire mentioned his hope for an annual snakehead ball and told Huslin that the summer of the snakeheads "will be in the hearts and minds of everybody for quite a long time. We're going to try to see to that."

On December 10, an article appeared in the *Daily Times*, a Pakistani newspaper, which amazingly enough linked the snakehead to Saddam Hussein. In his "Postcard USA" column, titled, "From Snakehead to Saddam," Khalid Hasan wrote, "Now that the most misunderstood fish in the world [the snakehead] . . . has been eliminated . . . it is only a matter of time before the glory boys in dirty green and brown go after that other monster in the American nightmare factory," Hussein. After harshly criticizing the Bush administration's policies toward Iraq and, in particular, Mr. Hussein, Hasan explained that the "one thing in common between the snakehead and Saddam Hussein" is that "both have been demonized in the U.S. media." What followed was a lengthy excerpt from an article by Stephen Braun that appeared in the *Los Angeles Times* on November 29 and that recounted the saga of the Crofton snakeheads and told of their demise and the federal action to ban the entire family of fish. Apparently satisfied that Braun's account proved his point, Hasan ended his article with a suggestion—"For snakehead read Saddam."

Given how much media attention the snakehead had received, it would be a shock if it didn't make year-end lists of one sort or another. And, of course, it did. In the *Capital*'s list of the top ten local stories of 2002, the snakehead came in at number seven. "Never has a creature," the paper said, "with the possible exception of Moby Dick or Jaws—aroused such excitement as did the northern snakehead." In *Baltimore Magazine*'s annual year in review article, Geoff Brown wrote that "the northern snakehead fish, a creepy-looking, slimy beast from the Far East, was welcome comic relief" in a year that boasted "lethal tornadoes . . . drought, banking scandals, the Catholic church's revelations," among other things. "That's why we love the Frankenfish," Brown continued. "These resilient, carnivorous fish were a bogeyman we could handle (and, eventually, even slay). Conquering the killer fish was one of the *good* things" that happened in 2002. *Parade* included the snakehead in an article in its December 29 issue, titled "The Best & Worst of Everything." Next to a picture of a man holding a snakehead, *Parade* wrote, "Victory Declared. State Biologists in Maryland announced that the northern snakehead—the most notorious of all invasive fish—had been eradicated." Interestingly enough the picture was not of a northern snakehead, which was after all the species that Maryland had vanquished. The man in the picture was James Scritchfield, and the fish he was holding in his hands was the giant snakehead he had pulled from Baltimore Harbor in September. In its year-end issue, *Fortune* magazine ran a series of articles reflecting on "What Went Right in 2002." In one, David Grainger praised the snakehead for creating a great summer distraction. "Were you not torn away from thoughts of impending war, corporate malfeasance, and J. Lo? . . .That's what makes a damned good distraction. Kill it, if you must, We wish it well."

On New Year's Day, Hank Stuever of the *Washington Post* offered up "The List" of things that were "in" and "out" for the 2003. There in the "out" column was the northern snakehead, accompanied by one of the most popular and least flattering snakehead images used by the media during the past summer. On the positive side, the northern snakehead was in good company. Others on the outs included firefighters, Harleys, and Donald Rumsfeld. But, in a turn that no doubt cast shame on the entire snakehead family, Stuever claimed that the northern snakehead had been dethroned by the lowly shad, a fish with not half the character of a northern snakehead. Ignominious defeat!

Although the northern snakehead was apparently out, it was not forgotten. A week later the *Washington Post* ran an article on the front page of the Food section, titled "Burma in a Bowl." After stating that Maryland officials responded to the appearance of snakeheads by poisoning the pond, the header for the article said that good cooks in Burma would have dealt with the snakehead in a different fashion, by making soup. "Sweet-tasting snakehead," continued the header, "as well as other types of mild, white-fleshed fish, is the key ingredient in mohinger (pronounced MOW-heen-ga), Burma's national dish."

The culinary connection took a turn for the stranger about a month later, when an Associated Press article on the virtues of snakehead ice cream appeared. The article focused on the Kasara Bakery, in Thailand, which seven years ago began its foray into fish-based desserts, with sweet snakehead fish cakes in the shape of a fish. The bakery's owner, Kasara Thepprasit, knew that if the cakes tasted too fishy, they wouldn't sell, so she blended in a proprietary mixture of herbs to eliminate the fishiness in the fish. The snakehead cakes were a big hit, so the bakery branched out with other products including snakehead fish cookies and pastries filled with fried snakehead bones. From there it was only a short evolutionary leap to snakehead ice cream. And we're not talking just a splash of snakehead. The Kasara Bakery's ice cream is 40 percent fish meat! The ice cream, like the cakes, is not the least bit fishy. "The bits of fish," the article said, "could easily be mistaken for coconut flakes." Kasara was proud of her snakehead confections, and she said she even turned down an offer from an Australian company to purchase her fish cake recipe for the equivalent of nearly $700,000. Praise for

Kasara's Bakery extends all the way to Thailand's royal family. "Every time the royal family comes here," Kasara told the reporter, "we give them snakehead fish cake, and they always stop to talk to me. They tell me that it's good to see Thais being so inventive and creating such strange foods with just local ingredients."

On January 22, Gale Norton, the secretary of the Interior, addressed the National Fisheries Leadership Conference. She told the audience that one of the jobs of the U.S. Fish and Wildlife Service was dealing with invasive species, and then she offered remarks that proved the sturdiness of the snakeheads' ambulatory and omnivorous reputation. "I came across one of the ugliest examples [of invasive species] this summer," Norton said, "when I met the snakehead fish. Here in the Washington, D.C., area, the State of Maryland was fighting the proliferation of this foreigner. . . . This singular snakehead could move on land from one body of water to another. It only served to make it more dangerous as an invasive species." Norton then added, "Steven Williams [the director of the U.S. Fish and Wildlife Service] describes it as—this fish that eats all the other fish in a pond and then crawls out and over to the next pond, where it also eats all the fish. He says, 'Maybe it does belong in Washington after all.'"

During the fall of 2002 the snakehead did develop a very interesting, albeit indirect connection to Washington, courtesy of Congressman Steny Hoyer, whose district includes a big chunk of Crofton. One of Hoyer's reelection campaign ads used the snakehead story as a way to highlight his commitment to a couple of hot-button issues. The ad, which is reproduced below, was created by MacWilliams, Robinson and Partners, an advertising and strategic communications firm that has produced media for Hoyer since 1994.

Male Announcer: They're big. [*Jaws* theme sound effect]
Female Announcer: They're mean. [*Jaws* theme sound effect]

Male Announcer: They swim in the water . . . [*Jaws* theme sound effect]

Female Announcer: . . . And walk on land.

Male Announcer: The snakehead fish. A clear danger to Maryland and our way of life. [*Jaws* theme sound effect]

Female Announcer: That we [*Jaws* sound effects cut out; chopping sound] exterminated.

Male Announcer: But just when you thought it was safe—[*Jaws* theme sound effect back in]

Female Announcer: . . . There are worse things than snakeheads lurking.

Male Announcer: The cost of prescription drugs is eating up pocket-books faster than piranhas. [*Jaws* theme sound effect]

Female Announcer: And some sharks on Wall Street want to take your Social Security money and gamble it on the stock market.

Male Announcer: Piranhas and sharks, they're harder to get rid of than snakeheads [*Jaws* theme out], but our congressman, Steny Hoyer, knows how to do it.

Female Announcer: Steny Hoyer is fighting to keep the cost of prescription drugs down.

Male Announcer: And Steny Hoyer will keep up the fight to prevent cuts in the Social Security benefits you earned.

Female Announcer: Steny Hoyer . . . a congressman on our side.

Steny Hoyer: Paid for by the Hoyer for Congress Committee.

As the snakehead story faded, the pond that had given birth to it regained its relative anonymity, if not in memory, then in fact. Gone were the crowds of people eager to connect the story with the place and perhaps catch a glimpse of one of the famed fish, alive or dead. Gone, too, were the anglers, for the poison had stripped the waters clean. The DNR would restock the ponds in spring 2003 and the fish would return, but not before. A visit to the pond on a cool, clear day in late October was a lonely experience. The orange plastic barricade remained at edge of the parking lot leading down to the water, although its work was through. A remnant of yellow police tape laid on the ground, close to where it had done its best to keep the milling media minions away from the action and safe from harm. A few pesticide application markers were strewn about, and a no-fishing sign stood guard a few feet out into the water. Most of the leaves had fallen and the air was still. Virtually all of the waterborne plants were gone, and the pond's glassy surface reflected the overcast sky and the denuded trees all around. At the corner of the pond nearest the Little Patuxent River, the row of sandbags, which appeared to be well on its way to becoming a permanent feature of the landscape, still created a line of defense between the pond and the river, but more than a few errant bags were slouching in this direction and that, faintly foreshadowing a less than upstanding future. The pond was much higher than it had been during the drought-stricken summer and the water rested against the lowest tiers of the sandbag wall. There was a shallow pool on the other side of the wall and few swampy areas between it and the river, which was just tens of yards away. This relatively narrow band between the pond and the river, once fretfully viewed as a potential getaway route for the notorious and, purportedly, ambulatory snakeheads, on this day looked merely like a common and unexciting, albeit quite wet, slice of Maryland woods.

Standing at the edge of the pond, it was hard to believe that it was, just months earlier, the focus of international attention. Surprisingly, for a pond that was so famous, it had no formal name. There was no handle, no shorthand, no nickname to apply. There was nothing to call it other than the pond, the unnamed pond, snakehead pond, the pond where the snakehead was caught, or sometimes, in the local press, MacQuilliam's pond, after its owner. Such anonymity is not surprising. Before the summer of 2002 there was no need to identify the pond. You either knew of its existence, or you didn't, and if you did you

This picture shows the area around and behind the sandbags during the fall of 2002 and was taken following a prolonged rainy period when the level of the pond was much higher than it had been during the previous summer and, quite likely, the previous couple of years, a time when the area was going through a prolonged drought. The picture offers evidence of why state and federal officials were concerned about the proximity of the pond and the Little Patuxent River. Had there been a major rain event prior to the time that the pond was poisoned, it is certainly possible that a water connection between the pond and the Little Patuxent River could have been created. If that had happened, one or more northern snakeheads could have made it to the river. Courtesy Eric Jay Dolin.

simply went there to fish. It was enough to say, let's go to the pond off Route 3, behind the mall. Soon, this might no longer be the case.

In 2001, Peter Bergstrom, then with the U.S. Fish and Wildlife Service's Chesapeake Bay Field Office, launched the stream-naming project, with the goal of formally identifying larger creeks draining to the tidal rivers in Anne Arundel County, Maryland. The rationale was simple. People tend to care more about things with names. It was hoped that by naming local creeks, and publicizing those names, stewardship of these important but too often ignored resources would increase. Soon after the project began, its purview expanded to include a few local ponds. When the unnamed pond off Route 3 catapulted to fame, Bergstrom decided that it was an excellent candidate for being named. So he called Danny MacQuilliam to see if he had any suggestions. As it turned out, MacQuilliam's oldest son, Wes (sixteen), also thought the pond should have a name and well before Bergstrom's call he told his dad what it should be— Walking Fish Pond. MacQuilliam liked the name and he passed it along to Bergstrom, who in turn submitted it to the U.S. Board on Geographic Names for adoption. If the name of the pond becomes official, it will provide a final irony to the story. Forevermore, the pond that became famous for harboring northern snakeheads will bare a name that reflects a characteristic that the fish never had.

The most important impact of the summer of the snakehead is how it raised the public's interest in the issue of invasive species. In among all the hype and exaggeration that attended the story, there was a large dose of good information and real stories about how invasive species have reworked our landscape and changed our lives, often for the worse. The snakehead story, in a sense, forced a public discussion, if not a public debate on the impact of invasive species and what we should be doing to address them. For many of the biologists who were deeply involved in the snakehead situation and who also care deeply about the issue of invasive species, it is this unintended by product of the summer that they found most gratifying. Although Courtenay felt that "in many cases some of the reporters overblew the story," leading to "too much hype," he also saw the coverage as a valuable means to an end. "A lot of people that had no idea about the dangers of invasive species have now learned something. The press did a great service in that aspect of raising public awareness about invasive species."

Similarly, Dr. Paul Loiselle, the curator of freshwater fishes for the New York Aquarium, viewed the media's presence as a double-edged sword. "It is unfortunate in a way that this thing became a source of humor because frankly this was not funny at all. If this thing had gotten established we would be talking about some serious economic impacts on both commercial and recreational fisheries. . . . The silver lining is that the import of snakeheads has now been banned. And what I hope it has done is sensitized various state fish and game agencies that the live fish for Oriental restaurant trade can also be a significant source of undesirable exotics getting established." According to Sharon Gross, the chief of the Invasive Species Branch at the U.S. Fish and Wildlife Service, as a result of the summer of the snakehead, "we've seen not only a rise in interest and awareness of the public, but also at the congressional level, the states, and within the agencies. . . . Even though the coverage was sensationalistic it really made people think about invasive species, their potential impact, what government is doing, what industry is doing, what can we do, what needs to be done in the future, and that has a very positive benefit to those of us who do this day in and day out, in making the work relevant." For Gross's colleague, Kari Duncan, the snakehead has become a symbol that will always serve as a convenient marker for getting people's attention. "Any time we do any kind of information write-up for any of our audiences on invasive species, we can refer back to snakeheads. There's name, brand, and image recognition. It will help us get the word out."

Getting the word out is especially important given the magnitude of the invasive species threat and our ability to counter it. According to a recent U.S. General Accounting Office report, "Scientists, industry officials, and land managers are recognizing that invasive species are one of the most serious, yet least appreciated, environmental threats of the twenty-first century." Although more than twenty federal agencies have some role or responsibility when it comes to invasive species management, and many states, too, have their own programs, the barriers that protect us from new invasions and the tools we have to fight invasions once they occur are seriously constrained by budgetary limits, a lack of coordination between organizations and levels of government, and gaps in existing laws. One major effort to address this situation is being spearheaded by the Invasive Species Council, which was created by Executive Order in 1999 and is comprised of representatives from ten federal departments and agencies. The council is charged with providing national leadership on invasive species and coordinating related federal activities. To that end, in January 2001, it published a management plan titled, "Meeting the Invasive Species Challenge," which, in effect, provides a broad blueprint for future federal actions. It is an ambitious document that focuses attention on a number of key areas, including bolstering and expanding efforts to prevent invasive species from becoming established; developing better means of detecting invasive species early and then rapidly responding to their appearance with eradication or containment measures; more effectively controlling and managing species once they are established; and improving education and the public's awareness of invasive species and informing them about what they can do to keep invasive species problems from getting worse. Implementation of the plan is an ongoing and evolving process, as it should be, for the threat of invasive species will likely never go away. Perhaps it is not just wishful to thinking to hope that the snakehead's meteoric rise and descent during the summer of 2002 will have a lasting and positive impact on the long-term battle against invasive species.

On October 2, just a few weeks after the northern snakeheads of Crofton had been vanquished, Congressman Bob Goodlatte, chairman of the House Agriculture Subcommittee, convened a hearing on invasive species before the Subcommittee on Department Operations,

Oversight, Nutrition and Forestry. A panel of experts, from a range of organizations presented their opinions and perspectives on the nature of the threat posed by invasive species and what should be done to address it. Understandably, given the purview of the subcommittee, most of the commentary focused on invasive plants and insects that negatively impact crops and trees. But Jill Stevenson, the deputy director of DNR's Fisheries Service, was on the panel too, and her topic was not plants or agricultural pests, but the northern snakehead. She walked the committee through the steps taken that summer to eradicate the fish and told them that one of the DNR's goals was to have nonnative species legislation introduced during the 2003 Maryland General Assembly session, which could help the state better cope with the introduction of other invasive species in the future. And indeed, the Maryland General Assembly did adopt legislation in 2003 aimed at giving the DNR expanded authority to prohibit the importation, possession, or introduction of certain nonnative acquatic organisms, as well as the authority, under specific circumstances, to enter and inspect private property for the presense of such organisms.

Next door to the hearing room was a display of invasive species, including two northern snakeheads—a baby pickled in a jar and a fourteen-inch adult sealed in a plastic freezer bag. Congressmen, panelists, members of the audience at the hearing, and other visitors waited in line for their turn to view the fish. According to a *Washington Post* reporter, who recorded the scene in a subsequent article, there were a range of reactions, from "that's ugly" to the more basic, "ew." One man, apparently amazed that these were specimens of the fish that had caused all the uproar this past summer, inquired, "*That's* the snakehead?" Indeed, it was.

EIGHT

MAKING SENSE OF THE
SUMMER OF THE SNAKEHEAD

If you set out to write a screenplay for a summer thriller starring a fish, you would be hard-pressed to create anything as compelling and fun as the story of the northern snakehead as it transpired during the summer of 2002. Candy Thomson said it best: "We can't make this stuff up. It is too good the way it is. That was the beauty of the story." First, of course, was the fish's name. "Snakehead" conjures up images of a cold, slithering, serpentine beast, with nefarious designs. As many observers noted, had the snakehead had a less menacing name, it would have been more difficult to demonize and satirize. However, a name does not a story make. Before the summer of 2002, snakeheads had cropped up in at least seven other states, and in none of those instances did the

242

fish's appearance create more than a ripple of news coverage, and in most cases there was silence. An errant snakehead, whether a northern, giant, or bullseye, simply was not newsworthy. But when the snakeheads hit Crofton, the media stars were aligned. A powerful combination of timing, information, misinformation, dramatic events, humor, memorable characters, geography, fishing history, and a desire to be distracted from more disturbing news is what gave us the summer of the snakehead.

For the story to be born it needed a spark, and that was provided by Thomson. She was at the right place at the right time. If Thomson hadn't been pursuing the nuclear worm story, if her contact at the U.S. Fish and Wildlife Service hadn't told her about the snakehead and forwarded her the e-mail traffic on that topic, and if she hadn't dug a little deeper, the summer might have played out much differently. But the messenger is only as good as the message, and here Thomson was given an incredibly important assist. The information about the snakehead that she gathered in those first few days of the story was truly scary. The e-mails and the other background materials painted a picture of a potentially invasive species, with alarming traits that might cause significant harm to the ecosystem were it to become established. Walter Courtenay, the man in charge of the government's risk assessment on snakeheads, who was arguably the country's leading snakehead expert, offered his opinion in no uncertain terms—get rid of that fish. Add to this Bob Lunsford's well-intentioned but ultimately mistaken and overly dramatic comments on the northern snakeheads' talents and it is easy to see why Thomson and her editors saw great potential in the story and ran with it. Thomson's articles and those that appeared shortly after in the *Capital* and on area TV were enough to get the ball rolling and generate local and regional interest, but it wasn't until Anita Huslin and the *Washington Post*, with its greater reach and national stature, latched onto the snakehead that the story caught fire.

One of the major reasons why the snakehead captured the public's imagination was because the first stories were so riveting. As is often said, you have only one chance to make a first impression, and the snakehead's first impression was amazingly memorable. Thomson's and Huslin's articles, appearing within a week of each other, as well as many of the other early media stories, presented a chilling image of the northern snakehead. In what could be termed the "Frankenfish trifecta," readers were informed that snakeheads could walk on land; survive out of water for days; and eat every other fish, and possibly every other living thing in sight. Reporters were not making up this stuff. Rather they were simply repeating what they had been told or read, albeit at times with some dramatic embellishment.

But the story was not completely accurate. The northern snakehead could not walk in the manner that was being portrayed and the fish's propensity to consume all other living things and turn ecosystems on their head was more hyperbole than scientifically based judgment. Still, first impressions count, especially with the news. The initial media reports on any subject provide a critical frame of reference in the public's eye. Once people have a basic image of a story it is hard to modify it with clarifications down the road, especially if such clarifications significantly alter or contradict the original story. This dynamic is most evident in big stories. If, for example, a string of articles identify a person as having embezzled $1 billion, only to be followed by a stories in effect saying, whoops, we meant $1 million, the stain of the larger, more dramatic amount will not be entirely washed away. It will linger on. To a considerable extent, such was the case with the snakehead story.

Throughout the summer and beyond, images of the ravenous snakehead, ready and able to gulp down almost anything in its path and then hike through the countryside in search of more to eat, remained burned into the public's collective consciousness. The image remained largely intact despite efforts of the DNR and others to correct certain exaggerations and inaccuracies in the northern snakehead's profile. Sure, there were reporters who clarified what was known about snakeheads as more information became available, but there were as many if not more who repeated the Frankenfish trifecta with little or no variation. It's hard to blame them for doing so. The story as first reported was just too good. And by the time clarifying information about the northern snakehead began surfacing the story had already been out for a couple of weeks, carried far and wide. Indeed, by the middle of July, the snakehead story had gotten so big so fast that in some sense, the story had become the story. Given the media frenzy in progress, one can understand how so many who covered the snakeheads got caught up in the hype.

It would be wrong to assume, however, that the staying power of the Frankenfish trifecta was solely the result of media types failing to take heed of new, more accurate revelations about the snakehead's prowess. Certainly, for example, some reporters and editors, hearing fisheries biologists say that northern snakeheads couldn't really walk on land, still chose to say that they could. But the truth about snakeheads was, as Thomson said, a moving target, and it wasn't always easy for the biologists and wildlife managers or those in the media to separate fact from fiction and hype. As late as July 23, well after the DNR had begun trying to dispel the mythology surrounding the snakehead, none other than the secretary of the Interior said snakeheads were "like something from a bad horror movie" and that they could "travel across land." And just two days later, the director of the U.S. Fish and Wildlife Service called the northern snakehead "an omnivorous critter that can eat everything in a small pond, then waddle off across land on its belly to find new waters and new prey." If the secretary of the Interior and the director of the U.S. Fish and Wildlife Service were making comments like this, then why should the media be expected to pitch the story differently?

To see how important the initial imagery of the snakehead was to the evolution of the story, assume that the media first heard about the snakehead from an official press release issued by the DNR that read as follows:

A northern snakehead, a fish normally found in Asia, was recently captured and then released in a pond in Crofton. The angler took a picture of the fish before releasing it, which is reproduced below. The northern snakehead, which can grow up to 36 inches long and weigh as much as 15 pounds, is a top-line predator, like a bass or pike, and its diet consists mainly of fish. It has a modified lung and can breathe air, and it can survive out of water for up to three days as long as it is kept wet. It is capable of surviving Maryland winters and becoming established locally, but only in fresh water. Northern snakeheads are not tolerant of salt water and would not survive in the Chesapeake Bay. How the northern snakehead got into the pond is unknown. Most northern snakeheads are imported into this country for human consumption and are sold at ethnic fish markets.

The northern snakehead is a potentially invasive species, and if it became established in Maryland it could have a negative impact on native fish populations. The DNR does not know if the specimen caught and released is the only one in the pond, but we have no reason to believe that there is more than one snakehead in the pond or that there are snakeheads in any other local bodies of water.

In the meantime, with the pond owner's consent, we are closing the pond to public access. That way we will be able to closely monitor the situation and develop and carry out a plan to eradicate any snakeheads in the pond. If you catch a fish in any other body of water that looks like the one shown below, please kill it, by cutting or bleeding it, place it in a plastic bag, and then contact the DNR.

Had this been the first information provided to the media, and had any subsequent public comments from the DNR and other government organizations been equally measured and devoid of any mention of "walking," it is certainly reasonable to conjecture that the story wouldn't have exploded the way it did. "If the snakehead was just something that ate a lot," said Thomson, "and it was penned up in this little scummy pond, I wouldn't have made a big deal of it." Even if the initial information about northern snakeheads mentioned that they could move a short distance over land by wallowing, it is hard to imagine that this would have caused any reporter's news antennae to shoot up. The attack of the wallowing or flopping snakeheads is not remotely as exciting as the attack of walking snakeheads. But being a Monday morning quarterback is easy. Living through a situation and responding in real time, when information is either lacking or not clear, is much harder. While it is true that the story of the snakeheads got an immense boost from mistaken assumptions and exaggerations that became public in the beginning, there is no value in casting blame. All of those involved were trying to do the best they could. The facts were hard to pin down, and in some cases unclear or unavailable.

The snakehead story not only benefited from the Frankenfish trifecta, but also from periodic rejuvenation. In a process akin to punctuated equilibrium, the story jumped from one evolutionary stage to another. Or, to tap the *Jaws* parallel, just when it seemed safe to go back in the water, the snakehead story came back for another bite. The first wave of articles focused on Paul DiMauro's catch and the mystery of what lay lurking in the Crofton pond. Then, while the media's gears were still engaging on the story, Joe Gillespie caught his fish and interest shot way up. Now that there were, apparently, at least two snakeheads in the pond, the plot thickened considerably. Another week passed, and just as the press was beginning to show fatigue, repeating the same old facts and interviewing the umpteenth angler bent on capturing another snakehead, Gillespie caught a handful of Frank juniors and the media and enraptured public went wild. And the hits just kept on coming. The DNR immediately closed the pond and announced the formation of the special snakehead panel. A few days later the agency announced that they had nabbed the guy who dumped the fish, and—surprise, surprise—the fish had been there for two years. At the same time, state and federal biologists caught ninety-nine baby northern snakeheads in the pond. Over the coming weeks and months, the snakehead story was kept alive and healthy by a series of events, including Secretary Norton's press conference announcing the ban on snakeheads, the snakehead panel meetings and reports, the appearance of snakehead T-shirts, the herbicide and rotenone applications, and the postmortems.

The story also had great characters. There was DiMauro, the quickly forgotten angler who caught the first northern snakehead and let it go; Gillespie, the family man, who not only landed and kept the second snakehead, but also was the first to capture babies; Schwaab, Early, Lunsford, Slattery, Surrick, Lynch, and other earnest government bureaucrats doing their best to keep the public informed and the fish contained; Berkshire and his daughters, the entrepreneurs who viewed the northern snakeheads as a marketer's dream; Koorey, one of Berkshire's T-shirt competitors who wanted to teach his boys about business and earn a little money; Courtenay (Dr. Snakehead) and Shafland, the two exotic species experts from Florida who provided their own unique experience and perspectives; Kim Klopcic and Jerry Trice II at the Yin Yankee Café, who saw in the snakehead a culinary oddity and advertising opportunity; and the eager local teenagers ready to either beat the snakehead to death or sell it at a profit. All of these people, as well as others, added depth, flavor, and human interest to the story that served to make it more interesting and, as a result, more worthy of coverage.

Ironically, part of the reason the snakehead story became larger than life is because it was contained. Had the snakehead gotten into the Little Patuxent River or become established in other bodies of water, it is unlikely that the media would have had so much fun with the story. As Huslin said, "I don't think it would have been handled as humorously as it was if the fish had escaped." It is one thing to have a cautionary tale of an invasive species possibly becoming established, and quite another to recount a story in which that species is here to stay, and could spread. Nobody laughs about the hundreds of millions of dollars of damage caused by zebra mussels or the thousands of acres of marshlands eaten into oblivion by nutria. The snakeheads, because contained, were manageable not only from the DNR's perspective, but also from the media's and the public's. We could laugh about them only because they didn't cause any damage worth crying about. And laugh about the story we did. The fish's name and awe-inspiring powers and the breathless media coverage lent themselves beautifully to satire. When the story ascended to the humorous heights of late-night talk shows that was proof that the snakehead had become a part of America's cultural landscape, if only for a fleeting moment. And that celebrity, in turn, helped fuel the snakehead story all summer long.

Although the snakeheads were contained, the threat of escape was real, and that too added to the excitement and newsworthiness of the story. Anything about fish in an area where people love to fish would elicit interest. This was not only a great fish story, but it was also taking place in Maryland, a state in which recreational fishing is big business. The possibility that a rapacious invader would make mincemeat of the regions' sport fish sent more than a few anglers' and fisheries managers' hearts racing.

One of the simplest reasons why the snakehead story became so big is timing. Traditionally, the summer is a slow news season and editors the world over saw the snakehead story as a way to fill space with a gloriously enthralling tale that kept on giving. The summer is also the time that the public is usually most receptive such stories. People looking to unwind, relax, and have fun, found that following the twists and turns of this story satisfied each of those expectations. But this wasn't just any summer. It was less than a year after the horrific terrorist attacks on 9/11, and emotions were still raw. The public was reeling from the collapse of corporate giants such as Enron and WorldCom and the related meltdown of the stock market. War drums were beating and it appeared as if the next stop for U.S. forces was Iraq. In short, it was a summer when many people had more than the usual reasons to take a respite from bad news. As Sue Bents, the administrative assistant at Crofton's Town Hall, observed, "With all the hoopla, and all the giggles and laughs, it was a tension breaker. . . . With everything that was going on with 9/11 and the follow-up, it was good to laugh about something stupid for a few minutes."

The geography of the story also played a key role in its rise. If Crofton had been located one hundred miles east of I've-never-heard-of-it, Idaho, it is likely that even the discovery of thousands of snakeheads breeding wildly and carrying on till all hours of the night would have generated no more media coverage than the harvesting of a three-pound potato. But the snakeheads were in Crofton, Maryland, just a hair's breath away from the U.S. capital, which arguably boasts the largest contingent of media in the world. When the first stories about the snakehead came out, there were plenty of reporters and camera crews ready and willing to take a jaunt to Crofton to see what all the fuss was about. And more than a few reporters saw this as a golden opportunity to step back from covering CEO "perp-walks" and the intricacies of prewar diplomacy to do an unusual and fun piece on the toothed terrors from Asia that had invaded suburbia. The DNR's John Surrick recalls a British reporter who was visiting the pond commenting, "I'm just so tired of this economic stuff that I had to do something interesting today."

While the snakeheads of Crofton are gone, a very important and serious issue remains. Every year, new species arrive in the United States and a few of them will ultimately become invasive. Over time, perhaps our ability to combat such species and keep them from gaining a foothold will improve. From that perspective, the summer of the snakehead is a positive sign. The invaders lost. The northern snakeheads were stopped dead in their tracks . . . in a manner of speaking of course.

BIBLIOGRAPHY

This is a list of the main publications used in writing this book, not a complete record of all the sources consulted. It is intended to serve as guide for those who are interested in delving more deeply into the summer of the snakehead and its aftermath. The gray literature I used, such as e-mails and other unpublished communications, is not listed here but was nevertheless critical to this project.

In writing this book I relied heavily on access to newspaper articles and other media accounts that were available on the Internet. Indeed, without access to such electronic information my task would have been much more difficult, for I would have been forced to find hard copies of a huge range of newspaper and magazine articles, as well as taped versions of numerous television broadcasts. This book is better as a result of the ease of research provided by the Internet, and because of that I want to thank all the people who have contributed to the creation of such a fantastic research tool.

Citing Internet sources is tricky. Information available at one time might not be available at another, and URL addresses often change or disappear. My goal was to give enough information so that readers could find the sources if they wanted to. Except when I felt that a URL address was critical, I have not included it. For example, in citing articles that appeared in newspapers and were also posted on the Internet, instead of listing the URL where the article was found, I cited the article much the same way I would had I found it in a hard copy of the publication, that is, using the name of the author and publication, the title, the date. Page numbers are for the most part not included because electronically posted articles usually do not include them.

253

For those who want to learn more about the general topic of invasive species, there are plenty of places to turn. If you have access to the Internet, go to www.invasivespecies.gov. This is a fantastically comprehensive, government-sponsored site that bills itself as "a gateway to federal and state invasive species activities and programs." There are also many books on invasive species. Other than the ones listed in the bibliography, I recommend the following:

Bright, Chris. *Life Out of Bounds: Bioinvasion in a Borderless World*. New York: W. W. Norton & Company, 1998.

Devine, Robert S. *Alien Invasion: America's Battle with Non-Native Animals and Plants*. Washington, D.C.: National Geographic Society, 1998.

McKnight, Bill N., ed. *Biological Pollution: The Control and Impact of Invasive Exotic Species*. Indianapolis: Indiana Academy of Science, 1993.

Mooney, Harold A. and Richard J. Hobbs, eds. *Invasive Species in a Changing World*. Washington, D.C.: Island Press, 2000.

Van Driesche, Jason, and Roy Van Driesche. *Nature Out Of Place*. Washington, D.C.: Island Press, 2000.

INTERVIEWEES

Sue Bents, William Berkshire, Erin Berkshire, Don Boesch, Scott Burke, Michael Cooke, David Cotton, Walter Courtenay, Paul DiMauro, Steve Early, Joe Gillespie, Don Kemp, Glenna S. Kidd, Steve Koorey, Anita Huslin, Paul Loiselle, Heather Lynch, Danny MacQuilliam, Tom Pittman, Chris Ramsey, Janice Saul, Eric Schwaab, Paul Shafland, Mike Slattery, Mike Smith, John Surrick, Michael Thomas, Julie Thompson, Candus Thomson, and Jerry Trice II.

1. MYSTERY FISH

Axelrod, Herbert R., and William Vordervinkler. *Encyclopedia of Tropical Fishes: With Special Emphasis on Techniques of Breeding*. Jersey City, N.J.: TFH Publications, 1958. 147.

Clemons, Alan. "Jungle Love: Of bass and grass." ESPN Outdoors, http://espn.go.com/outdoors/fishing/s/f_fea_bass_grass_Clemons.html.

Courtenay, Walter R., Jr., and James D. Williams. *Snakeheads (Pisces: Channidae): A Biological Synopsis and Risk Assessment*. Unpublished report to the U.S. Fish and Wildlife Service, Division of Scientific Authority and Fisheries Management, 2002.

Dickey, James. "Kudzu," in *The Whole Motion, Collected Poems 1945-1992*. Hanover, N.H.: Wesleyan University Press, 1994.

Elton, Charles S. *The Ecology of Invasions by Animals and Plants*. Chicago: University of Chicago Press, 1958.

Hoots, Diana, and Juanita Baldwin. *Kudzu: The Vine to Love or Hate*. Kodak, Tenn.: Suntop Press, 1996.

Howells, Robert G., James D. Williams, and Walter R. Courtenay, Jr. "Snakeheads Represent an Increasing Threat to U.S. Waters." *Aquatic Nuisance Species Digest* 4, 4 (February 2002).

Lachner, Ernest, C. Richard Robins, and Walter R. Courtenay, Jr. "Exotic Fishes and Other Aquatic Organisms Introduced into North America." *Smithsonian Contributions to Zoology* 59. Washington, D.C.: Smithsonian Institution Press, 1970. 1–29.

Laycock, George. *The Alien Animals*. New York: The Natural History Press, 1966.

Moser, Frederika C., ed. *Invasive Species in the Chesapeake Bay Watershed*. Maryland Sea Grant, August 2002.

National Invasive Species Council. *National Management Plan: Meeting the Invasive Species Challenge*. 18 January 2001. www.invasivespecies.gov/council/nmp.shtml.

Pimental, David, Lori Lach, Rodolfo Zuniga, and Doug Morrison, "Environmental and Economic Costs Associated with Non-Indigenous Species in the United States." Ithaca, N.Y.: Cornell University, College of Agriculture and Life Sciences, 12 June 1999.

Sagoff, Mark. "What's Wrong with Exotic Species?" Institute for Philosophy & Public Policy report, www.puaf.umd.edu/ippp/fall1999/exotic_species.htm.

Stone, Richard. "Fighting Back: Keeping Paradise Safe for the Natives." *Science* 285 (1999): 1837.

Todd, Kim. *Tinkering With Eden*. New York: W.W. Norton & Company, 2001.

U.S. Congress, Office of Technology Assessment. "Harmful Nonindigenous Species in the United States." Washington, D.C.: U.S. Government Printing Office, 1993.

2. "The Baddest Bunny in the Bush"

Burke, Scott. "Alien Fish Raises Concerns at DNR." *The Capital*, 24 June 2002.

———. "No Fish Tale: Anglers Take Hunt Seriously." *The Capital*, 30 June 2003.

Huslin, Anita. "Freakish Fish Causes Fear in MD." *Washington Post*, 27 June 2002, B3.

"Killer Fish Can Move on Land." NBC4.com, 28 June 2002.

Le Fish Corner. "Fish of the Week: Asian Snakeheads." http://www.seremban.net/fishcorner/fc250999.htm.

Neary, Lynn. "Evil Fish." "All Things Considered," National Public Radio, 27 June 2002.

Thomson, Candus. "It Lurks in Crofton's Waters." *Baltimore Sun*, 22 June 2002.

———. "Search Continues for Predatory Fish in Crofton Pond." *Baltimore Sun*, 26 June 2002.

———. "Wanted: The One That Got Away." *Baltimore Sun*, 30 June 2002.

"Wanted: Killer Fish That Walks." NBC4.com, 27 June 2002.

3. THEN THERE WERE TWO

Burke, Scott. "Crofton Fish Tale Goes National." *Capital*, 6 July 2002.

Dowd, Maureen. "Have You Seen This Fish?" *New York Times*, 7 July 2002.

Huslin, Anita. "Feared Fish Finds Its Way into Anglers' Net." *Washington Post*, 2 July 2002, B2.

———. "Freaky Fish Story Flourishes." *Washington Post*, 3 July 2002, B1.

Lynch, Dotty. "Summer Stories." CBSNews.com, 4 July 2002.

Mayell, Hillary. "Maryland Wages War on Invasive Walking Fish." *National Geographic News*, 2 July 2002.

MacGillis, Alec. "Amateur Anglers Aim to Hook a Snakehead." *Baltimore Sun*, 7 July 2002.

Ringle, Ken. "Stop That Fish!" *Washington Post*, 3 July 2002, C1.

Smith, Eric. "Cityscape: The Growing Fish Tale." *Capital*, 8 July 2002.

Thomson, Candus. "Pond Most Likely Has More Than One Snakehead." *Baltimore Sun*, 3 July 2002.

4. SPAWN OF FRANKENFISH

Barnes, Jeff. "Spawn of 'Frankenfish'?" *Washington Times*, 9 July 2002, A1.

Burke, Scott. "State Shuts Down Pond with Snakeheads." *Capital*, 10 July 2002.

Clines, Francis X. "Battling an Alien Predator in a Suburban Pond." *New York Times*, 13 July 2002.

Cowherd, Kevin. "Watch Your Arms, the Fish Are Biting in Crofton." *Baltimore Sun*, 13 July 2002.

Idyll, Clarence P. "New Florida Resident, the Walking Catfish." *National Geographic*, June 1969, 847–51.

Griffith, Stephanie. "Asian Snakehead, Dubbed 'Frankenfish,' Panics U.S. Naturalists." *Agence France Presse*, 13 July 2002.

Harper, Jennifer. "'Frankenfish' Sets Off Feeding Frenzy." *Washington Times*, 11 July 2002.

Huslin, Anita, and Micheal E. Ruane. "Spawn of Snakehead?" *Washington Post*, 10 July 2002.

Kobell, Rona. "All Things Snakehead Conquer Community." *Baltimore Sun*, 13 July 2002.

Maryland Department of Natural Resources. "DNR Officials Identify Source of Snakehead Fish." Press Release, 11 July 2002.

Mueller, Gene. "Area Fish Will Kill Imported Monster." *Washington Times*, 17 July 2002.

Perez, Luis. "Fierce Fish Dragnet." *New York Daily News*, 13 July 2002.

"The Things You're Searching For: The Fish That Ate Maryland." Lycos 50 Daily Report. http://50.lycos.com/, 18 July 2002.

Torode, Greg. "Snakehead Must Not Be the One That Got Away." *South China Morning Post*, 7 July 2002.

5. POISON 'EM

Biemer, John. "Northern Snakehead as Alien as It Looks." *Courier-Journal*, 21 July 2002.

———. "Snakehead Facts, Misconceptions." *Capital*, 26 July 2002.

California Department of Fish and Game. "The Threat from Northern Pike in Lake Davis to California's Fisheries and How Rotenone if Used to Help Manage Our Fishery Resources." www.dfg.ca.gov/coned/pikebooklet.pdf.

Chun, Diane. "'Frankenfish' Found in St. John's River." *Gainesville Sun*, 20 July 2002.

Courtenay, Walter R. "The Introduction of Exotic Organisms," in *Wildlife and America*, ed., Howard P. Brokaw. Washington, D.C.: The Council on Enviromental Quality, 1978.

Daley, Beth. "Asian Fish Spawned Local Scare." *Boston Globe*, 24 July 2002.

Dart, Bob. "Snakeheads Illustrate 'Invasive Species' Threat." *Cox News Service*, 25 July 2002.

"DEM Bans Aggressive Snakehead from R.I." *Providence Journal,* 28 July 2002.

Emanuel, Mike. "Sniggling Snakehead Ousted From U.S." Fox News Channel, 24 July 2002.

Grossberger, Lewis. "Fish Got to Walk." *Mediaweek*, 29 July 2002.

Harrop, Froma. "Free Market Offers All Kinds of Solutions to the Problem of the Northern Snakehead." *Asheville Citizen-Times*, 30 July 2002.

Harris, Edward. "Singaporeans Love Snakehead Fish." *Seattle Post Intelligencer*, 28 July 2002.

Huslin, Anita. "After Solving Snakehead Puzzle, Md. Moves in for the Kill." *Washington Post*, 19 July 2002.

———. "U.S. Moves to Ban Import of Snakeheads." *Washington Post*, 23 July 2002, B3.

Huslin, Anita, and Steve Vogel. "Test of Snakehead Poison Starts." *Washington Post*, 24 July 2002.

Jamaludin, Farid. "Asians See Snakehead as 'Healer.'" *Star Online*, 26 July 2002.

Kaur, Sharmilpal. "Monster Fish in the U.S., Tasty Delicacy in S'pore." *Straits Times Interactive*, 26 July 2002.

Kluger, Jeffrey. "Fish Tale." *Time* (5 August 2002) 50–51.

Kobell, Rona. "Florida's Dr. Snakehead Is Making a House Call." *Baltimore Sun*, 18 July 2002.

Kottelat, Maurice, Anthony J. Witten, Sri Nurani Kartikasari, and Soetikno Wirjoatmodjo. *Freshwater Fishes of Western Indonesia and Sulawesi*. Indonesia: Periplus Editions Limited, 1993.

Lampe, Jeff. "Latest Scourge of Nature Is the Snakehead." *Peoria Journal Star*, 23 July 2002.

Lee, Dennis P. "Northern Pike Control at Lake Davis, California." American Fisheries Society, 2001.

Little, Jane Braxton. "Detonation to Cut Pike in Lake Davis." *Sacramento* (California) *Bee*, 23 April 2002.

Maryland Department of Natural Resources. "Maryland Snakehead Fish Scientific Advisory Panel Assembled, First Meeting Planned." Press Release, 16 July 2002.

———. "Snakehead Scientific Advisory Panel First Report to the Maryland Secretary of Natural Resources." 26 July 2002.

Morin, Brad. "Snakehead Fish Fueling Fears." *Foster's Online*, 24 July 2002.

Mulligan, John E. "Gracious! It's Voracious!—U.S. Bans Importation of Fearsome Snakehead." *Providence Journal*, 24 July 2002.

Nieves, Evelyn. "Renegade Fish Is Outlasting Even Bombings." *New York Times*, 6 May 2002.

Oberg, Alcestis Cooky. "Exotics Chomp Up U.S. Wildlife." *USA Today*, 29 July 2002.

Rankin, Joe. "Northern Snakehead Not Found in Maine." MaineToday.com, 25 July 2002.

Ringle, Ken. "Gone Fission: The 'Nuclear' Worm." *Washington Post*, 27 July 2002.

Shogren, Elizabeth. "Fish and Game's Enemy No. 1: The Snakehead." *Los Angeles Times*, 24 July 2002.

"Snakeheads in the Grass." *Boston Globe*, 21 July 2002.

Thomson, Candus. "Biologists Fear Vietnamese Bait Could Harm Md." *Baltimore Sun*, 15 July 2002.

U.S. Department of the Interior. "Injurious Wildlife Species; Snakeheads (family *Channidae*). Proposed Rule." *Federal Register* 67, 144 (26 July 2002).

U.S. Fish and Wildlife Service. " 'Frankenfish': The Facts." Fact sheet accompanying the press release for the July 23, 2002, press conference with the secretary of the Department of Interior on the proposed ban of snakeheads, www.fws.gov/frankenfish3.htm.

———. "Interior Secretary Norton Proposes Ban on Importation of Snakehead Fish." Press Release, 23 July 2002.

Watson, Traci. "Aquatic Aliens Spawn Trouble." *USA Today*, 22 July 2002.

Wisby, Gary. "The Fish That Ate Chicago? Not Yet." *Chicago Sun Times*, 31 July 2002.

6. Going in for the Kill

"Alien Fish Found in Baltimore Harbor." CBSNews.com, 5 September 2002.

Bivens, Matt. "America's War on 'Frankenfish.'" *Moscow Times*, 26 August 2002.

Cowherd, Kevin. "This Hot Topic Soon Will Sleep with the Fishes." *Baltimore Sun*, 8 August 2002.

Crable, Ad. "'Frankenfish' Now Illegal in Pa." *Lancaster New Era*, 1 August 2002.

Davis, Robert. "Stalking Giant Snakeheads." *Bangkok Post*, 20 December 2002.

Doggett, Tom. "Snakeheads Put Small Maryland Pond on World Map." Reuters.com, 16 August 2002.

"Freak Fish Found in Two More States." CBSNews.com, 3 August 2002.

Huslin, Anita. "The Big One Doesn't Always Get Away." *Washington Post*, 24 August 2002, B3.

———. "Biologists on Mission to Kill." *Washington Post*, 18 August 2002, C3.

———. "Md. Snakeheads' Destiny Spawns Capitalist Spirit." *Washington Post*, 19 August 2002, B1.

———. "Md. War on Fish Just Might Get Ugly." *Washington Post*, 27 July 2002. B1.

Gross, Max. "Kosher Tale Nabs a 'Frankenfish.'" *Forward*, 9 August 2002.

Hiassen, Rob. "For a Change, Snakehead Run into Town on a Rail." *Baltimore Sun*, 22 August 2002.

Jackson, Sheila, and Faith Hayden. "Fish Has a Grip on Our Attention: Headlines About Snakehead Just Keep Hooking Us In." *Baltimore Sun*, 5 August 2002.

Julavits, Joe. "Jumping Sturgeon, Giant Carp, Frankenfish Starring In … Attack of the Killer Fish Don't Fret, Media Fright Nothing New." *Florida Times Union*, 4 August 2002.

Kiehl, Stephen. "Killer Fish Won't Say Die." *Baltimore Sun*, 30 August 2002.

Klug, Foster. "Giant Snakehead Fish Caught in Inner Harbor." www.Delawareonline.com News Journal, 7 September 2002.

Kobell, Rona. "Feisty 'Frankenfish' Now Fugitive in N.Y." *Baltimore Sun*, 3 August 2002.

———. "Fish Evade Death for Now." *Baltimore Sun*, 8 August 2002.

———. "A Pain in Pond, a Delight to Diners." *Baltimore Sun*, 24 August 2002.

———. "Snakehead Extermination Approved." *Baltimore Sun*, 16 August 2002.

MacCash, Doug. "Nu Attitude: Louisiana Doesn't Have a Nutria Problem; It Has an Attitude Problem." *Times-Picayune*, 20 August 2002.

McFeatters, Dale. "An August Fish Story." Scripps Howard News Service, 19 August 2002.

Maryland Department of Natural Resources. "Snakehead Scientific Advisory Panel, Second Report to the Maryland Secretary of Natural Resources." 1 September 2002.

Miller, S. A. "Officials Defend Snakehead Tactic; Discount Poison Woes Elsewhere." *Washington Times*, 22 August 2002.

Moss, Wayne, and Donna and Eve Shavatt. "He Said, She Said: Snakehead Full of Nonsense?" *Pittsburgh Post-Gazette*, 11 August 2002.

O'Sullivan, Michael. "Step Right Up! See the Snakehead!" *Washington Post*, 26 July 2002, T29.

Page, Clarence. "Fishy Story." PBS Online NewsHour, 1 August 2002.

Paumgarten, Nick. "And They're Off Dept. One Fast Fish." *New Yorker* (5 August 2002), 22–23.

Powder, Jackie, and Rona Kobell. "Area Merchants Are Unfazed by the Plan to Kill Snakeheads." *Baltimore Sun*, 9 August 2002.

Richardson, Michael. "Hitchhiking Species a Threat Worldwide." *International Herald Tribune*, 28 August 2002.

Rodricks, Dan. "Drought Can't Force Seniors to Water Down Their Plans." *Baltimore Sun*, 14 August 2002.

Rose, Derek. "Eco-invaders Go Hog-wild." *New York Daily News*, 21 August 2002.

Ross, Corey. "Pet Shops Say Ban on 'Frankenfish' Is Half-baked Snakehead Fish." *Omaha World*, 7 August 2002.

Sansone, Michael. "8 Ways to Improve Your Bottom Line." *Restaurant Hospitality*, November 2002.

Shaffer, Sarah. Snakehead article [unknown title]. *The Bowie Star*, 22 August 2002.

Smith, Stephen. "Mr. Smith Goes to … Find a Monster." *New Statesman*, 26 August 2002.

Sweeney, James F. "Waves of Fear Walk this Way." *Plain Dealer*, 18 August 2002.

Thomson, Candus. "Snakehead Netted by Inner Harbor Fisher." *Baltimore Sun*, 6 September 2002.

———. "Tougher Laws on Alien Fish Urged." *Baltimore Sun*, 20 August 2002.

Vergano, Dan. "120 Non-native Snakehead Fish Killed in Md. Ponds." *USA Today*, 4 September 2002.

Ward, Jon. "Pond Owner Says No to Snakehead Plan." *Washington Times*, 8 August 2002.

Wineke, William. "Nothing to Fear but Fish Itself." *Wisconsin State Journal*, 3 August 2002.

7. AFTERMATH

Associated Press. "DNR Confirms Snakeheads Gone from Crofton Pond." *Bay Journal*, December 2002.

———. "Thailand Bakery Adds Fish to Ice Cream." ABCNEWS.com, 13 February 2003.

"At Last, U.S. Hopes, Snakehead Is History." *Washington Post*, 3 October 2002, B3.

"The Best & Worst of Everything." *Parade*, 29 December 2002. 4–12.

Brown, Geoff. "Year in Review: 2002." *Baltimore*, December 2002. 118–29.

Grainger, David. "What Went Right in 2002, Distractions in Which We Praise the Tale of the Snakehead Fish." *Fortune*, 30 December 2002.

Hasan, Khalid. "From Snakehead to Saddam." *Daily Times*, 10 December 2002.

Huslin, Anita. "There's a Livelihood in That Dead Fish Yet." *Washington Post*, 28 November 2002.

Nicholls, Walter. "Burma in a Bowl." *Washington Post*, 8 January 2003.

Stevenson, Jill T. "Testimony of Jill T. Stevenson, Deputy Director of Fisheries Service, Maryland Department of Natural Resources, on the Experience of Maryland Natural Resource Managers with Aquatic Invasive Species." U.S. Congress, House of Representatives, Committee on Agriculture, Subcommittee on Department Operations, Oversight, Nutrition, and Forestry, 2 October 2002.

Stuever, Hank. "The List." *Washington Post*, 1 January 2003.

"The Top 10 Local Stories of 2002." *Capital*, 29 December 2002.

U.S. Department of Interior. "Injurious Wildlife Species; Snakeheads (family *Channidae*), Final Rule." *Federal Register* 67, 193 (4 October 2002).

INDEX

page numbers in *italics* refer to illustrations

"ABC Nightly News," 89

Agence France Presse, 88, 91

al Qaeda, 95, 147, 178, 226

Aquatic Nuisance Species Task Force, 13, 31

American Dime Museum, 159

Associated Press, 73, 142–43, 201, 233

Baltimore Magazine, 231

Baltimore Sun, 33, 36, 39, 40, 42, 52, 66–67, 76, 107, 109, 118, 136, 152, 154, 156, 158, 160, 185, 188, 193, 216

Bangkok Post, 66, 71, 180

Barry, Dave, 182–84

Berkshire, Erin 51, *176,* 212

Berkshire, William, 49–50, 77, 84, 125, 152–53, 155, 168, 170–75, *176,* 190–91, 198, 212–14, 230–31, 249

bin Laden, Osama, 72, 105

Boesch, Donald, 84, 115–16, 118, 120–21, 124–25

Boston Globe, 133, 138

BrainFang, 161–164

Burke, Scott, 40–41, 45, 48, 73, 273

Capital, 40, 49, 54, 63, 70, 143, 217, 231, 243

carp, 17–18, 134–35

"CBS Evening News," 66

Chicago Sun Times, 140

Chicago Tribune, 156

CNN, 88, 102, 105–7, 134, 168, 199, 216

Cooke, Michael, 57–61

Cooper, Anderson, 105–7

Courtenay, Walter, 9, 14–15, 25, 27, 37–38, 42, 44, 71, 83, 93–94, 100, 115, 118–21, 122, 128, 137, *174,* 202–3, 206, 217–18, 238, 243, 249

Crofton, Maryland, 1, 26, 36, 39–40, 44, 45, 50, 52, 71, 84, 94, 105, 109–12, *112,* 144, 168, 209–10, 250–51

Crofton Pond, 1–6, *2, 58, 68, 89,* 235–38, *237;* naming of, 237–38

"The Daily Show with Jon Stewart," 144–47, 150

Dickey, James, 18–19

DiMauro, Paul, 1–7, *5, 6,* 26, 38, 48, 64, 72–73, 75, 106, 215, 248

Early, Steve, 26, 63–64, 83, 100, 103, 124, 139, 150–51, 175, *194*, *195*, 206, *208*, 214, 248

Florida Times Union, 158
Fortune, 232
Forward, 159–60
Fox, Charles J. (Chuck), 84, 115, 126, 150, 152, 155, 166
Fox News, 88, 132, 168, 204
Frankenfish, 44, 45, 72, 77, 80, 81, 86, 88, 90, 105, 108–10, 127, 186, 202, 213, 244–45

Gainesville Sun, 137
giant African snail, 21
Gillespie, Caitlin, 52, 61, 211
Gillespie, Joe, 52–68, *60*, *62–63*, 73, 76, 78–83, 85–86, 89, *89*, 99, 111, 200, 203, 210–12, *211*, 215, 248. *See also color section*
Gillespie, Julie, 52, 61, 82–83
Gillespie, Mark, 52, 89, *89*, 95. *See also color section*
Griffith, James, 1–2, 4–6, 48
Guardian Limited, 178
gypsy moth caterpillar, 20–21, 74

Harkey, Jake, 54, 56, 89. *See also color section*
Helias, Jean-Francois, *180–81*
Hoyer, Steny, 234–235
Huslin, Anita, 42–45, 68, 90, 113, 123, 126, 132, 154–55, 177, 190, 216–17, 230, 244, 249
hydrilla, 22

The Independent (South Africa), 88, 134
The Independent (United Kingdom), 88, 91
International Herald Tribune, 178

invasive species, 15–25, 34, 133–37, 216, 238–41
Invasive Species Council, 16, 240

Kansas City Star, 66
Kemp, Don, 78–79, 200–1, 207, *208*, *211*
"Kirk, Mark & Lopez Morning Show," 164
Klauda, Ron, 26–27
Klopcic, Kim, 185, 189, 249
Kobell, Rona, 118, 152, 154, 156, 158, 188
Koorey, Steve, 169–75, *174*, 190–91
kudzu, 18–19, *19*

Lake Davis, California, 123–24, 194–97
Lancaster New Era, 157
"Late Night with Conan O'Brien," 148
"Late Show with David Letterman," 147, *149*
Little Patuxent River, 26, 30–31, 39, 41, 46, *47*, 50, 92, 122, 236, *237*, 249
"Live with Regis and Kelly," 91
Loiselle, Paul, 96–98, 239
Los Angeles Times, 128, 132, 231
Lunsford, Bob, 6, 26–27, 30, 35–38, 41, 44–46, 63, 72, 76, 100, 118, 155, 243, 248
Lycos 50, 98
Lynch, Heather, 62, 86, 91, 99, 101, 104, 150, 167, 199, 248

MacQuilliam, Danny, 113, 152–155, 214–15, 238
MacQuilliam Organization, 2, 84, 113
Madagascar, 97–98
Malaysian Star, 141
Maryland Department of Natural Resources (DNR), 6, 9, 10, 25, 27–28, 30, 32, 35, 37, 40–41, 44, 46, 53, 60, 62–65, 67–68, 74–75, 81–84, 86, 99, 100–3, 105, 115–16, 121, 124, 135, 139, 140, 150, 155–56, 175–76, 182, 188, 191, 197, 200–4, 206–9, 214, 235, 241, 246–47, 251

Maryland's Snakehead Fish Scientific
 Advisory Panel, 132, 191–93
"McLaughlin Group," 95–96
Mediaweek, 147
Moscow Times, 178
mosquitofish *(Gambusia),* 22
MSNBC, 66

National Geographic News, 66, 71, 88
National Public Radio, 45, 108, 166
NBC Channel 4, 44, 46, 69–70, 86, 88,
 90, 204–5
Newsday, 66
New Statesman, 184–85
"NewsHour with Jim Lehrer," 156–57
"News Night with Aaron Brown," 105–7
Newsweek, 102
New York Daily News, 96–97, 160,
 177–78. *See also color section*
New Yorker, 160
New York Times, 72, 88, 91
Ng, Peter, 38, 141
Nico, Leo, 8–9
Norton, Gale, 126–28, 135, *148,* 234, 248
nuclear worm, 33–35, 136
nutria, 24–25, 91, 179

Omaha World-Herald, 157
On Golden Pond, 59–60
The Onion, 147, *148*

Parade, 232
People for the Ethical Treatment of
 Animals (PETA), 157
Peoria Journal Star, 134
Pittsburgh Post-Gazette, 161
Plain Dealer, 178
Providence Journal, 132, 138
purple loosestrife, 22, 25

Ramsey, Chris, 51, *176*
Restaurant Hospitality, 189

rosy wolf snail, 21
rotenone, 31, 42, 121–22, 195, *196*
Reuters, 157

Saul, Janice, 57–61
Schenk, Ann, 7, 25
Schwaab, Eric, 26, 41, 46, 64–65, 73–75,
 82, 84–85, 99, 102–4, 128, 135, 145,
 150, 194–95, *195,* 207, 248. *See also
 color section*
Scotsman, 132
Seattle Post Intelligencer, 142
Seattle Times, 88
Shafland, Paul, *14,* 71, 94, 115, 118–22,
 124, 143, 206, 217–19, 227, 249
Slattery, Mike, 27–31, 41, 46, 64, 65, 68,
 112, 199, 215–16, 248
Smith, Eric, *48, 67,* 70
Smith, Mike, 169–72, 190
Somerville, Charles C., *87*
South China Morning Post, 66
snakehead: aquarium trade, 11, *12,* 42,
 157; Baltimore Harbor, 201–2, *202;*
 blotched, 13, 97, 128; bounty, 48–49,
 54, 63; breaking the story, 35–36;
 bullseye, 13, *14,* 218–19; cartoons, *48,
 67, 69, 87, 117, 131, 230;* characteristics, 9–15, 37–38, 74–75, 86, 92,
 127–31, 142, 160, 222–30, 244–47;
 chevron, 13, 97; Chinese, 11; culinary
 aspects, 9–10, 42, 71, 85, 91, 158, 222,
 224, 228, 233–34; emperor, *181;* federal ban, 10, 126–33, 219–30; first one
 caught in Crofton, 4, *5–6;* fishing, 10,
 179–84; giant, 7, 141, 179, *180,*
 201–3, *202,* 227; healing and medicinal properties, 10, 141–42; herbicide
 application, 156, 165–69, *167,* 176;
 human attacks, 140–41, 227; humor,
 72, 107–9, 144–50, 160–61; Japan, 12,
 39; juveniles, 79–80, *80,* 85–86, 125,
 248; misconceptions, 37–39, 142–44,

snakehead: (*continued*)
244–47; music, 161–65; native ranges, 10–12; northern, *5*, 8–9, 11–12, *13*, 35, 39, *62–63*, 74, *80*, 86, 94, *198–200*, *208*, *211;* purchasing, 158–59, 185; racism, 224, 228; risk assessment, 10, 12; rotenone application, 194–205, *194–96*, *198–200;* Saddam Hussein comparison, 231; second one caught in Crofton, 56–61, *60*, *62–63;* Soviet Republics, 12, 39; state bans, 12; T-shirts, 51, 169–75, *189*, 189–91, 212, 248; wanted poster, 41–42, *43*, 60; year-end lists, 231–32. *See also color section*
Stevenson, Jill, 26, 207, 241
Stossel, Sage, *131*
Straits Times, 88–89, 142
Surrick, John, 40, 44, 68–69, 81–82, 86, 100–1, 168, 202, 248, 251

Taylor, Alison Elizabeth, 117
Thompson, Edith, 27
Thompson, Julie, 27, 33–35
Thompson, Richard, *69*
Thomson, Candy, 28, 33–42, 46–48, 51, 65, 67–68, 71, 76, 100, 102–4, 136, 168, 175, 193, 202, 216, 242–44, 247
Time, 143
Times-Picayune, 179

"Today Show," 90
Trice, Jerry, 185–89, 249

Uncle Nicky's Fish'n Hole, 50–51, 109, *110*, 173
USA Today, 133–34
U.S. Department of Interior, 126, 133
U.S. Fish and Wildlife Service, 9, 13–14, 27, 85, 127–30, 139, 216, 217–30, 234, 237, 239, 243, 246
U.S. Geological Survey, 8, 14, 37

Versak, Beth, 6, 7, 8, 25

walking catfish, 92–95, *93*
Warner, Lisa, 7
Washington City Paper, 117
Washington Post, 42, 44, 66, *69*, 72, 90, 107, 132, 136, 162, 190, 216, 230, *230*, 232–33, 241, 243
Washington Times, 81–82, 84, 88, 90, 108, 152, 194
Williams, Jim, 8–9, 13–14, 127–128, 217
Williams, Steven, 139, 234
Wisconsin State Journal, 158
www.snakeheads.org, 224–25

Yin Yankee Café, 185–189, *186*

zebra mussels, 19–20, 73, 90, 135